The Damnation of John Donellan

Under the names Elizabeth McGregor and Holly Fox, Elizabeth Cooke has been writing for over twenty years and has published twelve novels. *Little White Lies* was televised by the BBC and in *The Ice Child* she turned to a historical theme for the first time with the story of the Franklin expedition. Elizabeth Cooke lives in Dorset.

ALSO BY ELIZABETH COOKE

As Elizabeth McGregor
The Ice Child
The Girl in the Green Glass Mirror
An Intimate Obsession
Learning by Heart
Little White Lies
Out of Reach
A Road through the Mountains
Second Sight
The Wrong House
You Belong to Me

As Holly Fox
This Way Up
Up and Running

First published in Great Britain in 2011 by
PROFILE BOOKS LTD
3A Exmouth House
Pine Street
London EC1R 0JH
www.profilebooks.com

Copyright © Elizabeth Cooke, 2011

1 3 5 7 9 10 8 6 4 2

Printed and bound in Great Britain by
Clays, Bungay, Suffolk

The moral right of the author has been asserted.

A CIP catalogue record for this book is available from the British Library.

ISBN 978 1 84668 482 1
eISBN 978 1 84765 752 7

The paper this book is printed on is certified by the © 1996 Forest Stewardship
Council A.C. (FSC). It is ancient-forest friendly. The printer holds FSC chain of custody
SGS-COC-2061

FSC
Mixed Sources
Product group from well-managed
forests and other controlled sources
Cert no. SGS-COC-2061
www.fsc.org
© 1996 Forest Stewardship Council

The Damnation of
JOHN DONELLAN
A Mysterious Case of Death &
Scandal in Georgian England

ELIZABETH COOKE

P

PROFILE BOOKS

Contents

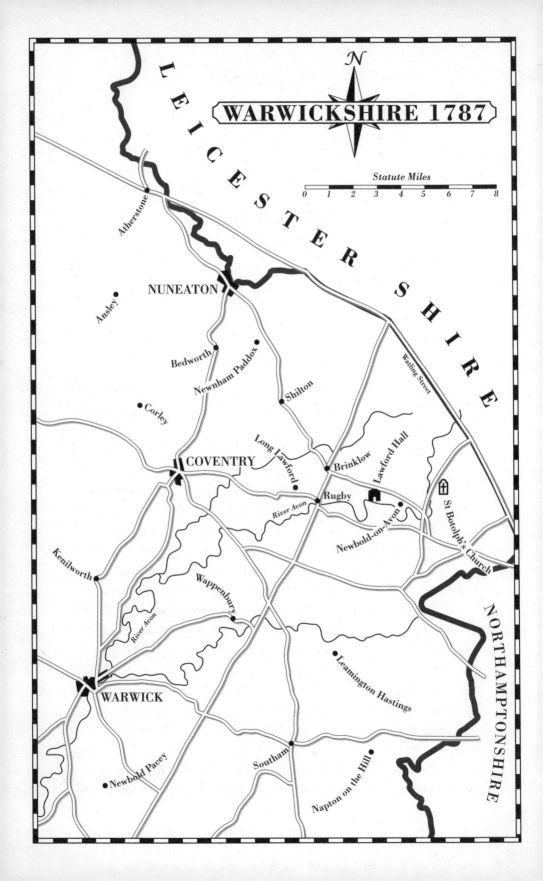

Prologue

IN THE FIFTEENTH-CENTURY CHURCH in Newbold-on-Avon, Warwickshire, is a curious monument. Mounted high on the chancel wall to the right of the altar is a visored helmet, the crest of which shows a disproportionately heavy long-necked bird, marked with a double chevron and holding a struggling serpent in its mouth. The ancient armour is believed to be a relic of the Boughton family.

Through the leaded glass windows, the bird faces a Boughton vault under the yews of the churchyard; but to the south side is a much older tomb, a more probable last resting place of Theodosius Boughton, once the heir to a vast fortune and the seventh Boughton baronetcy. Theodosius was barely twenty when he died suddenly, after taking a prescribed physic, on 30 August 1780. He was buried in the tomb a week after he died; but his body was exhumed three days later when rumours began to circulate the parish that the apparently fit and healthy young man had been poisoned. His body was brought out from the tomb into the sunlight of an exhaustingly hot September day, and a belated autopsy was conducted before 500 ghoulish spectators on the grass in front of the vault.

The surgeon, Samuel Bucknill, was well prepared for the stench of his unsavoury task: to protect himself against the odour he wore a waggoner's apron soaked in vinegar with a napkin, also dipped in vinegar, tied around his mouth and nostrils. Bucknill had to be given a glass of strong wine after his job was done, and for weeks afterwards denied that he had rushed from the scene out of fear.

Other 'gentlemen of the Faculty' (according to the *Northampton Mercury* of 23 April 1781) examined the body. They concluded that it was in a 'mortified state' and added: 'when it is considered how long Sir Theodosius had been dead, the excessive Heat of the Weather at that Time, the Circumstance of the Body having been heated to the Degree it was six Times by the soldering and unsoldering of the Leaden Coffin ... the Body was not more mortified than might be expected.' This measured response was not reflected in the *Gentleman's Magazine*; 'The whole corpse,' it reported, 'was a spectacle of horror scarce to be endured.'[1]

The mortification was reported in careful detail. The corpse's face was black and its tongue protruded until it almost touched its nose. Dr Rattray, one of the attending doctors, noted that there were no maggots on the face, as he had noticed when called to view the body five days previously, but the teeth were black, the throat and chest were also black and the body had swelled considerably. 'It rather put on the appearance of gangrene,' he commented. Bucknill had pointed out that there was a quantity of thick fluid in the stomach but when it was removed from the body and examined closely, no grainy particles were discerned. When the chest was opened, 'a pint of extravasated [*sic*] blood appeared on each side of the thorax or breast'. 'The contents of the stomach were about a spoonful and a half of a slimy reddish liquor which I rubbed between my finger and thumb and it contained no gritty substance,' Rattray observed. He also added enigmatically, when asked later, 'There was another circumstance which, for decency, I have not mentioned.'

In fact, decency had nothing to do with this dreadful public inspection. Nothing decent at all was left of the careless, headstrong boy who only a fortnight previously had ridden out to go fishing the night before his death.

Theodosius's mother, Lady Anna Maria Boughton, was also in the churchyard. The same article from the *Northampton Mercury* attests that she 'viewed the melancholy operation performing upon the Corpse of her Son without betraying the least appearance of Feeling or Affection'. But Anna Maria's calm would not have been unusual in a woman of her rank. An heiress in her own right before her marriage, for eight years now she had been the widow of the sixth Baronet Boughton, and, until Theodosius attained his majority at twenty-one (an age he would now never reach), in control of a valuable estate. A dignified appearance was second nature to her; however, she might have been forgiven for displaying some emotion in the face of the events of the previous ten days, in particular those of the morning of her son's death.

Theodosius had been given a phial of liquid to drink at around 7 a.m. that day. He had complained at the sickening taste of the mixture, and tried to put it down. Yet the person standing by his bed that morning had insisted that he drink it all, despite having smelled the concoction and realised that it had an aroma of bitter almonds.

Within the hour, the heir to the extensive estates of Lawford Hall had died in convulsions. And the person who had insisted that he take every last drop of the physic had been his own mother.

Anna Maria turned from the scene at the opened coffin on that stifling afternoon and returned to her carriage. Inside the church, a vast monument to Theodosius's great-grandfather and step-great-grandmother bore mute testimony to the Boughton name while in the main body of the church lay the fourteenth- and fifteenth-century tombs of their ancestors. The inscription on the tomb of Sir William Boughton and Catherine Shukburgh spoke of 'valuable qualities, the esteem and favour of County ... steady and untainted principle ...' Anna Maria had a role to play, one foisted upon her by marriage: to maintain that untainted principle, whatever serpent might attack.

FROM THE 4ᵗʰ BARONET BOUGHTON OF LAWFORD TO THE 10ᵗʰ BARONET (1663–1856)

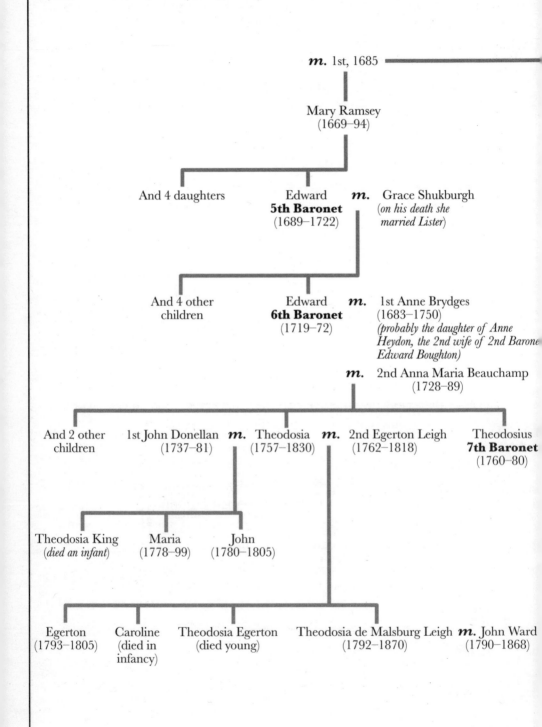

m. 1st, 1685

Mary Ramsey
(1669–94)

And 4 daughters

Edward
5th Baronet
(1689–1722)

m. Grace Shukburgh
*(on his death she
married Lister)*

And 4 other
children

Edward
6th Baronet
(1719–72)

m. 1st Anne Brydges
(1683–1750)
*(probably the daughter of Anne
Heydon, the 2nd wife of 2nd Barone
Edward Boughton)*

m. 2nd Anna Maria Beauchamp
(1728–89)

And 2 other
children

1st John Donellan **m.** Theodosia **m.** 2nd Egerton Leigh
(1737–81)   (1757–1830)   (1762–1818)

Theodosius
7th Baronet
(1760–80)

Theodosia King
(died an infant)

Maria
(1778–99)

John
(1780–1805)

Egerton
(1793–1805)

Caroline
(died in
infancy)

Theodosia Egerton
(died young)

Theodosia de Malsburg Leigh **m.** John Ward
(1792–1870)   (1790–1868)

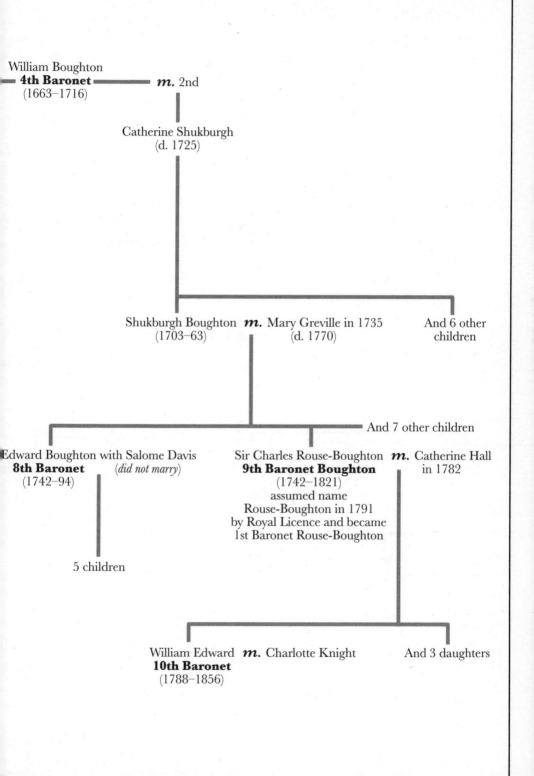

William Boughton
4th Baronet
(1663–1716) ═ *m.* 2nd

Catherine Shukburgh
(d. 1725)

Shukburgh Boughton *m.* Mary Greville in 1735
(1703–63) (d. 1770)

And 6 other
children

And 7 other children

Edward Boughton with Salome Davis
8th Baronet *(did not marry)*
(1742–94)

Sir Charles Rouse-Boughton *m.* Catherine Hall
9th Baronet Boughton in 1782
(1742–1821)
assumed name
Rouse-Boughton in 1791
by Royal Licence and became
1st Baronet Rouse-Boughton

5 children

William Edward *m.* Charlotte Knight
10th Baronet
(1788–1856)

And 3 daughters

THE EARLY BOUGHTON LINE

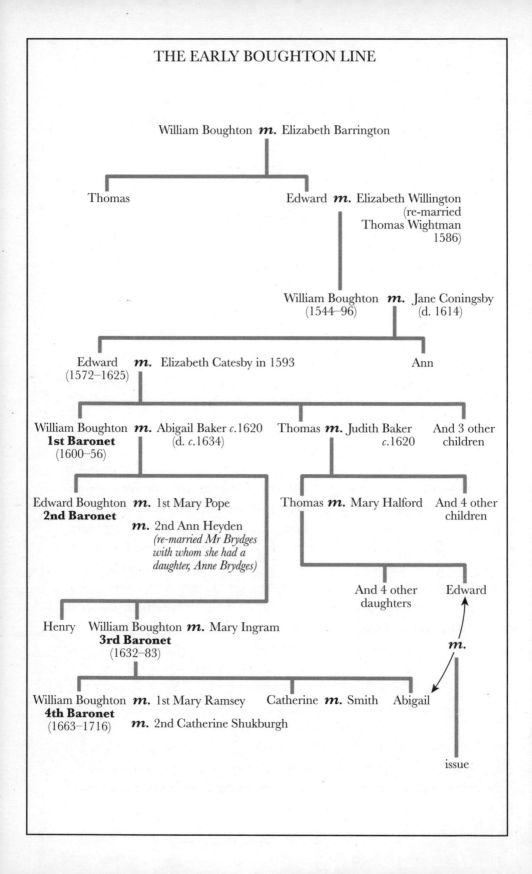

William Boughton **m.** Elizabeth Barrington

Thomas

Edward **m.** Elizabeth Willington
(re-married
Thomas Wightman
1586)

William Boughton **m.** Jane Coningsby
(1544–96)   (d. 1614)

Edward **m.** Elizabeth Catesby in 1593
(1572–1625)

Ann

William Boughton **m.** Abigail Baker *c.*1620
1st Baronet   (d. *c.*1634)
(1600–56)

Thomas **m.** Judith Baker
*c.*1620

And 3 other
children

Edward Boughton **m.** 1st Mary Pope
2nd Baronet

m. 2nd Ann Heyden
*(re-married Mr Brydges
with whom she had a
daughter, Anne Brydges)*

Thomas **m.** Mary Halford

And 4 other
children

And 4 other
daughters

Edward

Henry   William Boughton **m.** Mary Ingram
3rd Baronet
(1632–83)

m.

William Boughton **m.** 1st Mary Ramsey
4th Baronet
(1663–1716)   **m.** 2nd Catherine Shukburgh

Catherine **m.** Smith   Abigail

issue

1

Poison

'She carved thee for her seal, and meant thereby
Thou shouldst print more, not let that copy die.'

William Shakespeare, 'Sonnet XI'

IN 1780 THE BOUGHTON FAMILY occupied an enviable position
in Warwickshire society. Lawford Hall stood near the River Avon,
surrounded by meadows and its own formal and informal gardens
– a graceful and imposing house built on three sides of a square,
the longest side facing the meadows and with a curved wall protecting the garden. Tall chimneys flanked each end of the Hall;
relics, perhaps, of an earlier building on the site, with a whisper of
the Elizabethan about their design. The land on which Lawford
Hall stood had once belonged to Pipewell Abbey, but Henry VIII
had ordered the abbey's closure and, in 1542, had given its lands to
Edward Boughton and his wife Elizabeth Willington.

Today, the village close to where Lawford Hall once stood,
Newbold-on-Avon, is surrounded by nineteenth- and twentieth-
century housing, a drawn-out extension of the industrial sprawl
of Rugby. In 1780, however, both Newbold and Rugby existed in
rural idyll: a quiet, undulating county of newly enclosed fields,
and of farms and cottages. The fine church predominated, rebuilt

on the site of a much earlier Anglo-Saxon building on top of a hill within walking distance across the fields of Lawford Hall.

Since the death in 1772 of Sir Edward Boughton, the Sixth Baronet Boughton, Lawford Hall had been the residence of his widow Anna Maria, and their children. Now, in at the end of August 1780, Theodosius Edward Allesley Boughton had just celebrated his twentieth birthday. His sister Theodosia, who was three years older, had married at the age of eighteen and, since the summer of 1778, had also lived at the Hall with her husband, Captain John Donellan. In 1780 their two children were two-year-old Maria and newborn baby John.

August had been extraordinarily warm, but it had been a peculiar year altogether for weather, more unpredictable than most. Seventeen-eighty was the year of the Great Hurricane in the Atlantic and Caribbean; eight different relentless storms had battered the American coast. The turbulent forces in the Atlantic by the end of the year, reached their peak in October, when 22,000 people were to die as the Great Hurricane raced through the Antilles, and a hundred British merchant ships and the 74-gun HMS *Cornwall* would sustain heavy casualties. On 22 August, Captain Cook's ship, the *Resolution*, had at last sailed into Stromness harbour, Orkney, after a four-year voyage round the world, in the teeth of a fierce gale which had prevented the vessel from entering the English Channel. Scapa Flow proved to be the only shelter that the *Resolution* could find.

By the end of the month, however, Warwickshire was enjoying a belated period of summer calm, sheltered in the heart of England. On the afternoon of Tuesday 29 August, a young servant boy, Samuel Frost, returned from running an errand for Theodosius: he had been sent to the local apothecary, Mr Powell, some three miles away, for a bottle of medicine. Powell had visited Lawford that same morning for the second time in three days and prescribed a different physic for Theodosius, one designed not to be as nauseating as the draught that had made him sick the previous Saturday. Samuel Frost swore later that this new bottle had been delivered to Theodosius directly, and that he had seen him put the medicine into his pocket.

It was about five o'clock when Lady Boughton and her daughter, who were walking in the garden, saw Theodosius; he was on horseback and passed by the wall of the garden not far from them.

'Where are you going?' called his mother.

'A-fishing,' came the reply.

As the evening darkened, Lady Boughton and Theodosia went to the parlour; John Donellan entered later. He drank a bowl of milk that had been prepared for him, and left the room. His wife followed him.

There was a staircase outside the parlour which led directly up to the Donellans' bedroom and to two others, which were not used; there was no connecting landing or staircase to any other part of the house. Theodosius's room was on the other side of the building, along an 80-yard passageway. Anna Maria would have been able to hear, firstly, that the Donellans were in the room above her and, secondly, that no one came down the stairs again and along the passageway.

By now it was dark in the house; candles were lit. Theodosius returned around nine o'clock, after Lady Boughton had sent word to him to come home. He was seen by his mother, but not by his sister or brother-in-law, and he went to his room. Lady Boughton went up to hers soon after. In the stables William Frost, the coachman, would still have been occupied for a few minutes attending to Theodosius's horse (unless Theodosius had done it himself, which was unlikely). Night fell, and silence.

It was six o'clock when Anna Maria woke the next morning. By her own account she did not move from her room until seven, when she intended to go and visit her son.

There was much of his father in Theodosius. Edward had been only fifty-three when he had died 'of apoplexy' eight years before; he had not been, like so many of his ancestors, a man of high government or ministerial office, but a country gentleman. He had been fond of the traditional country pursuits of hunting, shooting and fishing, and his son likewise. However, the boy preferred to adopt the least strenuous methods for all three. He hunted the old-fashioned way, driving the game into nets and then taking a few pot shots at whatever had been caught; and as for fishing, a contemplative few hours sitting on the river bank was not for Theodosius. His main purpose in fishing was to net his catch as soon as possible, then split open the fish and bait them with arsenic for the rat traps around the house.

At six o'clock that morning, Theodosius was awake like his mother. Samuel the servant boy (who was probably a relation of the coachman William) knocked on Theo's door. When called in, he asked if the young master had the straps to some nets which were to be used later in the day.

Theodosius jumped out of bed and went into his inner room, bringing out the straps. He was, according to Samuel, 'in a very good state of health'. Theo was looking forward to the visit that day, or perhaps later in the week, of a friend of his, Fonnereau. Perhaps he spoke to Samuel about the fishing trip they had both undertaken the night before – Samuel would later testify that he had met his master at the river.

That morning, other members of the household would also have been awake at six. Certainly the cook, Catharine Amos, who had been helping with the household wash the evening before, would have already been in the kitchen, checking that the fire was still in place in its huge hearth and asking one of the gardeners or maids to bring a further stock of coal. The fire in a Georgian kitchen had to be kept going twenty-four hours a day, even if one of the new-fangled ranges had been installed.

It was also likely that William Frost was once again busy. He knew that Lady Boughton and John Donellan intended to go riding that morning, and would have been back at the stables attending to the horses. No one would have eaten yet. Breakfasts were not usually eaten in the house until nine o'clock or so, and the servants would have taken the opportunity to have theirs at the same time.

It is hard to be sure how many other servants were in or around Lawford Hall that day. Anna Maria kept a very tight ship, employing a surprisingly small staff. Of those servants who were certainly in the house that morning, we know only seven by name: William

Frost and Samuel Frost; Catharine Amos, and the gardener Francis Amos; the maid Sarah Blundell; the nursemaid Susannah Sparrow; and a footman, John Yateman.

The family's bedrooms were on the first floor. Theodosius may have inherited his late father's suite of rooms, which would have reflected his masculine, even boyish, tastes: in the main room a plain four-poster bed and probably pale green walls (the colour of most earlier Georgian interiors). His personal effects would have been in the inner room, which also contained a washstand and a chamber pot. The function of the inner room was as a place to keep valuables under lock and key, but Theodosius was not renowned for being careful with his belongings. He probably had keys to the inner door, but rarely would have bothered to know where they were.

His mother had a separate suite, which would have consisted of a bedroom and at least one other room, but more probably two. The dressing room and washing room would have been intricately decorated with all the fashionable clutter that mystified most Georgian gentlemen. She would have had a wash cabinet and a four-poster bed, or perhaps the more fashionable 'tester' bed. A tester was to die for in 1780, the more ornate four-poster curtains having been truncated to become heavily festooned drapes above the head of the bed. She may well have had a 'Turkey' carpet on the floor, probably made in the new Wilton factory. And, aside from these practical elements, the room would have been heavily furnished with her porcelain and 'treasures', including her own needlework and craftwork.

Theodosia did not rise at the same time as her mother. Although her husband John was due to go out riding with Anna Maria, she was not seen downstairs until almost nine, when there is the first mention of her standing on the steps of the house. Nothing at all is known of the whereabouts of the children, and the nursemaid is not mentioned in any account of the day.

Anna Maria finally left her room an hour after waking, and went to see Theodosius. It was seven o'clock.

Anna Maria knew that her son was not well – and certainly not in the 'very good state of health' that Samuel Frost later described under oath. If pressed, however, she would only ever refer to Theo's illness as 'a particular complaint'. For Theo had contracted venereal disease at Eton when he was only fifteen and, to Anna Maria's revulsion, did not seem to be clear of it even now. She had employed a local apothecary to prepare physics for the lad, which Theodosius took with bad grace, often forgetting where his medicine was, refusing it entirely or leaving it to stand on a chimneypiece alongside a mixture of other bottles. For the last month or so, John Donellan had been warning Anna Maria ominously that Theodosius was ruining his health, and her son-in-law was plainly anxious. The apothecary had been called back and had prescribed a concoction of medicines – which seemed to have at least brought down Theo's florid, flushed appearance – and then, after a gap of a fortnight, another purgative.

That summer Anna Maria had bought Theodosius a book about family health which she had encouraged him to read – to very little apparent effect. Even more recently, Donellan had told her that Theodosius's health seemed to be getting much worse, and rapidly so: the boy had lost weight and now had a swelling in his groin. Only the previous Saturday, Donellan had told the local priest, the Reverend Newsam, that Theo was skeletally thin and would not be long for this world if he did not mend his ways. The boy had become reinfected even since coming back to live at Lawford.

Anna Maria probably did not want to think too much about either the complaint or the way it had been caught. But the one thing she could do, even if she could not control her irrepressible boy, was to make sure that he took his medicine.

According to her later testimony, while Theodosius propped himself up in bed, Anna Maria asked where the medicine bottle was.

'On the chimneypiece,' he replied.

After hunting through the various bottles there, she found it and took it down.

'Read the label,' Theodosius told her.

She did so. 'Purging draught for Sir Theodosius Boughton.'

Theodosius seemed satisfied. 'Get me a piece of cheese,' he said.

'The stuff tastes vile.' Anna Maria cut him a piece, and then poured some of the medicine into a glass.

'You did not shake the bottle first,' Theo pointed out.

Anna Maria shook the rest of the bottle and, in doing so, spilled a little on the table. She noticed a grainy residue in the bottom of the phial. Then she handed the glass to her son.

He swallowed half of it. 'My God,' he exclaimed, pushing the glass away from him, 'it tastes sickening. I won't keep it down.'

Anna Maria was probably wise to this ruse. The previous Saturday, Theodosius, when pressed to take the physic, had vomited it straight back up. This new mixture, only brought from the apothecary the night before, was designed to be less nauseating.

Theodosius ate another piece of cheese, but after a moment spat it out. His mother probably guessed that she had a fight on her hands. She smelled the medicine; the odour reminded her of bitter almonds. Nevertheless, she made Theo drink the remainder.

Grimacing and complaining, her son washed out his mouth with a little water, then lay back down on the bed. A report published the following year said that he 'fell back on the bed with his arms extended', but that was not verified by any other testimony.

By now, it was ten minutes past seven.

Two minutes later, as Anna Maria hovered by the bed, Theodosius began to groan. His stomach heaved. It was to be said later in court that he seemed in a 'very considerable degree of agony'[1] and that 'his eyes seemed much affected'. But the mother stood by. She did not call a servant or her daughter or Donellan. In fact, she claimed that she took 'no further notice of him at that time'. In another ten minutes or so, Theodosius seemed calmer. So calm, in fact, that his mother thought he was going to sleep. Satisfied that the medicine had been taken, she left the room.

Returning five minutes later, at about twenty past seven, she found a scene of horror. Theodosius was heaving, groaning, his hands clenched. He was frothing at the mouth and unable to speak. Anna Maria ran out on to the landing, calling out for the maids. When Catharine and Sarah appeared, she told them to send William for the apothecary, Powell.

'William is at the stables,' she was told.

'Tell him to go and get Powell!' was Lady Boughton's reply. She ran back upstairs to Theodosius's room, Catharine Amos and Sarah Blundell following her. The boy was rigid, panting, his eyes rolling. Catharine at once knelt by the bed and tried to wipe the froth from Theo's face. But she was not there long. After a moment or two, she left the room and went back down to the kitchen.

In a few minutes, John Donellan was at the bedroom door, having met William Frost in the stable yard and, on hearing that Frost had been sent to get Powell, given him his horse. 'What do you want?' he asked Lady Boughton. At the threshold Donellan stopped, on seeing Sarah Blundell by the bed, the prone boy and the expression on his mother-in-law's face.

'Good God!' Anna Maria gasped. 'What medicine can Mr Powell have sent?' She lowered her voice. 'I am certain it would have killed a dog if he had swallowed it.'

Donellan looked from Theo to his mother, and around the room. 'Why the devil did Powell send such a medicine?' he demanded. 'Where is the bottle?'

Anna Maria simply pointed to where she had replaced it on the shelf. Donellan walked over to the chimneypiece, glanced through the bottles and held up the one she had used. 'Is this it?'

She nodded. Donellan poured water into the empty bottle and shook the liquid into a basin of dirty water nearby.

'You should not do that,' Anna Maria objected.

He took another bottle from the shelf and did the same.

'What are you doing?' Anna Maria asked. 'Let everything remain the same until Mr Powell arrives. Don't touch the bottle.'

Donellan turned to Sarah Blundell and, thrusting the bottles into her hands, told her 'with some warmth' to take them away.

Anna Maria moved forwards. 'Let things alone,' she told the frightened girl, snatching the bottles back again and putting them on the table.

'The room should be cleaned,' Donellan insisted. 'Put the dirty clothes into the inner room.'

Anna Maria walked past the bed where Theodosius lay immobile. The boy had not said a single word since swallowing the second draught of medicine. A seemingly erroneous report published in 1781 claimed that Theodosius now said, 'Who gave me this draught?' but this is not corroborated by any witness.[2] While Anna Maria had her back turned opening the door to the inner room, Donellan gave the bottles to Sarah and motioned her to leave the room. Then he went after her; in the passageway downstairs that led to the kitchen, he met Catharine Amos, the cook, who was hurrying between the kitchen and the hall.

'Sir Theodosius was out very late overnight fishing,' Donellan said, unprompted. 'It was very silly of him, because he has been taking physic again as he had taken previously.'

Catharine Amos seems to have taken this as evidence that the young master was not as ill as she had assumed. She did not go upstairs.

Next Donellan went out into the garden, evidently searching for something. On seeing the gardener Francis Amos, he walked over to him. 'Gardener,' he said, 'you must go and take a couple of pigeons directly.'

The gardener was perplexed. 'They are not fit to eat, sir.'

'It will make no odds if they are not,' Donellan replied. 'They are for Sir Theodosius; we must have them ready against the doctor comes.'

Amos hesitated. Putting dead birds at the feet of an invalid was an old wives' remedy; it was meant to draw the bad vapours from the body. But it was an almost comical last resort. 'Is Sir Theodosius ill?' he asked.

'The poor fellow has a damned nasty distemper,' Donellan told him.

It was almost an hour later before the panic-stricken apothecary, Powell, arrived in the stable yard. Beside him was William Frost, the coachman sent to get him, still on Donellan's horse. Frost had not been able to give Powell any details of what had happened; only that Lady Boughton had demanded that he come immediately.

John Donellan was waiting in the yard.

A curious atmosphere had descended on the house. Powell

could hear no familiar sounds as he dismounted: no clattering from the kitchens, no sweeping out of the passageways. The last time that he had been here, the previous day, Theodosius had complained that his medicine had made him vomit. Powell had made up a new draught, even though the boy seemed to him to be in pretty fine fettle, and Samuel had collected it the afternoon before. It was made up of fifteen grains each of jalop and rhubarb and twenty drops of lavender water mixed with two drams each of syrup and of nutmeg water and an ounce and a half of plain water. It ought to have been drinkable, and effective. It would have had the boy rushing to the chamber pot, but nothing more dramatic.

Theodosius had not been the easiest or most biddable of patients; he complained a lot and resisted treatment. The boy admitted that he often forgot to take his purges, and that Captain Donellan had encouraged him to keep them in his bedroom so that he would see them and remember. Despite all that Captain Donellan had done to help him, though – including rescuing him from a few scrapes in local taverns – the boy was a force of nature, a true Boughton. Above all, he would not leave the women alone who kept reinfecting him.

At the same time, Lady Boughton was both an overbearing mother and a powerful woman. One word that she disagreed with Powell's treatments, or that they had made her poor boy persistently sick, could cost him the rest of his patients – his whole livelihood.

As Powell dismounted from his horse, Donellan walked across to him. He looked expectantly in John Donellan's face for confirmation that he still had both a career and a patient.

'Sir Theodosius is dead,' the captain told him.

2

The Following Days

'The doctor is often to be more feared than the disease.'

French proverb

ACCORDING TO POWELL'S LATER TESTIMONY,[1] he was taken by John Donellan straight to Theodosius's room, where he reported vaguely that 'some servant' was present, though he could not say who.

He inspected the body but saw 'no distortion' and, more astonishingly, 'nothing in particular'. He noted that Theodosius had been dead 'near an hour'. When asked how the young man had died, Donellan replied, 'In convulsions.' Powell later said that John Donellan also tried to persuade him that Theodosius had caught cold the night before, but he could not recall his exact words.

At some unspecified time later that same morning, Powell saw Lady Boughton, who told him that Theodosius 'was convulsed soon after he took the medicine'. But there is no mention at all by anyone else in the house, when under oath later, of Powell having been questioned about what he had put in the prescription or why Theodosius had reacted as he did. No hint of blame, confusion or anger from anyone who spoke to him that day, in the family or beyond.

It was after Powell's visit that John Donellan sat down to write to Theodosius's guardian, Sir William Wheler (Anna Maria had appointed him to this role some years earlier). Like Theo's father, Wheler was a baronet; his Leamington Hastings estate lay about six miles from Lawford Hall across rolling, open country. Leamington Hastings had been described in 1629 as an extensive estate of 'forty messuages' (defined by law as dwelling houses with adjacent buildings and land), 'forty gardens, two dovehouses, one thousand acres of land, two hundred acres of meadow and fifty acres of pasture', and it had been added to since then.

Donellan wrote:

Dear Sir,

I am sorry to be the communicator of Sir Theodosius's death to you, which happened this morning; he has been for some time past under the care of Mr Powell of Rugby, for a similar complaint to that which he had at Eton. Lady Boughton and my wife are inconsolable. They join me in best respects to Lady Wheler, yourself, and Mr & Mrs Sitwell.

I am, dear sir, with the greatest esteem, your most obedient servant, J.D.

Lawford Hall, August 30th, 1780.

At the time, Wheler and his wife were staying with their friends the Sitwells, who had been recently bereaved, at Leamington (now Royal Leamington Spa). No mention had been made of how Theodosius had died. No reply was received that day.

'Some time afterwards', according to Lady Boughton, Donellan, Theodosia and herself were in the downstairs parlour. Donellan raised the subject of the medicine bottles.

Anna Maria later testified that 'Donellan in her presence had said to his wife that her mother [meaning herself] had been pleased to take notice of his washing the bottles out; and that he did not know what he should have done if he had not thought of saying he put the water into it to put his finger to it to taste'. Donellan's words and actions – if Anna Maria's version is accurate – smack of self-defence. Anna Maria testified later that she could not trust herself to reply; she turned away from him to the window. In the face of his mother-in-law's rebuff, Donellan repeated what he had just said. Still getting no reply from her, he asked Theodosia to call a servant, who was asked to go and fetch William Frost.

Now came one of the major – but by no means only – divergences between Donellan's account and Anna Maria's later testimony. In her deposition to the coroner on 14 September, Anna Maria made no mention whatsoever of having seen Donellan in the house prior to his entering Theodosius's bedroom at approximately half past seven. Donellan's version was quite different.

According to Donellan's later published *Defence*, he and Lady Boughton had made an arrangement the previous day that they would ride out together that morning to take the waters at Newnham Wells, a little way across the fields. Donellan had gone downstairs and was waiting in the yard with the horses when at some time between seven and seven fifteen he glimpsed Anna Maria through a window. He had called to her, asking if she was ready to leave; she had replied that she was about to change her clothes. When she did not appear after some minutes, Donellan had ridden out alone, returning at about ten minutes to eight.

Next, according to both Anna Maria's trial testimony and Donellan's *Defence,* William Frost was called into the parlour to verify this.

Donellan asked the coachman, 'Will, don't you remember that I set out of these iron gates this morning about seven o'clock?'

'Yes, sir,' Will replied.

'You remember that, don't you?' Donellan persisted.

'Yes, sir.'

'And that was the first time of my going out. I have never been on the other side of the house this morning.' Donellan was careful to drive the point home, repeating, 'You remember that I set out there at seven o'clock this morning, and asked for a horse to go to the Wells?'

'Yes, sir.'

'Then,' Donellan replied, 'you are my evidence.'

'Yes, sir,' Frost answered.

It was the first time that the word 'evidence' – to play such a major part in the months to come – was uttered.

Nothing else is recorded of the events or the emotions of that day or of the following one, 31 August, in Anna Maria's testimony other than that she instructed that two women be sent for to lay Theodosius out.

It was the evening of the thirtieth, the day of Theo's death, that Francis Amos, the gardener, said that John Donellan came into the garden. Seeing Amos, Donellan called to him, saying, 'Now, gardener, you shall live at your ease, and work at your ease; it shall not be as it was in Sir Theodosius's days. I wanted before to be master; but I have got master now, and shall be master.'

There were no witnesses to this remark, to which Amos testified in court; at no time did Donellan confirm it.

On Friday 1 September, Theodosius's friend Fonnereau arrived and was allowed to view Theo's body. Fonnereau himself remains a shadowy figure. It was said that he lived in Northamptonshire, and there was certainly a Claude William Fonnereau, born in 1761 to William and Anne Fonnereau in Clapton, Northamptonshire, who would have been nineteen in 1780 and so would have been a contemporary of Theodosius. His brother, Charles William, was only sixteen, but could have been a riding or sporting companion to Theo. It was later implied by the prosecuting counsel that Theodosius was interested in Fonnereau's sister, and that the possibility of marriage had been mentioned, a marriage which would have certainly – if the couple had had children – taken the inheritance away for ever from Theodosia. Charles and Claude had two sisters, Harriet and Mary-Anne, but no other mention of Fonnereau's family was ever made and Fonnereau's connection to Theodosius ended after this visit. He was not seen again; he was not called to the trial; he did not give a deposition to the coroner.

On this Friday, however, no matter how silent Lawford Hall

appeared to be, the countryside around it was not. The first of the persistent rumours began to spread. Sir William Wheler, still at Leamington, testified at the trial that 'it was intimated to him … a suspicion of Sir Theodosius having been poisoned'.

Curiously, it was a full twenty-four hours before Sir William acted on this information. And, although a guardian to the dead boy, he did not go to Lawford Hall to see what was happening for himself or to comfort Anna Maria and Theodosia in their grief. Instead, on Saturday 2 September, he wrote his reply to Donellan's first letter telling him of Theo's death. It had taken Sir William three days to respond.

But most curious of all, considering that he had already been given a 'suspicion' of poison, was the text itself.

Lemington, September 2nd, 1780

Dear Sir,
I received the favour of your letter the day after my return to Mr Sitwell's. The sudden and very untimely death of my poor unfortunate ward gives me great concern, and we condole with lady Boughton, Mrs Donellan, and yourself, for his loss. I send a servant with this, to know how Lady Boughton and Mrs Donellan do after so sudden and great a shock. Please make our respects to them; at a proper time I shall make my respects to them and you in person.
I am, sir, your obedient and humble servant, Wm Wheler.

It was at best a holding letter, and one which was by now several days overdue; the sympathies were extended more to the ladies than to Donellan, as would have been proper. Perhaps Wheler's attentions were divided between two grieving families, his friends the Sitwells and the Boughtons? It would not have been expected of him to descend without invitation or notice; nevertheless, his concern for Anna Maria in particular is distant, bearing in mind that she had lost her only son and had no husband to support her. Interestingly, although Sir William notes that the death was 'sudden and very untimely' he does not ask for the exact details.

Wheler did nothing more that day. It was on the Sunday, 3 September, that he was really stirred into action.

The local vicar, the Reverend Piers Newsam – the same priest who had been seen speaking to John Donellan on the Saturday before Theodosius's death – arrived at Sir William's house with a letter (which was not available at the trial) from the Earl of Denbigh. Lord Denbigh, alias Basil Feilding, lived in the mansion of Newnham Paddox at Monks Kirby, equidistant between Lawford Hall and Wheler's own residence.

The arrival of such a letter from a superior being, one who was used to being both heard and obeyed, would have acted as a sharp warning. The Denbighs were aristocracy of a different calibre to the Boughtons: Basil Feilding was an earl whose title dated back three centuries. Earls could literally lord it over baronets. The Denbighs were also superior to the Boughtons in property, and their home – Newnham Paddox – was huge. (It was demolished in 1950, the then countess condemning it as a '365-room monstrosity'). Days of destruction were far away, however: in 1780 Newnham, then a superlative Palladian mansion, dominated the countryside.

And when the Denbighs spoke, the countryside listened.

To Sir William's consternation, the earl had picked up on the rumour of poison, a rumour that he himself had not yet acted upon. (There is no actual written or recorded evidence of the rumour or 'report' – other than what Wheler says in his letters and what he and others refer to at the trial.) In a flurry of sudden activity, Wheler sent for the apothecary, Powell. And then he wrote to Donellan.

Wheler's letter bears all the hallmarks of a man who has been, metaphorically at least, shaken by the scruff of his neck; he suddenly remembered that he was supposed to be looking after Theodosius. But again, it is quite remarkable that Sir William did not write on the day that the Reverend Newsam visited him. With Theodosius's body deteriorating quickly in the heat, and every hour precious if an autopsy was to be carried out with any accuracy, Sir William took another day to put pen to paper. His next letter to Donellan is dated 4 September:

Dear Sir,

Since I wrote to you last, I have been applied to, as the guardian of Sir Theodosius Boughton, to inquire into the cause of
his sudden death; and the report says that he was better the
morning of his death than he had been for many weeks, and
that he was taken ill in less than half an hour, and died in two
hours after he had swallowed the physic. There is great reason
to believe that the physic was improper … I find I am very
much blamed for not making some enquiry into the affair …

Next he went on to explain why he had called Powell:

… his character is at stake; I dare say it will be a great satisfaction to him to have the body opened … it will appear from the
stomach whether there is anything corrosive in it.

From here, the letter takes on a note of near panic:

As a friend to you, I must say … it is reported all over the
country that he was killed either by medicine or by poison. The
country will never be convinced to the contrary unless the body
is opened, and we shall all be very much blamed …

The body was still at Lawford Hall, about to be sealed in a lead
coffin.

Wheler then told Donellan that he had asked that 'Dr Wilmer
of Coventry or Mr Snow of Southam, in the presence of Dr Rattray
or any other Physician that you and the family think proper' should
perform an autopsy.

He added:

Mr Powell is now with me, and from his account it does not
appear that his medicine could be the cause of death; he has
not given him any mercury since June … Mr Powell says it will
be a great satisfaction to him to have the body opened, and for

the above reasons, I sincerely wish it. I will only add that this affair makes me very unhappy … I beg of you to lay this affair before Lady Boughton … to point out to her the real necessity of complying with my request, and to say that it is expected by the country.

I am … your sincere friend and obliged humble servant,
Wm Wheler.

One thing is very clear from this letter. Wheler's tone is not accusatory; there is no hint that he might hold Donellan responsible. The sense is that between the two of them, they must now contain a rapidly spreading lie. Wheler is 'very unhappy' but a very long way from crying 'Murder!' The letter is an attempt to make the family see and hear what he had been seeing and hearing outside Lawford Hall. The opening of the body was to quell rumour, a rumour that contended that Theo was 'killed either by medicine or by poison'; but the tone is all about containment of a rumour, not investigating a crime. And even if a crime were uppermost in Wheler's mind he did not at this stage suspect Donellan of having a part in it – or he would hardly have warned him, asked for his help or referred to him as a 'friend'.

It is also interesting that Wheler had been contacted by Lord Denbigh rather than Anna Maria. If her suspicions had genuinely fallen on her son-in-law, it is reasonable to suppose that she would have asked Wheler for help herself, or told him of her suspicions – after which Wheler would naturally have bypassed Donellan. But she remained silent.

One other element is also disturbing.

If Donellan himself believed that Theo had been poisoned, why didn't he himself act? Why didn't he tell Wheler how Theo had died in his first letter? Did he believe, instead, that the death had been natural? And what exactly was going on at Lawford Hall as the rumours spread about the countryside?

Donellan did not waste a moment in reply. He responded to Sir William the same day, telling him that the whole family 'most cheerfully' wished for the body to be opened. That afternoon

Wheler answered: two surgeons and Mr Powell should open the body as soon as possible. He continued, 'I hope that you understand it is not to satisfy my curiosity, but the public', adding, for the third time, his usual anxious proviso: 'to prevent the world from blaming any of us'.

It was getting dark that evening when the physician and the surgeon nominated by Sir William, plus another unidentified man, arrived at the house; they later testified that Powell, the apothecary, was already there.

David Rattray is listed in the Universal British Directory for Coventry in 1791 as a 'Doctor of Medicine'. According to the E. H. Cornelius Library of the Royal College of Surgeons, Rattray was forty-one years old at the time of this case and practising in Coventry, having obtained his degree from Edinburgh. In the Coventry Directory, Bradford Wilmer is listed as a 'Surgeon'. Having trained at St Bartholomew's Hospital in London, Wilmer went on to practise in Coventry for forty years. He had been – interestingly as regards the subsequent trial – a pupil of Sir John Hunter, the renowned anatomist. He had also become famous locally for reporting the curious case of Mary Clunes of Coventry: Mary, an alcoholic, had been found in her bedroom completely consumed by fire, 'leaving only the legs and all the other bones covered in a whitish ash' but with very little damage to the rest of the room.

But in 1780 neither a surgeon nor a doctor of medicine – no matter how lurid or famous their cases – were as we would recognise them today. The practice of medicine was largely uncontrolled by any official body – it was not until the Medical Act of 1858 that a register of qualified practitioners was published nationally and, even of those named then, only 4 per cent had a medical degree from an English university.

Surgeons such as Wilmer were licensed *only* to perform surgery, and then only in the presence of a physician like Rattray, who was *only* qualified to diagnose internal problems and was therefore there to act as his assistant. The whole profession was an overlapping medley of barber surgeons, surgeons, doctors, 'men-midwives', unqualified and untrained midwives, apothecaries and druggists, many of these jobs having sprung up in the previous century when medicine had been routinely combined with other employment – innkeeping and distilling among them. The profession of medicine was rising, but in 1780 it stood somewhere on the boundaries between experiment, folklore and scientific discovery. Donellan was opening the door to a profession – but not to professionals as we would recognise them.

In evidence later, cranking up the mystery a notch, Rattray said that he had received an anonymous note asking him to go to Lawford and 'open the body of Sir Theodosius Boughton'; it asked that he take Mr Wilmer with him.

The three men were met by Donellan – 'in the passage with a candle in his hand' – in the hallway of the house, where they noticed that Powell, the apothecary, was standing by the great table reading a letter. Turning to Powell, Donellan took the letter and saw that it was addressed to him. Apologising, Powell said that he had opened it by mistake (according to Donellan's later written *Defence*).

All five men went into the parlour while, upstairs, the lead coffin was being unsoldered. They were offered supper and, while they were eating it, Rattray read the letter that had been taken from Powell. It was from Sir William, saying that he himself would not come to see the autopsy because he 'conceived no person was proper to be there but the surgeon and physician sent for'. (There is no record of Wheler coming to Lawford until the funeral; a curiously detached response but one that would make sense if he had confidence that his instructions were being carried out by Donellan.)

Donellan was, meanwhile, searching in his waistcoat pocket for another letter, but instead pulled out an empty envelope. Afterwards, he insisted that he was looking for some more correspondence from Sir William which proved that he had the guardian's full confidence.

Rattray grew impatient. It was late; he 'wished to get over such little matters as these'.

Obeying Wheler's instructions that only the doctors should examine Theodosius's body, Donellan stayed at the foot of the stairs while they went up to perform the grisly task of viewing the corpse.

It did not take long.

Wilmer went into the room first; but he came back out again quickly. He had only looked at Theo's face, and 'expressed surprise that the body was so putrid; it would serve no purpose to open it'. But the other two wanted to form their own opinions, so the three men returned to the laying-out room together, only for Rattray to agree: 'the body seemed to us to be in such a very disagreeable state that we did not like to enter into the investigation of it, not knowing that any particular purpose was to be answered by it, except the satisfaction of the family.'

An amazing admission to modern ears: a doctor employed to carry out an autopsy says that a body is so revolting that he does not want to examine it. However, in 1780 it was believed that the odours alone from a corpse could be fatally infectious. More interesting is Rattray saying that he did not know that the purpose of the autopsy was to dispel the rumour of poisoning. Donellan had said nothing about that; nor had Sir William's letter, but it is odd that neither Wilmer nor Rattray nor their anonymous friend had heard the rumours. Wilmer later said that he would have certainly opened the body, 'disagreeable state' or not, if poison had been mentioned.

They went back downstairs to speak to Donellan, who quite correctly did not ask for their conclusions – those were for Sir William to hear first – and asked them instead, 'Shall you see Sir William Wheler?'

The two medical men disagreed later on what their reply was. Rattray insisted that he told Donellan that he had to go to somewhere called Brookswell the next day and so would not be going home that night; Wilmer flatly contradicted this, testifying that Rattray said he would see Sir William and 'give him an account of the business'. At any rate, Donellan was satisfied that one or both of the doctors would tell Wheler their conclusions, which he took to be that nothing could be proven by opening the body because it was too far decayed.

At the front door of the Hall, according to Donellan's *Defence*, Wilmer and Powell were given five guineas each for their trouble, and Rattray two guineas, as he had been perceived to be acting merely as an assistant. According to Donellan, Anna Maria appeared to bid the men goodbye, but she refused to pay them, saying that she carried no money with her. Donellan obliged instead.

The next morning, Donellan wrote again to Sir William:

Dear Sir,
I sent for Dr Rattray and Dr Wilmer; they brought another gentleman with them; ... upon receipt of your last letter, I gave it to them to peruse and act as directed ... I wish you would hear from them the state they found the body in, as it will be an additional satisfaction to me that you should hear the account from themselves.

The 'other gentleman' may have been Wheler's apothecary, Bernard Snow, but this was never specifically confirmed. Donellan then, for the first time, described what he thought was the cause of death:

Sir Theodosius made a very free use of ointment and other things to repel a large boil which he had in his groin. So he used to do at Eaton ... I repeatedly advised [him] to consult Dr Rattray ... but ... you will not wonder at his going his own way, which he would not be put out of ... Lady Boughton expressed her wishes to Sir Theodosius that he would take proper advice for his complaint; but he treated hers as he did mine.
John Donellan.

If this letter betrays a growing defensiveness on Donellan's part, and the first complaint at Theo's own difficult character, the day was not over yet. Donellan had another cause for distraction: the servants announced that yet another surgeon was at the door.

This was someone that neither Wheler nor Donellan had asked

for: Mr Samuel Bucknill, a local surgeon who had turned up of his own accord.

'I have heard that Dr Rattray and Mr Wilmer have been here,' Bucknill explained. 'I heard that they declined opening it on account of the putrid state it was in. If it is of any satisfaction to the family,' he went on, with some evident enthusiasm, 'I will at all events take out the stomach.'

Here was someone with no introductory letter, no invitation from the family; someone confident enough to knock on the door of Lawford and bulldoze his way through to Theo's corpse, dissecting instrument in hand. But Donellan had no knowledge of how well qualified Bucknill was to perform an autopsy; more importantly, he did not have Wheler's permission to use him. He prevaricated. 'It would not be fair,' he said, 'after Dr Rattray and Dr Wilmer had declined it, and they so eminent in their profession. It is impossible.'

Bucknill's reaction to Donellan's rejection of his services was to leave as abruptly as he had arrived; it is certain, given what happened the following day, that he went the six miles straight across the fields to Sir William Wheler.

Wednesday 6 September was the day scheduled for Theodosius's funeral. The latest fashion was for burial at night, but Theodosius's cortège was organised for three o'clock in the afternoon. It is likely that Donellan was responsible for the arrangements, as women were not usually welcome at such events – they were thought to be too emotional.

Donellan, by his own testimony, thought that he had fulfilled all that was required of him: he had allowed Wheler's nominated physicians to see the body and had given them the opportunity for a dissection. He had also confirmed, or so he thought, that Rattray would visit Sir William and tell him what they had found. Apart from that, he had no other instructions, so he went ahead and arranged bearers and stewards, and the coffin was re-soldered. The weather had not changed; it was still very hot.

Despite having taken charge of arrangements at Lawford Hall

since Theodosius's death, Donellan's position was uneasy. His mother-in-law was of no help; she had left everything to him to sort out. She had even refused to pay Rattray's and Wilmer's fees and, by her own admission at the trial, had not written to Theo's guardian. Nor had she asked Powell about the medicine; instead, she had questioned Donellan about his washing out the medicine bottles. Donellan's position was further undermined at the house when the servants were told by him – or so it transpired at the trial – to wash out a still that he had kept in his rooms for distilling rose and lavender water (a still that the prosecution would later contend had been used to distil lethal laurel water).

And then another letter arrived.

Lemington, September 6th, 1780.

Dear Sir,

From the letter I received from you yesterday morning, I concluded that the body of the last Sir Theodosius Boughton had been opened ... but find that they found the body in so putrid a state that they thought it not safe to open it ... I likewise find that a young man of Rugby, Mr Bucknill, did attend and offer to open the body, but it was not done ...

One can almost hear Wheler fuming with frustration. He added that he had not heard from either Rattray or Wilmer and that it had been Bucknill who had told him the story. As if despairing of Rattray and Wilmer, Wheler went on to tell Donellan to let Bucknill dissect the body, with a Mr Snow. He then jumped to the conclusion that Donellan or the Boughtons must have been afraid of the dissection being carried out in the house:

If there is any danger in opening the body, it is to themselves and not to the family. The body may be taken into the open air. Mr Bucknill is or was very desirous of opening the body.

I am, with respects ...

William Wheler.

His postscript had an even more frustrated urgency:

If Snow is from home, I do not see any impropriety in Bucknill doing it, if he is willing.

Bucknill had obviously made an impression.

Donellan replied at once, in a letter dated 'a quarter before one o'clock, Wednesday'. The house was full of mourners, and the drive with carriages and horses. He referred 'you, or anyone that pleases' to his previous letter, saying that he had let Wheler's doctors see the body alone and he asked that they let Wheler know what they had decided. He agreed that Bucknill had been at Lawford Hall, but that Sir William had not introduced him for, if he had, Donellan would have let him see the corpse. The letter was hurried, fraught:

The time fixed for burial is three o'clock today, if you please order to be postponed until the state of the body is made known to you … please let me know … if we do not hear from you we conclude you have seen some of them [the physicians] …

Not a word of reply was sent to Donellan by Sir William, even though a rider would have been able to reach him, and bring back a response, before three o'clock.

But a greater question remains.

As Theodosius's guardian, why wasn't Sir William Wheler at the house to attend the funeral? Had he been there, the authority to carry out the autopsy and to delay the funeral would have been his, and Donellan would have been relieved of this onerous – and soon to be damning – burden.

At two o'clock, with the lead coffin already brought downstairs and standing in the hall, Bucknill arrived back at Lawford.

Neither Rattray nor Wilmer came back, despite Donellan sending a servant out looking for them with a letter asking them to do so. There is no record in the trial transcript or in Donellan's *Defence* to suggest that Donellan ever received a reply; but the *Scots Magazine* of 1781 (edited by James Boswell) quotes a letter sent from the doctor, Wilmer, on 6 September in which he politely excuses himself from responding immediately, pleading an urgent 'midwifery case', but saying that he would go and see William Wheler if he got back from Coventry in time.

Rattray had only returned to his own home that morning after his visit away, and testified later that he had received a letter from Donellan begging him to go and tell Sir William the circumstances of the night of 4 September.

Oddly, Rattray did not reply to his messages, but at some time on the same day he did meet up with Sir William, at the 'Black Dog tavern'. In court later, he did not say when, nor did he say what kind of conversation they had. But neither he nor Wilmer went back to Lawford that day. Why Wheler did not absolutely insist on the doctors returning to the Hall to do their job is a puzzle.

Bucknill, of course, was a different matter. He turned up three-quarters of an hour after Donellan had sent his servant off to look for the other two doctors, saying that he had received a message from Sir William to come to Lawford and meet Mr Snow there so that Snow could open the body.

Donellan was standing in the hall.

According to later testimony, Bucknill asked, 'Has Snow arrived?'

'No,' replied Donellan. He must have hesitated or seemed confused, for the doctor's reply was impatient. 'Pray sir,' Bucknill insisted, 'have you received any message or letter from Sir William Wheler?'

'I have.'

'I have to meet Mr Snow here, and we are to get Sir Theodosius's body into the garden, or any convenient place we think proper, and we are to open it.'

Donellan made no move to comply. 'I have written to Sir William,' he said. 'And to Doctors Rattray and Wilmer. I am waiting for Sir William's orders.'

Something was awry here. Donellan *had* received Sir William's orders in his postscript: 'If Snow is from home, I do not see any impropriety in Bucknill doing it ...'

Bucknill was beside himself with impatience. He had a very ill patient two miles away; the funeral was not for another hour; Donellan would not give permission for the autopsy to go ahead until Snow arrived, and Snow was not there. He decided to go to his patient, saying that he would be gone at most an hour and a half.

But he was 'not ten yards' out of the door when a messenger arrived with the news that his patient appeared to be on the verge of death. Riding on with all haste, he was nevertheless overtaken within a mile by a servant who had galloped at breakneck pace from Lawford. Mr Snow had arrived at the house, he was told. They had missed each other by about three minutes. Bucknill now had to choose between the dying and the dead. He chose his living patient, rode on, and sent the servant back saying that he would return within the hour.

It was almost exactly three o'clock when Bucknill arrived back at Lawford Hall.

He was met again by John Donellan. 'Is Mr Snow here?' Bucknill asked.

'He is gone,' Donellan replied.

Bucknill, by his own testimony, was speechless.

'He has given us orders what to do,' Donellan said. 'I am sorry that you should have given yourself all this unnecessary trouble.'

Samuel Bucknill took his horse in utter disgust and 'rode away as fast as I could'.

Theodosius Boughton was not taken from his coffin that day. There was no dissection. The pallbearers hoisted the heavy lead coffin on to the carriage, and the procession to Newbold church began in the sweltering heat.

He was buried as arranged.

3

The Major Players
The Boughtons

'Nobility is a graceful ornament to the civil order'

Edmund Burke

'Those comfortably padded lunatic asylums which are known, euphemistically, as the stately homes of England'

Virginia Woolf

IT IS NOT OFTEN THAT A FAMILY DECIDES to put one of their relations in a bottle and throw them into a pond. Of course, if they are causing trouble in the neighbourhood, it is an interesting solution. The best thing to do is to herd twelve clerics together, each with a lighted candle, and have them exorcise a particularly haunted bedroom; after a few minutes, during which time all but one candle is blown out by the incensed ghost, the priests will succeed in cramming the ancestor into a glass phial. Then everyone can rush outside and throw the bottle into the bottom of a flooded pit.

It seemed to work for Sir Edward Boughton in the 1770s. Until then his ancestor One-Handed Boughton (he had lost an arm in an accident) had run riot in the darkened lanes around Lawford Hall. The story went that, in life, he had been fond of ravishing young women and 'acquiring neighbours' lands by fair means or foul'.[1] His ghostly arrivals were heralded by the noise of a cracking whip and loud shouts, followed by a phantom coach and horses hurtling past, One-Handed Boughton at the reins, resplendent in scarlet hunting jacket.

Time tends to distort. However, whether the legend of the thundering carriage was true or not, this Elizabethan Boughton seems to have caused some disturbances at the Hall. His locked bedroom, which no one would occupy come the eighteenth century, resounded with loud scrapes and bangs; servants – when any could be persuaded to enter – would find that the furniture had been mysteriously rearranged. In despair, Edward Boughton, the Sixth Baronet and Theodosius's father, had employed the twelve clerics to carry out the extraordinary ritual. And he really believed that it had worked. Out walking one day with his neighbour Sir Francis Skipwith of Newbold Hall, he refused to fish in the marl-pit pond, saying 'the spirit of his ancestor lay there.'[2] The colourful, tragic and complicated nature of the Boughton family, however, encompasses far more than just a troublesome ghost.

The Boughton baronetcy had been created in 1641, a gift from Charles I to William Boughton for his support during the Civil War. The title lasted 322 years. Although the first three generations of Boughtons had established a progressively powerful line, from the time of William Boughton, the Fourth Baronet, the dynasty was destined to be fraught with division, feud and scandal.

The Fourth Baronet – whose portrait reveals a fleshy face with irregular features, not improved by his supercilious stare – was born in 1663. He married twice, effectively creating two families: the children from his first marriage, to Mary Ramsey, and the children from his second marriage, to Catherine Shukburgh, existed on either side of an ever-expanding gulf, united by name alone. While Mary, having provided an heir, died young and quietly sank without trace from history, Catherine was an altogether different proposition. Seeing what she perceived as weaknesses in Mary's children, particularly the eldest son, she set out to exploit them.

Catherine had been in her early twenties when she had married William, twenty years her senior. Having come from a whole tribe of sisters, she was used to large families, but she had also learnt to 'divide and rule'. Having lost her own mother when she was barely five years old, she had grown up with a step-mother, Diana Verney. Whatever ploys she might have learned from Diana, she now used them to manage her own step-family, and she promptly engaged her own step-mother to look after William's children. William's eldest boy, Edward, was only twelve years old, but he grew up with little paternal influence; cosseted by his grandmother, Abigail, he had been left alone with her and his four sisters.[3]

Young Catherine now found herself as the matriarch of a family steeped in history. This was familiar territory: the Shukburgh family itself was influential. For centuries, the Boughtons had been high-profile figures at Court: the first baronet's grandfather had been 'Esquire of the Body' to Henry VIII, for which the parishes of Bilton, Dunchurch, Long Lawford and Newbold had tumbled satisfyingly into the Boughton coffers. Born in 1544 but fatherless by 1548, this ancestor – another William – had moved stratospherically up through society, his status propelled by confiscated lands.

He also married fantastically well; Jane Coningsby came from glamorous stock. Her father, Humphrey, was Gentleman Treasurer to Queen Elizabeth I, and her brother, Thomas, had been knighted after mustering troops in Normandy on Elizabeth's behalf. Thomas Coningsby's alpha-male stories were so famous that they had influenced an up-and-coming playwright, William Shakespeare, to write *Henry IV Part II*, after having read Coningsby's diary of the Siege of Rouen in 1591. The Boughtons were now allied with a powerful clan; the Coningsby estates included an imposing fifteenth-century castle on the river Lugg in Herefordshire, lucratively framed by 60,000 acres. William's wife remained more Coningsby than Boughton, however, all her life. When she died, Jane was not buried in the Boughton vaults in Newbold church, but in the exclusive enclave of Westminster Abbey, as was her daughter Ann. The slim, pale face on a Nicholas Hilliard miniature of Jane shows an expression of wry amusement – whether in judgement of the ambitious Boughtons, or simply satisfaction in her own sense of destiny, is debatable.

Like his Coningsby brother-in-law, William Boughton performed important duties for his monarch. In September 1586, after the Babington Plot to murder Elizabeth had been revealed, William Boughton was one of the men nominated by the Court to 'remove the Scots Queen'.[4] He dutifully shooed a distressed and disorientated Mary through Warwickshire, constantly moving her to prevent her supporters from finding her, obeying the chilling instruction to 'Remove without giving to her … any warning longer than two or three days and not shewing to her what place certain she shall go … according to the Queen's Resolution'. A month later, Mary went on trial for treason.

The Boughtons had always been stubbornly loyal to the Crown, even when it might have put their own lives in danger. The first baronetcy – two generations further on than the Coningsby–Boughton marriage – was a gift to a man who had stood by the doomed monarch Charles I even though support of the Royalist cause in Parliamentarian Warwickshire was folly (or courage, whichever way one prefers to look at it). Sir William had waved the Royalist flag just twenty miles from the Parliamentarian stronghold of Northampton, and the bloody conflict of Edgehill had been fought in October 1642 only twenty-five miles from Lawford Hall. It was said that Warwickshire was haunted by the screams of 30,000 men for a year afterwards, as a spectral battle raged nightly over the rolling countryside. But this was a haunting that William's wife would neither see nor hear; she died in her thirties, probably in childbirth.[5]

Catherine Shukburgh therefore married into a family with a mixed history: it is to be wondered which type of Boughton she saw when she looked at her new husband. Was this William an obsequious servant obeying every royal command, or a courageous man outfacing any opposition? Was he cast in the mould of the raping-and-pillaging One-Handed Boughton or the upwardly mobile William who had married Jane Coningsby? Was she to be the wife of a hero, or a fool? A countryman or a courtier? Her husband soon provided an answer. He refused a peerage, saying merely that he 'preferred the life of a country gentleman'[6] to that of Court. From this point onwards, the Boughtons were destined to be courtiers no longer.

Peerage or no peerage, Catherine demonstrated a keenly defined sense of reputation. On her instructions, a monument to both herself and William was raised in Newbold church, and the fourteenth-century tombs of Thomas Boughton, his wife Elizabeth de Allesley and Elizabeth's parents were moved into side aisles. On this Rysbrack memorial, William and Catherine stand side by side; between them sits a fiery urn, and three cherubs look affectionately down, representing three sons who died in infancy.[7] On the top of the memorial the Boughton coat-of-arms dominates, the three crescents echoing the design given to William's great-grandfather over eighty years before. 'Sir William Boughton,' reads the inscription, 'descended from an honourable and ancient family, but far greater in worth than pedigree, for he has left to posterity an example of a tender and most endearing husband, a kind and provident father, a generous neighbour and a constant reliever of poor at his gate.' It goes on to record his 'steady and untainted principle' as an MP and his 'zeal for the established church'.

Catherine and William's marriage was fruitful. They had seven children: Richard, Thomas, Katherine, Eliza, William, Charles and finally Shukburgh Boughton, born in 1703, the only son to survive beyond early adulthood. In the last days of 1708, William drew up a draft will.[8] It makes remarkable reading.

By this time, only two of his daughters by Mary Ramsey were still alive, but if they had hopes of sharing in their father's wealth with their step-brothers and sisters, they were to be disappointed. William left these eldest girls, Mary and Anne, 'all my Moneys and Efforts in Chambers in London divided between them' (this would have been a property occupied while he was in Parliament) but Catherine Shukburgh's children fared considerably better. Daughters Katherine and Eliza were each to receive £1,000 (equivalent to £78,000 today) when they reached twenty-one or on the day of their marriage (whichever happened first) and until then £50 (£4,000) a year 'for her maintenance'. William's eldest son by Catherine, Richard, was to receive £80 annually and a property called Bilton Hall (a home he was never to enjoy to the full, as he died in Lyons as a young man). As a kind of postscript, William remembered his own sisters Katherine and Abigail, giving them £80 a year for life. Everything else he left to his eldest son by Mary Ramsey, Edward, born in 1689 and now sixteen years old.

But even more astonishing than the vast gulf in the bequests are the alterations made to them subsequently. Still on the draft will, the generous amounts given to Catherine's daughters were left intact, but the bequests to Anne and Mary were crossed out in ink; the £80 per annum to William's sisters was an amendment, a previous sum which appears to begin with the letter 'h' (hundred?) being just visible beneath. There is also another puzzling omission: no mention was made of Shukburgh Boughton, Catherine and William's youngest son, even though he was five years old at the time.

William died eight years later, in 1716, by which time the will had been drafted yet again. This 1716 version stood. His sisters, who were by then both married, received £30 (not £80) a year; but his daughters by Mary Ramsey received nothing at all.[9] By contrast again, his daughter Katherine, by Catherine Shukburgh, received even more than in the first draft - £2,000 (£170,000) on the day of her marriage and £2,000 thereafter to be given to her as his executors saw fit.[10] The division in the family developed still further.

Edward, the heir from his father's first marriage, was now twenty-seven, and received all his father's estate. There was nothing that Catherine could have done about this: if Mary Ramsey's daughters had vanished from their father's bequests, Edward - as the first-born son - had to inherit. Edward subsequently married Grace, the eldest daughter of Sir John Shukburgh, Catherine's niece. Grace was at least ten years younger than her husband, and it is probable that Shukburgh family machinations, rather than romance, were behind the marriage.

Poor Edward had not had an easy life. Having lost his mother when he was five, he had then all but lost his father to Catherine Shukburgh a few short years later. He was the heir, but he was second best: by the time of his father's death his position in the household had been usurped by his half-brother Shukburgh, Catherine's adored only surviving son, who was by then thirteen. Edward rattled around Lawford in the company of his grandmother and older sisters; he was hardly the stuff of which Boughton legends were made. The fact that he was due to inherit everything in preference to darling Shukburgh reputedly drove Catherine to extreme measures. She hatched a plot, it was claimed, to bring Edward's life to a hasty close, whose details were alleged after his death.[11]

Edward collapsed and died, aged only thirty-three, in 1722. He and Grace had three surviving sons: Edward, William and Francis, of whom the eldest, Edward, was only three years old – another boy left without a father. Worse was to come, however, for the young boys. Grace, whose relationship with their father was later proved in court to have been unhappy, re-married within the year.[12] It is not known if she immediately moved out of the family home; but she rapidly began a large second family with her new husband, Matthew Lister.[13]

Grace's eldest son Edward was only seventeen, and at Oxford University, when he met his future wife. She was called Anne Brydges and to the dismay of the family she was thirty-five years his senior.[14] Within two years they were married, thus propelling the family into a legal battle where Catherine Shukburgh's influence was revealed. Before Edward's father had died so suddenly, he had rendered invalid his wife's jointure to various estates in Little Lawford, Newbold, Bretford and Little Harborough. Grace had not disputed this when he died, possibly because she had re-married so quickly, possibly because she felt that her young son would still look after her interests when he was an adult. However, she had not foreseen his marrying Anne Brydges. Grace seems to have had an ally in the Shukburghs, for it was Catherine's family who initially took up her cause, bringing a lawsuit to try and keep Grace's estates from Edward's wife. They evidently loathed her, blaming her for the public scandal.[15] 'The true reason for these lawsuits have been occasion'd by the Plaintiff's wife who by her cunning and artifice drew him in while he was at Oxford to marry her ... although she was then above sixty years of age, and without the knowledge of any of his friends or relations who afterwards were so exasperated with the old lady who is three years older then his grandmother ...' the Shukburghs ranted on, adding years to Anne's real age and finishing their accusation with the flourish: 'She stirred up these Unnatural Suits.'

At least they admitted they were 'unnatural'. The lawsuits were aggressively divisive, pitting mother against son. Edward was forced to defend his own father's actions, while the Shukburghs and Listers tried to argue that there was a simple, overwhelming reason why Edward Senior had disinherited his wife. It was not that he had been unhappy with her, they said, but because he had been a raging alcoholic and out of his mind. Edward was forced to rally a number of friends to testify that, although his father had indeed liked a drink, he had been sane. The depositions make jaw-dropping reading.[16]

'Sir Edward was always of good understanding,' testified Thomas Kipwell and James Caldecott, though adding, 'except when he was in Liquor when he was as all men are.' The local vicar agreed. 'The Plaintiff's father was a person of sound mind,' he said, 'but a little whimsical when in Liquor.' Richard Williams phrased it slightly more strongly: Edward used to drink to excess, he admitted; but he had 'good judgement'.

Edward himself was forced to testify as to his own father's character, even though he could not possibly have remembered much about him; and, in doing so, he made an astounding accusation. While agreeing that his father, when drunk, 'would remit some indiscreet notions', he claimed that the only reason that his father drank at all was because of his step-mother, Catherine Shukburgh. 'Lady Boughton,' he said, 'used all possible endeavours to keep him in liquor – with a view as is apprehended to kill him so that her own children which she had with Sir William might inherit his estate it being settled upon them upon failure of issue.'[17] He went on to say that his father had only been saved from drunkenness by going to stay with Catherine's father, Sir John Shukburgh, 'where he lived a sober life and behaved himself as well as any gentleman in the County'. The defence documents, however passionately phrased by Edward, still do not disguise the fact that his father had a serious problem. 'He was reputed a madman,' another less-than-helpful deposition asserts.

The lawyers' comments on these documents are almost as entertaining as the depositions themselves. Attached to the brief is a bill of their expenses for a single month, showing that they consumed £5 6s. 5d.-worth (£460 in today's money) of 'breakfasts, wine, cyder, ale and tea in the afternoon'. In the margin of the brief, one wrote, 'If (the opposition) should try to prove that Sir Edward rode from Bath without his hat or wig and in his mother's night-gown, contradict them.' They added that they knew that Edward had spoken to the 'lowest servants', adding, 'when intoxicated with liquor he would speak to any person'. It is a desperately sad description. Edward, hounded by his step-mother and married to a woman who seemingly had little respect for him (to judge by the court documents), remained forever a man capering about the countryside dressed in women's nightwear, being 'whimsical' with his friends and 'speaking to low persons'. However, whether he was alcoholic, indiscreet or just plain mad, Catherine's alleged ambition was achieved. Edward dropped dead at thirty-three.

His son did win the legal battle, but the parting was bitter.[18] His mother eventually left the area with her husband and was buried far from the Newbold family vault, at Burwell in Lincolnshire, in 1779. Edward and Anne were free to continue their married life in peace. His written household accounts demonstrate his attachment to her, but we shall never know the real reason why he chose such a mature woman as his first wife. Anne, although she had been married before to a Mr Arthur 'from London', had no children of her own, so perhaps her relationship with him was not so much as a wife as a surrogate mother to the teenaged Edward and his younger brothers. She may well have been in the house even earlier than 1738, as is suggested by a strange letter published in a newspaper by Edward when he was sixteen.[19] In this he offers a reward for the true identity of 'Tobias Swill', the author of a threatening letter which read: 'Sir Esquire, this is a warning to you that if you will not banish that damn'd old bitch of a housekeeper in less than a week, your house, your buildings, cattle, corn and fish ponds shall be utterl'y destroy'd and, if possible, your own great person … ' One wonders who was the 'housekeeper'? And who hated her enough to want her thrown out of Edward's house?

Sadly, but perhaps predictably, Edward and Anne's marriage did not last long. Anne Boughton neé Brydges died and was buried at Newbold church on 15 January 1750. She was sixty-seven, and Edward was thirty-one. Whether Anne had been truly loved as a wife, or rather more pragmatically as a surrogate mother, Edward's reaction to her death is clear from his notebooks: they descend into an illegible scrawl, and then lie empty. His life was, literally, a blank: a telling testimony to his loss.

By 1750, Catherine Shukburgh, who had been such a huge influence on the Boughtons, was also dead. Her son Shukburgh, the darling boy, had married Mary Greville in 1735 and they had already produced a large family, including four sons, of whom the eldest would take the Boughton baronetcy if Edward did not have children of his own. They lived at Poston Hall in Herefordshire, their progeny growing by the year, their eyes fixed on Warwickshire and Edward's alluring wealth and title. So, unless Edward now produced offspring of his own, Catherine Shukburgh's ambition to have her own son inherit the baronetcy would be fulfilled from beyond the grave.

By 1752, Edward Boughton started looking for a second bride.

4

The Major Players
The Cursed Quartet

'Men are what their mothers made them.'

Ralph Waldo Emerson

EDWARD BOUGHTON, born in 1719, was a countryman to his core. In the year in which he married Anne Brydges, 1738, his personal account books reveal his interests: he bought 'a great dog' for 10s. 6d.; a 'rule and compass' for 3s.; he repaired his carriage for 17s.; and he paid the blacksmith £2 2s.[1] A few repairs to the house by the carpenter cost him 3s. 10d.; he had a window box made for 10s., and he bought a brazier for £2 os. 6d. The only concessions to his having married Anne seem to be, later in the year, 'a box of soaps' bought for £1 3s. 6d. (which must have galled him, as it was more than he paid the butcher) and sixpence for 'a fiddler'. It is to be hoped that Anne retained some income of her own, because Edward was not exactly generous with his cash. She must have been underwhelmed by the lack of jewellery, clothes or furnishings. For a supposedly 'conniving woman', a box of soap is not much of a prize.

Even two years later, Edward's parsimony towards Anne does not seem to have improved. In May alone, he spent a vast amount on wine and cider - £16 9s. (£1,460 in today's money) - and £11 6s.

(the equivalent of £945) on himself; but the only feminine buy was 'a petticoat' for 9s. 6d. (£40), and even then it could have been for a servant.

There is a curious little anomaly, however, to this seemingly austere lifestyle. Someone at Lawford liked big gestures. Sometime between 1729 and 1739, two large paintings were commissioned from the Italian painter Jacopo Amigoni. Their subjects, Venus and Adonis and Flora and Zephyr, were depicted in an unashamedly romantic and sensual way, as barely draped figures locked in loving embraces beneath suspiciously English-looking oak trees. Did the otherwise undemonstrative Edward commission them for Anne; or did she commission them for him? Or were they ordered by that grande dame of the family, Abigail Shukburgh, who had looked after Edward as a child?[2]

Whoever commissioned them, the paintings were hanging at Lawford by the time Edward married his second wife Anna Maria in 1754. Perhaps they inspired him to be a little more outgoing. Whether from passion or just a desire to impress, he appears to have been more extravagant in his spending habits. The year shows a flurry of expensive buys: £13 8s. for 'a Turkey carpet'; £10 5s. for '2 mahogany chests'; £4 18s. for 'a screen'. In these accounts there are none of the scrawled, ink-blotted or even empty pages that followed Anne's death in 1750; rather, they are neatly written. In May, the month of his marriage, Edward dutifully notes payments to bell ringers and hired coaches, handkerchiefs, stewards at the church, ducks and chickens and fish for the wedding feast, together with a generous milliner's bill for £3 (over £270 today).

But most impressive of all was his purchase in March 1754 of the most luxurious item recorded in his account books: a diamond buckle costing £40 (£3,400 in today's money), presumably a gift for Anna Maria. This one item far exceeded his household bills for the month; the coachman, the housekeeper and the huntsman all earned less than £5 each in the first six months of the year.

In 1760, Edward prefaced his account book with a proud note of 'My Estate'.[3] It reads:

Warwickshire	£629 17s. 6d.
Northamptonshire	£37 8s. od.
Michaelmas rents	£644 14s. 4d.
Adson & Potterspury	£37 8s. od.

In fact, Edward had entered the estates brought to him by marriage twice. He made a correction, and totalled his 1760 income as £1,349 4s. 10d. This would be just over £100,000 in today's money – not poor by any standards, but comfortably off rather than very wealthy. His income had been reduced by his having to pay a land tax on Brownsover of over £71 a year, and it appears that he had also borrowed some money, as he had to pay a Mr Lamb a massive £560 (£48,000) in interest in 1744.

Nevertheless, the Boughtons seemed to live well. Their household bills covered the purchase of rabbits, lobster, salmon, fish, chickens, pigeons, eggs and a beehive; they paid washerwomen, labourers, coachmen, a weeding woman and a boy to deliver letters. They attended race meetings and balls; they gave 5s. regularly to the church collection plate; and they made a point of giving to the poor. 'Gave a poor man 6d.,' reads one entry on 28 July 1755, and 'gave a poor man 3d.,' writes Anna Maria a few weeks later.

But by far the most expensive household bill was for alcohol. In April 1755 alone Edward paid 15s. for ten pints of brandy. Comparing 1741 to 1755, Edward seems to have routinely spent over £1,300 in today's money at regular intervals for wine or spirits. However, this was not unusual; liquor was relatively cheap then and Georgian men had a rich diet and drank heavily – hence the preponderance of gout. Alcohol was a domestic and social given: in neighbouring Northampton, for instance, in 1750 there were sixty inns and alehouses for a population of 5,000.

Anna Maria's life was less concerned with the household bills; her entries list dressmakers, fabric, needles, ribbon – and 5d. for a pair of scarlet garters. In the year that her second son was born, she gave the nursemaid £1 4s. ('her second month's pay') and 2s. to the apothecary ('vials at Mr Powel's') who would figure so dramatically in years to come.

The overall expenses for the year 1761 were £1,475 7s. 2d. – over £110,300 in today's money. Expenses were exceeding income by over £100 a year.

The purpose of Edward's remarriage was to provide an heir, and the couple set about this task immediately. For 250 years, the name of the son and heir to the Boughton fortune had been either William or Edward – but it was a tradition that Anna Maria Beauchamp was not prepared to follow.

Anna Maria, described universally as 'an heiress', had been born on 22 October 1728, the eldest daughter of John Beauchamp and Elizabeth Shipton of Northampton.[4] The Beauchamps' second daughter, Elizabeth, named for her mother, was born in August 1729. Both girls were fit and healthy; but unfortunately the sisters that followed were not. Theodosia was born in September 1731 and died five months later. The following year, another child was born, in August; she too was baptised Theodosia, but her life was even shorter. She was buried in December of the same year. It seems that these deaths had a great impact on Anna Maria; when her own children were born she named them either Theodosius or Theodosia. Her influence on Edward must have been quite strong to overturn centuries of tradition in this way. Sadly, however, the pattern of early death was due to repeat itself.

Edward and Anna Maria's first-born little girl, Theodosia Beauchamp Boughton, was baptised at Newbold on 6 July 1757. The next child was another daughter, and she too was christened Theodosia: Theodosia Anna Maria Ramsay Boughton. Baptised on 2 September 1758, this second daughter tragically only lived three months. Two years passed, then, in August 1760, Theodosius Edward Allesley Boughton was born; a year later a brother arrived. Sadly Theodosius Willington Boughton, like his sister before him, lived only twelve weeks and was buried at Newbold on 2 December 1761.

Edward drew up his will, and did not alter it again.[5] To 'my dear wife Dame Anna Maria Boughton I leave all and every lands and common in Long Lawford … that my wife may enjoy the premises free and discharged.' On the event of his son Theodosius reaching the age of twenty-one, or being married before he was twenty-one, Anna Maria was to receive Brownsover Hall, 'with the gardens, orchard, grounds and meadows, and the Close and the Cottage Pasture'. This was to ensure that Anna Maria had a property of her own once Theodosius inherited. To his son, Edward left 'all my Real Estate' but, if he died, then it went to his daughter Theodosia – making Theodosia a potential heiress.

The unusual legacy of Edward's estate to Theodosia in the event of her brother's death was to seal the fate of John Donellan twenty-one years later.

However, no matter how 'dear' Anna Maria was to Edward, he was not the best of husbands to her in later years. While some of his time was respectably occupied as a JP for Warwick, the remainder was taken up with less admirable pursuits. Edward was fifty-one years old and had been married to Anna Maria for sixteen years when Abraham Turner, a tenant at Brownsover Hall, wrote to Shukburgh Boughton's wife, Mary Greville, in January 1770 about Edward's behaviour.[6] The emphasis by underlining is his:

> … I have parted with all my land at Brownsover except for 70s. a year and will get rid of that as soon as your <u>Good Nephew</u> gives me leave. I am informed his Lady lately catched him shut up with one of the maids which brought on a Violent Quarrel. Her Ladyship took an opportunity when <u>His Honor</u> was out to pack the maid off. Upon his return home and finding the maid gone, he went to bed in a great hurry by himself and would eat no supper. A great deal more is said but I believe what I have before say'd may be depended upon.

The situation had not improved six months later. In fact, it had become markedly worse. Abraham Turner continued his correspondence with Lady Boughton with a piece of sad gossip: 'your nephew Sir Edward keeps a mistress publickly and breaks his wife's heart.'[7]

Edward did not, then, set the best example to his son Theodosius, who was now ten years old and at Rugby School. Rugby was only four miles from Lawford Hall, so whether at home or at school, the public parading of his father's mistress, and the consequent misery of his mother, could not have escaped the boy.

Looking back to the First Baronet, Sir William, who was born in 1600, and through to his great-great-grandson Edward, the male Boughtons, with just one exception, all died at roughly the same age: William at fifty-six, Edward in his fifties, William again at fifty-two, and son William at fifty-three. One of the First Baronet's sons, Henry, had died in his thirties, but it was not until the Fifth Baronet, Edward, that we see an exceptionally early demise, at thirty-three. And so Sir Edward Boughton, Sixth Baronet, was following a family precedent when he, like his grandfather, died at fifty-three.

On 3 March 1772, two years after Abraham Turner's reports of his philandering, Edward had taken supper with the Reverend Hall – the same Reverend Hall who had officiated at the unusual exorcism of One-Handed Boughton just a couple of years previously. After they had eaten, the two men had decided to take a walk in the grounds of Lawford Hall. A local newspaper, the *Northampton Mercury*, reported on 16 March: 'They took a walk in Sir Edward's yard when Mr Hall perceived some signs of Uneasiness which led him to ask, what was the Matter? But, before any Answer could be given, Sir Edward dropped down dead.'

The *Coventry Mercury* reported five days later: 'Died suddenly at Lawford Hall Sir Edward Boughton, Bart. One of his Majesty's Justices of the Peace for the county of Warwick.'

However, the newspapers may not have been quite accurate in their reports. Many years later, the prosecution brief against John Donellan noted a potential witness called William Marriott: 'Marriott says that he was with Theodosius's father when he died and that he was a short-necked, full-blooded man and died as he was returning home from a Justice's meeting in a fit without any struggles or convulsions whatever.'

Whether it was Marriott or Hall who witnessed his demise, however, it is indisputable that Edward Boughton died very suddenly. Theodosia was fifteen and Theodosius was twelve. Their mother, who, until Theodosius came of age, was mistress of her own fortune again, as well as that of her deceased husband, was a widow at forty-four.

Lawford Hall entered a period of seemingly slow decline. On her husband's death, Anna Maria found that, although they owned extensive lands, much of the property was mortgaged. Alone and with two children to provide for, her financial situation clearly preoccupied her. Her son-in-law would later call her 'covetous', obsessed with money, and slow to pay. She appears to have employed a relatively small number of household servants for a titled estate: one coachman, one footman, one cook, one gardener and a few maidservants are all that are mentioned at the subsequent trial (although there may well have been more – normally it would have taken more than one coachman to run the livery for a country estate, for instance). When medical care was needed, Anna Maria turned to a local apothecary, Powell, rather than have a surgeon or doctor as her first recourse.

If an anecdote about a Mr Powell quoted in a book about the area at the time, M. H. Bloxam's *Rugby*, regarding the years beginning 1777, relates to *the* Powell in this case, it is revealing. The story, referring to a house used as accommodation for boys at Rugby School, relates: 'the house belonged to one Powell, a country apothecary, who went about in a drab suit of clothes, cauliflower wig and black-topped boots. Old Mother Powell was a regular skinflint.'[8] Thomas Powell and Thomas Clare are the only apothecaries listed in *Simmons' Medical Registers 1779–1783* for Rugby, so it is likely that the shabbily dressed man described here is the same Powell that tended Theodosius Boughton on his mother's instructions. Again, hardly the type of medical man one would associate with a baronet's family, but no doubt cheaper than a physician.

Although her prosecution lawyers later described Anna Maria's wealth as 'splendour', that was not accurate. She seems to have provided none of the extensive hospitality that Sir William and Catherine had once shown to their neighbours; Anna Maria went to Bath occasionally, and possibly to London for the season – it was necessary to put her daughter on display for the marriage market

– but there is no suggestion of Anna Maria being part of 'society'; no balls, no entertainments at Lawford are mentioned. Whether Anna Maria even kept up the age-old suppers and fairs for her tenant farmers at harvest time is also questionable. She was respectable, and she doted on her son. That much, at least, was accepted locally.

In 1775, Anna Maria decided to send Theodosius, then fifteen, to Eton. Until now, he had gone to Rugby School, where he had been first admitted in 1767, aged seven. The school had been founded in 1567 by Lawrence Sheriff, to whom Anna Maria's family, the Beauchamps, were distantly related: Anna Maria owned much of the land around Brownsover where Sheriff had been born. After a period of decay in the early 1700s, Rugby School moved to new premises twenty-seven years before Theodosius registered, by which time it had expanded to a roll of about 200 boys from all over England. Although the education that the boys received was well respected, discipline was severe and their living accommodation spartan: the Birching Tower and the old outdoor wash-houses attested to that. An old boy of the school, Albert Pell, was to describe it as 'cruelly comfortless' in his autobiography.

'Public schools are the nurseries of all vice and immorality,' wrote Henry Fielding in *Joseph Andrews* (1742). Many titled ladies resolutely refused to put their sons into what they considered to be harm's way: Lady Leicester of Holkham, for instance, insisted that her nephew take the Grand Tour and £500 a year rather than go to a public school that was, as she put it, 'a school of vice'. Theodosius would have entered Eton as a senior, where he would have expanded upon what Rugby had already taught him: a basic classical education accompanied by harsh discipline.

Eton exercised the law of survival of the fittest. It was physically demanding, not least in its punishments, and flogging by both masters and seniors was routine. The school was well known for its beatings. In the sixteenth century, Friday had been set aside as 'flogging day'; from 1809 to 1834 the headmaster, John Keate, used the birch unmercifully – on one occasion he is supposed to have publicly flogged eighty boys. In addition to this, the oldest self-electing society at Eton, 'Pop', administered private canings, known to be the severest punishment at the school.

At all boys' public schools at the time young boys were expected to 'fag' for the older ones in a form of humiliating domestic slavery. The poet Samuel Taylor Coleridge complained that at his school, Christ's Hospital, 'the boys tormented me' ; another pupil reported that he was woken regularly by a senior boy stubbing out his cigar on his face. Gambling, drunkenness and violence were commonplace, but occasionally the boorish behaviour overstepped even Eton's boundaries: the militia were called in more than once to keep order. The historian Edward Gibbon commented sourly, 'the mimic scene of a rebellion displayed in their true colours the ministers and patriots of the rising generation.'[9] These were boys from privileged backgrounds who, to keep up appearances and status, created mayhem, running up bills that their parents were expected to pay at the end of each term. Theodosius, however, was kept short of money; in the *Defence* Donellan noted that 'Lady Boughton allowed her son 18 pence a week when first there and half a crown thereafter … an allowance not suitable to his birth and fortune,' adding that, as a result, Theodosius borrowed money locally, thereby increasing his debts.

But Theodosius's debts were the least of his problems. He 'sank into debauchery'[10] and contracted venereal disease in his first year at Eton. In July 1777, the newly married Donellans visited him at school, and, according to an article in the *Northampton Mercury* of 23 April 1781, found him lodging at the house of one Mrs Roberts where he was 'in a deep salivation from the Venereal Disease whilst under the care of a Mr Pearson, Surgeon'. 'Salivation' – by which mercury was given in sufficient quantities to produce sweating and large quantities of saliva – was the standard treatment for the disease at the time.

A horrific case of the effects of mercury was reported in the *Hull Packet* newspaper of 1 November 1803. A child of three, Thomas Clayton, had been given Ching's Patent Worm Lozenges containing a white panacea of mercury, despite the travelling salesman who had sold them to his parents insisting that 'not one particle of

mercury' was in them. The poor child went into a state of high salivation – drooling, flushed and spotted complexion, convulsions
– and died in 'indescribable torments'.

Self-medication was common enough at the time and the newspapers were full of patent remedies, the sale of which was unregu-
lated by a government which none the less levied a duty on every
bottle sold. Nor did medical care improve with any noticeable
rapidity in Warwickshire in the late eighteenth century. A document
now in Warwick Records Office records one doctor's prescriptions
to the Ward-Boughton family in 1790: 'a halfpenny-worth of black
treacle applied to each side of the head until the rag drops off' for
violent headaches and 'a fresh ivy leaf applied with fasting spittle
each morning' for corns on the feet.

In the *Northampton Mercury* of 7 May 1781, 'anti-venereal diuretic
vegetable drops' were advertised, 'famous in curing every species
of venereal infection in bottles at 10s. 6d., 6 shillings, 4 shillings
and two shillings each'. In October of the same year, the newspaper advertised Fothergil's Chymical Nervous Drops, supposedly a
cure 'for those who have polluted themselves with Secret Venery',
who 'may have their Constitution Strengthen'd for 10 shillings 6d.'.
More chilling is the advertisement for Leake's Pilula Salutaria in
December 1773, in which a Mr Marshall of Northampton claimed
an absolute cure for venereal disease 'should the Malignancy be
ever so great. Effecting a cure where salivation fails in boxes for 2s.
6d. each.' Mr Marshall, in common with all his colleagues and com-
petitors, did not say what was in his super-strength 'Pilula Salutaria'.

These are the types of self-medicating 'cures' which Theodosius
would have bought or had prescribed to him, and which Donellan is supposed to have referred to as reported in the *Northampton
Mercury* of 23 April 1781: 'On the Saturday preceding the Death of
Sir Theodosius, The Rev. Newsam took Notice to Mr Donellan
that Sir Theodosius appeared much worse than usual, which Mr
Donellan, by Way of Reply, said he did not wonder at, for that he
was continually quacking himself with Mercury.'

In the summer of 1777, when Theodosius was almost seventeen and very soon after the Donellans' visit to Eton, Anna Maria

brought her son home. It was reported in the newspaper that 'Mr & Mrs Donellan received several letters from Lady Boughton in the first of which she tells them that she had fetched her son from Eton, and had placed him under the care of a Mr Clare, an apothecary at Rugby, plain proof that he was not then well; and in all the rest she complains of her son's irregularities and says that blotches appeared upon his Face, and that he had lost his fine Complexion and that he was taking Things for his Complaint.'

A letter survives which shows that Theodosius also went to stay with the Donellans in Bath for a while.[11] It seems that Theodosius was not interested in education. What he *was* interested in was hunting and fishing, drinking and fighting, brawling over imagined insults and generally running riot in the countryside. In the same article, the newspaper continues that 'he was engaged in several disputes and quarrels, one or two of which were near to be carried to serious lengths had not Mr Donellan stepp'd in and prevented them.'

Following several requests from Anna Maria, the Donellans left Bath in June 1778 and went to live at Lawford Hall. The *Northampton Mercury* reports that Anna Maria employed a tutor, a 'Mr Jones, near Northampton', for Theodosius for five months, until November 1778. But when Theodosius returned to Lawford, his health was no better. The newspaper goes on: 'On Sir Theodosius's return from Mr Jones's, he was so much altered in his Countenance and Person that Mr Donellan suspected he had contracted a fresh Venereal Complaint; and therefore, merely with the View of recommending a skilful Surgeon to him, he took an opportunity of questioning him ... At first he seemed unwilling to give any answer, but at length confess'd that when he went to Mr Jones's he was not well in his Old Complaint, and that while he was there he used a great Deal of Mercurial Ointment.' The paper adds the rather poignant detail that Theodosius admitted to using so much that he wore flannel drawers in bed every night 'in Order to prevent a Discovery upon the Sheets'.

John Donellan, the newspaper concludes, was convinced that Anna Maria would not employ a reputable surgeon to help

Theodosius; instead she bought him a book called *The Family Physician*, from which Theodosius 'was continually quacking himself' – in other words, dosing himself up with inappropriate 'cures'. But Theodosius compounded his problem by contracting another infection and, according to Donellan, 'had nearly destroyed his Constitution' by 'unfortunate Connections with different Women'.

The 'unfortunate Connections', quarrels and scrapes continued at Lawford. In his written defence published after his trial, Donellan gave an example of his care for the boy. One afternoon, Theodosius had asked the vicar of Newbold for the key to the church tower, saying that he wanted to climb to the top. Donellan went with him and, when they reached the top, Theodosius decided to try and turn the weathercock. As he climbed up, his foot slipped and he fell; Donellan reached out to catch him, but Theodosius fell backwards on to Donellan, winding the older man severely. On the way home in the coach, Theodosius told his mother what had happened, adding, as Donellan writes, 'he must have been killed, if his brother had not saved him.'

Theodosius Edward Allesley Boughton was a worrying, obstreperous boy. His royal confidant ancestors were a distant memory; even his great-grandfather's 'valuable qualitys so effectually recommended to the esteem and favour of the county' – an inscription on the Rysbrack memorial which Theodosius would have seen in church every Sunday at home – rang hollow now. Theodosius was the son of a father who had broken his wife's heart, and the grandson of a man who had dropped dead of alcoholic excess aged thirty-three.

The Boughtons were a family of dramatic opposites, of glorious highs and ignominious lows. Unfortunately, it looked as if Theodosius was set on the latter course.

While Theodosius was at Eton, his sister Theodosia had continued to live at home with her mother. The future for a sister whose brother was due to inherit the estate on which she lived could be a precarious one. Gertrude Savile, for instance, who lived in nearby Nottinghamshire in the early 1700s, complained of 'the baseness of the dependence on my brother'. Left penniless when her brother had inherited everything, she had been 'forced to grovel to Sir George for every gown, pair of gloves, every pin and needle', and complained that 'If it was possible to get my bread by the meanest and most laborious imployment [*sic*] I would without dispute choose it.'[12]

Dependent sisters were also a drain on finances. If Theodosius had ever married, Theodosia would have fallen even further down the food chain, behind his wife and their children, an embarrassment and a financial liability. She might have moved out to live with her mother in Brownsover Hall, but even then both women would have looked to Theodosius for money to maintain their family name.

Anna Maria, therefore, was faced with more than one problem. Not only did she have a son whose sole purpose in life seemed to be to keep bad company – which did not bode well for the Boughton fortune – but she also had a daughter whose reputation she must protect. Theodosia, if married, would at least have a husband to look after her; and Anna Maria no doubt gave some thought to the idea that a full-grown man with some sense of the world could give proper guidance to the fatherless Theodosius as well as – most importantly – provide for her daughter.

Theodosia would not have had much of an education, but, bearing in mind her brother's track record at Eton, she was probably better informed than him. Ladies were expected to be proficient in needlework and craftwork (there was a strong fashion at the time for the latter in particular); and they would have been schooled in a little French (but not the classics). Theodosia would have been expected to learn from other society ladies how to deport herself, dance, hold a lively conversation, and to know something of the arts. The aim was to charm general company, keep chaste until marriage (though not necessarily faithful after it) and be well schooled in 'the graces'.

As early as 1774, however, the *Lady's Magazine* railed against sending a girl away to be 'educated' in this way: 'Nothing can justify such monstrous indifference! What is called a genteel education by some, which is very different from a good one, can only prepare a young person for an early defeat.' In the same vein, it struck out against vacuous preening, as opposed to skills: 'She never hears a syllable about her understanding, judgement, or mental endowments.' Proto-feminist Mary Wollstonecraft went further: '[Girls] are only anxious to inspire love, when they ought to cherish a nobler *ambition, and by their abilities and virtues exact respect.*'

It was an age of the kind of display of which Wollstonecraft despaired. Lord Chesterfield, writing to his illegitimate son Philip Stanhope, in *Letters to His Son: On the Fine Art of becoming a Man of the World and a Gentleman* (1749), while insisting that Philip should be of a responsible, serious frame of mind, nevertheless encouraged him to develop a certain artful playfulness, the code by which high society operated. He repeatedly recommended 'graces' that a gentleman should refine. Quoting the philosopher John Locke, he advised, 'You will find the stress that he lays upon The Graces, which he calls good breeding ... Study hard; distinguish carefully between the pleasures of a man of fashion, and the vices of a scoundrel; pursue the former and abhor the latter, like a man of sense.' Theodosius's behaviour fell very short of that.

Chesterfield's opinion of women, however, was low. 'Vanity is their universal, if not their strongest passion,' he wrote. Money was not to be wasted on educating them or sending them on the Grand Tour; they were only important as introductions into the *beau monde* and, as such, they had to be flattered and cajoled into acting with sense.

Girls like Theodosia usually 'came out' into society aged about fifteen or sixteen, sometimes younger (in Eliza Haywood's didactic novel *The History of Miss Betsy Thoughtless* (1751) the heroine's adventures begin when she is fourteen). In the 1720s Daniel Defoe had already sneered at the 'daughters of the gentry carrying themselves to market',[13] while Lady Mary Wortley Montagu's description of Sir John Vanbrugh's attempts at finding a wife in 1713 is not flattering: 'I believe last Monday there were 200 pieces of Woman's Flesh, both fat and lean.'[14] Some writers, like Mary Wollstonecraft in her 1792 pamphlet *A Vindication of the Rights of Women*, condemned the flagrant sexual parading of single women and their mothers: 'What can be more indelicate,' she asked, 'than a girl's coming out in the fashionable world?'

Young women were certainly preyed upon at public gatherings, and a mother had to distinguish between the admiration of a gentleman and the leering advances of an adventurer. Society in Bath was no exception. Tobias Smollett's character Matthew Bramble complains that it was crowded with 'Vulgars … a very inconsiderable proportion of genteel people are lost in a mob of impudent plebeians.'

At least Anna Maria had relations in Bath on whom she could rely: her sister and brother-in-law, the Shiptons. And Bath *was* exciting, compared to Warwickshire. The city was in communication with a wider world: coaches ran daily to all the major areas of population. The place was buzzing with entertainments; beside the regular assemblies, parties and balls the *Bath Journal* in the 1760s advertised such delights as a 'Troop of Equestrians in Egyptian Pyramids', stage plays at the Lower Rooms and the Theatre Royal, a display of 'Fireworks by Signor Invetto', 'Dancing Displays by Master and Miss Michael', and 'Miniature Portraits Painted by a certain Mr Lightfoot' ('whose performances need no comment'). There were all kinds of things to lavish money on, too: from gold and silver writing pens, harpsichords and Dutch tulips to the more mundane 'elastic saddles' and 'shamoy leather socks for the prevention of chilblains'.

It is quite probable that Anna Maria and Theodosia also visited London; the season began in the New Year and went on until the end of April or so. It was considered that any gentleman of note had a 'town house' and a 'country house'. The Shukburgh side of the family certainly had a place in London; and in later years Theodosia herself would live in Portland Street and her cousins the Rouse-Boughtons in Devonshire Place during the season.

Georgian society was quite different in character from the public restraint and industry of the Victorians, and the hub of it all, London, was a very seductive lure for minor gentry from the provinces, male and female alike. At the head of London society was the

Prince of Wales, son of George III; by the time he had reached the age of eighteen in 1780 he had already set the tone for gambling, whoring and drunkenness. By the mid-eighteenth century London society was gripped by gambling fever: fortunes were both made and lost at pharaoh, quinze and piquet – thousands of guineas changing hands every night. The prince also led by example when it came to women: he publicly frequented brothels and early in his life had affairs with other men's wives, the Duchess of Devonshire and the Countess of Salisbury among them. Following his example, male members of the aristocracy frequented prostitutes as a matter of course.

But Anna Maria would not have taken Theodosia to London just to see and be seen; she would have been looking for a wealthy man for Theodosia to marry. London was the heart of government, and the aristocracy had a stranglehold on public finances and appointments. By 1720, a quarter of the peerage held government or Crown office, and being appointed to public office made the fortunes of men like Marlborough, Cadogan and Sir Robert Walpole. James Brydges made a profit of £600,000 from his time in the post of Payments General of Forces Abroad from 1705 to 1713. Anna Maria may have seen that there might be rich pickings to be had, and she would have leapt on invitations to dine and socialise, if only in the cause of a good marriage for her daughter.

If this was her aim, however, it fell rather short. In the season of 1777, it did not reach the peerage. It fell instead on a lowly commoner, although a glamorous one. Into the Boughtons' world stepped Captain John Donellan, Master of Ceremonies at the fashionable Pantheon Assembly Rooms in Oxford Street. He was a man of the world who had returned from soldiering in India with a reputation for both bravery and fortune-hunting. He was about to use both attributes to devastating effect.

5

The Major Players
John Donellan

'Money's a horrid thing to follow, but a charming thing to meet.'

Henry James

'LONDON,' WROTE THE DIARIST BOSWELL in December 1762, 'is undoubtedly a place where men and manners may be seen to the greatest advantage. The liberty and whim that reigns there occasions a variety of perfect and curious characters …' If London was driven by liberty and whim, and populated by curious characters, John Donellan must have felt quite at home. Not that he wanted to stand out as a curiosity; rather that he was perfectly placed to take advantage of the time and the place. A former officer in the Indian Army, he still went by the title of captain when he met Theodosia. She and her mother would have seen a man in the prime of his life: slim, handsome, sociable, a 'gallant', a man of the world. And, if his stories were to be believed, an outstandingly brave one, too, who had gained a reputation for courage in the service of the East India Company.

John Donellan was also a good storyteller – and he had to be. Back in England in the mid 1760s, he had had to fight for his entire reputation. Having served in the Indian wars with the French, he had argued his case against a court-martial ruling made against him for accepting bribes for passing on looted goods that had resulted, according to Donellan, from a chain of misunderstandings.

In his evidence to the directors of the East India Company,[1] he presented a version of the battle of Masulipatnam in the Indian province of Golconda in 1759 – and, tellingly, a version that appears in no other record of the event – that showed him in an extraordinary light. He had, he said, rescued his commanding officer, Lieutenant-Colonel Francis Forde, from a tight spot during the battle and then had, with the aid of a French spy, entered the French headquarters and single-handedly persuaded its commander, the Comte de Conflans, to surrender.[2] Donellan admitted in his statement to the court that his version might sound immodest – 'how ill a grace [is] a man who is the blazoner of his own deeds,' he acknowledged, 'but there are occasions where modesty would be culpable and silence an injustice to oneself.'

His story was not just immodest, it was unbelievable. But then Donellan was nothing if not imaginative – inventing and reinventing himself was one of his major skills. His version of events was not quite the one that made it to the history books. The battle was a decisive victory for the English, after which Forde negotiated with the Indian ruler, the Nizam of Hyderabad, to maintain the territory free of French troops in return for an annual income of 400,000 rupees. The region thus secured, the English went on to win the Siege of Madras, and the French were subsequently driven from India, allowing the English Crown to seize this massive and lucrative subcontinent.

In his evidence to the directors, Donellan undoubtedly felt that he ought to be given considerable credit for the victory, and was evidently prepared to face down any gasps of astonishment. 'Mr Donellan,' he said, referring to himself in the third person and as Mr, not Captain, 'cannot but consider this important service as principally resulting from his presence of mind.'

He then went on to justify his subsequent actions, for which he had been brought to court. He and some fellow officers had commandeered a large cache of valuables and 'were proceeding to turn them to best account for their employers [i.e. the East India

Company] when they received a verbal order from the Colonel to deliver certain black merchants such effects as they should claim for their property.'

Donellan claimed that these men were not Armenian traders caught in the conflict, as Forde suggested, but French in disguise. He refused the order. 'A warm altercation ensued', and it became obvious that the 'order' was a ruse by the Bannyan[3] and the 'merchants' to obtain the booty. Nevertheless a written order came back from the colonel, and vast amounts of loot, 'some marked with the cipher of the French East-India Company, and chests of treasure', were taken away.

In court Donellan protested that this was an outrage; to make things worse, Forde would not speak to him. Although the goods were returned to the merchants, Donellan accepted £50 from them for his trouble. It was for this that he was being court-martialled. He could be forgiven here for feeling that he was being unjustly treated – the booty of war was considered fair game for the badly underpaid British army officers in India.[4]

Donellan then testified to a really extraordinary twist of events. The defeated French general, Conflans, apparently asked him to join his own army. Conflans made 'many tempting offers and opened to him the most alluring prospects', Donellan insisted, but despite all the injustices he had suffered, he stayed loyal to the British Crown. He paints a noble picture of himself: 'But neither the resentment for the wrongs that had been heaped upon him – over-looked, degraded, every studied indignity thrown upon him – could make him for a moment forget his duty to the Company or his allegiance to his natural Sovereign.'

Donellan, along with several other officers, was found guilty and stripped of his rank. Although the others were later reinstated to their rank, Donellan was not. He returned to England. For a while he nursed his 'injustices' – for, it would appear, at least eight years – but then he decided to try for a commission in the cavalry in 1767 or 1768. He could not, however, obtain this without a clean bill of military health. The East India Company sent a verbal message that his conduct had been considered blameless in India.

His commission was returned; however, he still needed his commanding officer Forde's 'certificate of good behaviour'. He wrote to Forde saying that he hoped 'a trifling misconduct would not bar his advancement in life'. But Forde refused to endorse him.

It would not be the last time that Donellan pleaded his innocence in the face of intransigent authority.

Donellan was put on the half-pay list and for ever afterwards referred to himself as captain; but he never completely removed the stain to his character. Forde, in opposition to his senior commanding officer, Lord Clive, would not say outright that Donellan's behaviour was unacceptable; but neither would he put pen to paper to agree that Donellan had been 'courageous'. (Clive, at least, did send a letter to Donellan in September 1761 saying that he had showed courage in an expedition to Golconda.) There is no evidence that Forde ever supported Donellan, or even forwarded the verdict of the original court martial at Masulipatnam to the East India Company. As a result, Donellan did not apply for another military posting: his career as a serving officer was over.

He was now forced to apply his talents in another direction.

John Donellan had been born on 6 November 1737 in County Clare, Ireland, the illegitimate son of Colonel Nehemiah Donellan who was the commanding officer of the 39th Regiment. The O'Connor Donellan estate papers of County Galway list the family pedigree: one James Donellan was Nehemiah's father, and Nehemiah himself pursued an active military career, having been wounded at the battle of Fontenoy in May 1745 in the War of the Austrian Succession. John Donellan was acknowledged and treated well by his father, who obtained him his post in the East India Service.

A surviving print of Donellan, drawn at the time of the Boughton trial, with the title 'Published as the Act directs, 1st May 1781 by I. Walker' shows him in profile: he has a clean-shaven and youthful face, with a high forehead, and he is wearing a fashionable cutaway coat and a white stock with a small frill at his throat. Another pen-and-ink drawing shows him facing the artist with a rather bemused smile. Donellan looks like an intelligent, even kindly, person. In

1882 Edward Allesley Boughton Ward-Boughton-Leigh, Theo-dosia's grandson, described him as a 'good-looking man ... very handsome'. Another print, currently in the Lewis Walpole Library at Yale University, of the Pantheon Assembly Rooms shows a figure leaning on a column in the left foreground who is generally believed to be Donellan. Rather shorter than average and slight in stature, he stands with one hand slightly behind his back and the other in his breast pocket, reminiscent of popular depictions of Napoleon. He is looking towards a couple who are talking to his left; his air is proprietorial, and he has the same slight smile on his face.

The London that Donellan returned to from India in the 1760s was a place of marked contrasts. Visiting the city in 1780, the Prussian traveller Johann Wilhelm Von Archenholz wrote that London was markedly divided between east and west: to the east, along the Thames, were old, narrow streets of cramped houses, the scene dominated by wharves, and yards. 'The contrast between this and the West End is astonishing,' he wrote,' the houses here are mostly new and elegant, the squares superb, the streets straight and open.'[5] Now was the time when Georgian London's most imposing developments came into being: Portman Square, Bedford Square and Portland Place were all built between 1764 and 1778.

London was crowded, rapacious, bawdy. The seat of royalty and at the very heart of trade and government, it was, at the same time, a city of drunks, whores and desperate poverty. Its houses were overcrowded and its slums, like St Giles, stank; its roads were mostly unpaved and unlit. It was a place where children as young as seven or eight were plied as prostitutes, where Hogarth's Gin Lane was a living reality, and street singers on every corner were applauded for songs that would be regarded as obscene even today. There were, Von Archenholz records, 8,000 alehouses and over 50,000 prostitutes in the city.

Yet the capital city also had a spirit of grace, of Reynolds beauties, of ceremony and wealth, and it prided itself – as all England did – on being strong and powerful. England had the largest navy in the world and was engaged in wars on various fronts; it was a fighting machine, hardy and ingenious. Its countrymen were represented not only by the swagger of the ex-military man, but also by the rake and the fat alderman gorging himself on beefsteak and porter at breakfast. Visitors to London were sure to see three qualities that summed up England: a fighting, brawling, industrious spirit; conspicuous greed and sensuality; and abject poverty.

More than anything else, London was a city of social mobility at every level. But you would have had to have been a very dull man indeed not to understand that every strata of society had its grades. There was a gulf between the lowly baronet and the elevated duke, between the poor curate and the bishop, between the colonel and the foot soldier: but the hurdles were there to be jumped. Most difficult of all to bridge, however, was the chasm between an ordinary gentleman and a titled aristocrat. There was one obvious way to circumvent that: marry into a titled family.

Marriage might have been an alluring passport to high society for a man like Donellan, but it was not needed at all for a few low-born girls. These rose to fame, if not a lifetime's security, as the mistresses of wealthy men. In the Restoration Court of Charles II a hundred years before, it was said that no man could achieve power or recognition unless he had a mistress. That air of manly potency was vital to his reputation. In the Georgian era, a wife's infidelity was grounds for divorce, but a man's was not – although divorces were rare, since they required an Act of Parliament. Mistresses were widely accepted, even for men of the church. One astonishing example was Archbishop Blackburne, who brought his mistress, Mrs Cruwys, to live under his own roof, where she queened it at the head of the table whenever his wife was absent. Man of letters Horace Walpole recalled an occasion on which Cruwys was at dinner with Blackburne's illegitimate son by another liaison. Blackburne's affairs were ignored, however: he was chaplain to royalty. According to Walpole, the illegitimate son later became the Bishop of London.

So illegitimacy was not frowned upon then as it was to be in later years. As mentioned, John Donellan himself was illegitimate; Philip Stanhope, the adored son to whom Lord Chesterfield addressed his numerous letters, was illegitimate; Joseph Addison, friend of the Boughton family, had a son by the Countess of Warwick; Lady Harley had so many children by her various lovers that her offspring were called 'the Harleian Miscellany'; and the illegitimate daughter of Sir Edward Walpole married Lord Waldegrave and, later, the Duke of Gloucester.

Marriage among the aristocracy was rarely an affair of the heart – the idea of romantic love had yet to take precedence as a reason for wedlock – and when that new form of entertainment, the novel, talked of romance the very concept was howled down as derisory and dangerous. Marriage in high society was an alliance of families designed to ensure that land, revenue and power remained within the grip of the few. An aristocratic woman was required to be chaste before she married, but in society in 1760 she was merely required to be discreet after the wedding; husbands maintained mistresses and wives took lovers, and the whole understanding of the way society worked was based on a wife providing heirs rather than emotional support, and of husbands procuring, maintaining and often abusing ordinary women.

The Victorians did indeed subsequently feel ashamed of the raucous sensuality of their ancestors, and tried to erase it. Leading radical Francis Place, born in London in 1771, spoke in his autobiography of conversation even in his home being 'coarse and vulgar' and 'remarkably gross'. His son actually tore some pages from his papers when they were donated to the nation, leaving the embarrassed comment 'much licentiousness'.

Women who made their name through sex dominated society and were known as the 'Toasts' – the toasts of the town. They are relevant to Donellan in more ways than one, for the work that he was about to become engaged in required that he knew the distinction between aristocrats and fantastically wealthy courtesans.

The captain did not go unnoticed. In fact, he deliberately drew attention to himself. Although he maintained that he was not in any way at fault during his time in Masulipatnam, and was prepared to testify that not only did he take no booty of war from the city but he had also had his £50 fee taken from him at the court martial, he seemed to have enough money not only to mix in high society in London and dress well, but also to sport a large diamond ring that earned him the nickname 'Diamond Donellan'. At the trial, local Warwickshire and Northamptonshire newspapers would say that this ring was part of his spoils of war from India. 'He returned to Europe with a large sum of money and several valuable gems,' noted the *Nottinghamshire Gazette* in 1781. 'To his companions he used to boast of Secret Services ... ambition was his ruling passion ... play and gallantry he pursued ...' However he had come by his money, Donellan was now wealthy enough to buy a part share in a new business venture – the Pantheon.

The Pantheon had been devised and the process of building it begun by Philip Elias Turst, the owner of some land on the south side of Oxford Street, and a 'lady of means', Margaretta Maria Ellice. Ellice claimed that she had been connected with another extravagant place of entertainment just a few hundred yards away, Carlisle House in Soho Square, which had been started by a famous courtesan, Teresa Cornelys, in 1760. Initially, Carlisle House had the relatively innocent objective of providing genteel entertainment for the aristocracy, but it rapidly became as infamous as its occupant as the delights turned from dancing and card-playing to exotic masquerades. Capable of holding 500 guests in its mirrored rooms hung with chandeliers and Chinese wallpaper, for luxury it 'surpassed all description'.[6] In the previous decade, the *Gentleman's Magazine* had said of such establishments: 'Masquerade houses may be called shops where opportunities for immorality and almost every kind of vice are retailed.' They were right.

Probably the most famous masquerade of all was held in 1779 by the notorious brothel-keeper Mrs Prendergast of King's Place, near St James's Park. She came up with the idea after revealing in court that the Earl of Harrington had routinely visited her establishment every Sunday, Monday, Wednesday and Friday, enjoying the lowest kind of rough girl. This public revelation had sent him into a hypocritical rage ('he flew into a great passion, stuttering and swearing, waving his cane and shouting, Why! I'll not be able to show my face at Court!') not just at the bawd's casual admittance that he was a customer, but, far more damagingly, that he was often impotent.[7]

For Prendergast had declared that no one in her establishment could arouse the earl and that she had had to send out for two other girls, who had spent nearly an hour 'with great labour and much difficulty bringing his Lordship to the zest of his amorous passion'.[8] These two girls, on returning to their own madam, had been so fed up at their less-than-interesting hour and a fee of only three guineas that they had refused to pay their own house 25 per cent commission. The resulting uproar made the newspapers and culminated in Harrington's outburst. To make amends to him, and to repair the amorous reputation of her own girls, Prendergast organised the 'Grand Bal D'Amour' – the lewdest public event that year in a very lewd city.

She invited subscriptions for the night's events, to include famous beauties displayed '*in puris naturalibus*'. Harrington himself paid over 50 guineas when he heard what she had in mind; in all, she raised over £84,000 in today's money from Harrington and his friends, all of whom were agog at her plans. She also recruited female aristocrats such as the Hon. Charlotte Spencer (who charged £50 a night), the courtesan Harriet Powell and Lady Henrietta Grosvenor to entice further customers. It is not known whether Harrington's wife attended, who had an even worse reputation than her husband: her nickname was 'The Stable Yard Messalina', after the nymphomaniac wife of the Roman Emperor Claudius, and she had both male and female lovers.

The night was a wild success. The ladies danced nude, except for their masks, while an orchestra played facing the wall to spare any blushes the women might still have left. Afterwards the entire throng retired to couches provided 'to realise those rites which had been celebrated only in theory'. In the midst of the orgy it is said that Lord Grosvenor enjoyed his own wife by mistake, but was so pleased with her performance that the couple – previously separated – were reconciled. After their exertions the guests were treated to a banquet. The evening was deemed such a success that the aristocratic whores donated their fees to the servants, and the lower-class girls were given three guineas each and their cab fare home.

But masquerades were not the only kind of entertainment that high-class brothels could offer to gallants like Donellan – especially those like him, who were keen to flash their money around. In 1772, the notoriously successful bawd Charlotte Hayes threw a 'Tahitian Feast of Venus' to celebrate Captain Cook's revelation that the natives of the newly discovered Pacific island made love in public. (It was also her commercial response to the opening of the Pantheon.) She invited twenty-three 'gentlemen of the highest breeding' to watch as twelve athletic young couples provided a floorshow. Hayes was a canny administrator as well as an impresario: unlike most of her contemporaries she retired with a reputed fortune of £20,000 (£1.27m), all of it gained from gentlemen of breeding blessed with considerably more money than sense.

The Pantheon opened on 27 January 1772. Occupying a prime position on Oxford Street between Poland Street and Ramillies Street (the site now occupied by Marks & Spencer's Pantheon store at 173 Oxford Street), it had fourteen vast and richly decorated rooms, although its mock Roman and Byzantine style was criticised by some as being cold and 'church-like'. It was supposed to be not only a more refined version of the rapidly degenerating Carlisle House, but a winter version of the famous Ranelagh Gardens, whose season ran from April to November. During its building, however, the scheme had run into financial trouble, and its founder, Turst, lost his control of it to a committee of eleven men, Donellan among them.

In late 1771 the committee published a plan of how the Pantheon would be run. They would open three nights a week only, on Mondays, Wednesdays and Fridays, to provide musical concerts, balls and card-playing – although high stakes would not be allowed. It seems that the proprietors were trying to establish a respectable venue for the aristocracy, and to this end they devised a system whereby only peeresses or their nominated guests could be admitted – a kind of elite backstage pass on which the lady had to write the name of the person she was recommending.

The plan backfired in a most dramatic way. On the first night, it was obvious that some of the prized tickets had found their way into the hands of 'ladies of easy virtue' (according to the magazine *Town and Country*). The following Wednesday, this was confirmed by the arrival of the actress and singer Sophia Baddeley. Baddeley was wildly famous: the Duke of Ancaster had said that she was 'one of the wonders of the age' and Lord Falmouth had told her, 'Half the world is in love with you.' One night in 1771, the audience at the Little Theatre in the Haymarket had risen to applaud her beauty in a standing ovation that lasted fifteen minutes. But despite rumours that Lord Melbourne was wont to leave wads of banknotes under her pillow, she was always short of money. When, during a temporary lapse of funds, it was suggested that she cut down her clothing allowance to £100 a year (£6,300), she retorted, 'Christ, that is not enough for millinery!' A mercurial spendthrift, spoiled, over-generous, rapaciously sexual and extremely high-profile, the early years of the 1770s belonged to Sophia.

It says something for Donellan's own reputation that he knew Baddeley well enough not only to approach her when she entered the Pantheon but to take her to one side and tell the goddess that she was not welcome – a daring move which shows the expectations that the proprietors had of him as well as their own inflated ideas of their influence.

It did not work. Baddeley was back the following week, this time with George Hanger in tow. Hanger, who was actually the son of Lord Coleraine, would become a favourite of the Prince of Wales, visible in many caricatures and cartoons of the age. In a Boyne drawing of 1786 he is shown in a boat with the Prince being shipped off to Botany Bay as a debtor; in another one he cavorts about while the Prince spanks one of the society beauties, Mrs Sawbridge; in a Townly Stubbs drawing of 1786 Hanger is shown pimping for the Prince and distributing his 'favours' in the form of feathers he is taking from a handcart, while the Prince is depicted as a balding cock of the walk.

In 1772, Hanger was in his early twenties, and Sophia Baddeley was just a little older. At the doors of the Pantheon, surrounded by a crowd of friends who had drawn their swords in defence of Sophia, Hanger demanded that the proprietors explain why she had been excluded. Neither the proprietors nor Donellan were willing to do so in public, and Baddeley was admitted. The *Town and Country* recorded soon afterwards that 'ladies of easy virtue were indiscriminately admitted without any interrogatories concerning their chastity'. In one stroke, Donellan had been demoted to a mere doorman, and not a very effective one at that. (Baddeley's glory, incidentally, was to be short-lived. She died aged only forty-four in Scotland, impoverished, debt-ridden and addicted to laudanum. Hanger had set up home with her in Dean Street, but had left her when the money ran out.)

Donellan's position as moral guardian of his customers was probably untenable from the start. When the *Town and Country* reviewed his life after his trial, they said that he had been promoted to Master of Ceremonies at the Pantheon because he had been having an affair with the wife of one of the other proprietors, who presumably had pressured for his appointment: 'It is believed that whilst H … was devoting a building to the gods, Donellan was devoutly sacrificing at the altar of Venus and fabricating for him a pair of antlers' – in other words, making a cuckold of him. Similarly, an article in the *Nottinghamshire Gazette* of 4 April 1781 says revealingly: '[Donellan's] universal intercourse with polite prostitutes was well known … his connexion with Mrs H … in the vicinity of Rathbone Place is on the recollection of most people. The house, the table, the servants, the carriages of this lady were at the captain's constant disposal; and it is suspected that his attendances were rewarded in the most liberal way, which enabled him to continue his appearance in public and gave him the opportunity of being acquainted with the unhappy family into which he married.'

This single article brings Donellan to life in an unparalleled way. The picture of the badly treated but noble patriot painted by Donellan himself to the directors of the East India Company fades; he becomes not only a gallant, a rake and a frequenter of brothels, but a kept man.

But who was Donellan's lover, 'Mrs H'? The *Town and Country* identifies her only as the wife of one of the Pantheon's proprietors – one of the original builders, in fact. But there was no obvious 'Mr H' among either the builders or the known subscribers. The newspaper article suggests that 'Mrs H' was perhaps a 'polite prostitute' living near Rathbone Place – either the mistress or the wife of a man wealthy enough to run liveried servants and carriages, or a bawd running one of the dazzlingly wealthy brothels in the area, with income in her own right.

There are several contenders. Rathbone Place is on the north side of Oxford Street directly opposite Soho Square. Teresa Cornelys ran Carlisle House from Soho Square. Lady Harrington, the 'Stable Yard Messalina', was one of her patrons. But even if the indefatigably lecherous Lady Harrington was not Donellan's protector, there were plenty of other candidates among the courtesans and society women who frequented the place.

Donellan's lover might have been Charlotte Hayes (then in her late forties), who had set up a successful brothel in Great Marlborough Street in 1761, just south of Oxford Street and a little to the east of Soho Square; but Charlotte was never directly identified with the Pantheon. She and her husband did, however, have many influential friends, including the Duke of Richmond and the Earls Egremont and Grosvenor, all of whom paid 50 guineas a night for Charlotte's girls. Charlotte and her husband were said to have been worth £40,000 (£2.55 million) in 1769 – more than enough for her to pay for a little pied-à-terre for a favourite captain in Rathbone Place.

There were other prostitutes who might also fit the bill as Donellan's lover, though the connection is tenuous at best. *Harris's List of Covent Garden Ladies* records two working out of the narrow streets abutting Rathbone Place: Mrs Lowes ('she expects three guineas for a whole night') and Miss Townsend ('she refuses no visitors that will afford a couple of guineas and a bottle').[9] Though a street of respectable houses to the front, Rathbone Place housed poorer communities at its rear and came to be known as a haunt of artists, engravers and sculptors. The girls who worked the area, however, were not always 'happy with a pretty fellow': *Harris's List* of 1773 also mentions the pathetic, abused Polly Jackson, 'a little fluttering child about fourteen years of age debauched about ten months ago … under the direction of a lady who directs her to play her part'. Polly sold herself – or was sold – at No. 22.

Two women do, however, stand out above all others as Donellan's possible mistress. One is the actress Elizabeth Hartley. The incomplete list of investors in the Pantheon in 1770–71 might well have included Mrs Hartley's husband, an actor. As the actor-manager David Garrick described their relationship: 'She has a husband, a precious fool, that she heartily despises …' In fact, there is no record of any marriage, but Elizabeth had been with him for some years and they had toured the provinces and Ireland together. As Elizabeth seems to have been that rare breed of actress/prostitute, one who actually saved her money, it is quite feasible that her 'husband' thought it a good investment to buy a share in the Pantheon. A 'Mr Hartley' was certainly well-heeled enough to have his portrait painted by George Romney in 1785 and pay £18 18s. for it.

Elizabeth had been born in 1750 and had made her debut in Covent Garden in 1772. She was a stunningly beautiful woman whose appearances on stage sent the audience into raptures – until she opened her mouth, that is. The *Covent Garden Journal* actually described her voice as 'monstrous'. But she exuded sexual availability, with her 'slovenly good nature that renders her prodigiously vulgar', according to Garrick, who became her employer.

However, Elizabeth's story exudes more than sex. She had sense. She had started her career in Little St James Street, Haymarket, with the bawd Mrs Kelly and, as bawds did not give free lodging, it is likely that Elizabeth earned her keep. When Kelly moved to Arlington Street, in Piccadilly, in 1771, the painter Joshua Reynolds noted that Hartley was with her; but Elizabeth was soon to move on. Once she had been spotted by Garrick, she took her own lodgings in Queen Street, Haymarket. Reynolds used Mrs Hartley as a model several times, reinforcing the sexual titillation by painting her both as a Madonna in 1772 and as the fifteenth-century courtesan Jane Shore in 1773.

By 1773, Elizabeth Hartley was pursued wherever she went. One night at Vauxhall Gardens – the ultimate place for fashionable assignations, where a woman could be manhandled or worse in the suffocating crowds – she was jostled by several men. The character who came to her rescue – it is not clear whether he was already with her or not – was Sir Henry Bate. Bate held several church livings but left most of the work to his curates: he was far more interested in stirring up controversy in London. Bate knew Elizabeth's employer Garrick well, and had written some moderately successful farces for the stage, but he had made his name principally as the editor of the scandal-touting *Morning Post*. In the fracas at Vauxhall Gardens, Bate accepted a challenge to a duel thrown down by one of Elizabeth's assailants. The next morning, his rival substituted a professional boxer, but Bate was not to be outdone: he stripped to the waist and pummelled the man into submission, thereby earning himself the title of 'the fighting parson'.

Bate's relationship with Elizabeth Hartley lasted for years – in fact, he married her sister – but he also had a strong link to John Donellan. In January 1777, just eighteen months before Donellan married Theodosia Boughton, Bate had a duel with the notorious Andrew Robinson Stoney, and John Donellan was his second, even lending Bates his own sword for the purpose. The duel, over the honour of the heiress Mary Bowes, has the hallmarks of being set up between Bate and Stoney so that Stoney could fake a life-threatening injury that would bring Mary running to his side. But even if Bate and Donellan were perfectly innocent of the ruse, it still shows them conducting battles of 'honour' in the mainstream of society – or rather, battles engineered by cash-poor gallants to part wealthy young women from their money and potential rivals.

By 1775, Elizabeth Hartley, now firmly placed in Garrick's favour and a well-known figure about town, had a lover, a fellow actor called William Smith; by 1778 she was reported to be living in Bath recuperating from an illness (the same year that Donellan married Theodosia, also in Bath). The rest of her life fades from public view, but, in contrast to the sad end of someone like Sophia Baddeley or Teresa Cornelys, who died in the Fleet Prison, she kept her finances and emotions under control. The 'prodigiously vulgar' Elizabeth Hartley died in her own home in King Street Woolwich in 'easy circumstances'.[10]

The other woman who fits the bill as Donellan's mistress was Anne Parsons (nicknamed Nancy). Born in 1729, she was the daughter of a Bond Street tailor. In her late teens or early twenties she had married a slave trader, a Captain Horton, and had gone to live in Jamaica. But by 1764 she was back in London and mixing in aristocratic company. Although her reputation was racy, she was not a common-or-garden whore; she was much cleverer than that. In the late 1760s, she became the acknowledged mistress of the Duke of Grafton, with whom she lived openly from 1764 to 1769. The noble duke became prime minister when William Pitt fell ill in 1768, although he was outstandingly useless in the post. The *Spectator* magazine said of him that he was 'unsteady, capricious and indolent, with 'hardly any quality of a statesman'. Nevertheless, George III liked him and awarded him the Order of the Garter. He was married to Anne Liddell, daughter of the First Baron Ravensworth, but unhappily, and the affair with Mrs Horton finished off the relationship. The couple divorced in March 1769.

For a while, Mrs Horton ruled all she surveyed, despite a lack of aristocratic title. Society was hardly likely to snub the companion of the prime minister. A portrait by Reynolds shows her leaning reflectively on her left hand as she gazes away from the viewer: even-featured and pale-skinned, she is no roaring beauty, but she has a certain acute, intelligent look about her. This cool charm had obviously carried her far, and it did not desert her when a series of obscene verses called *Henry and Nan*, about herself and Grafton, circulated London in 1769. Grafton went to pieces and resigned from office in 1770. But he did not marry Mrs Horton. Pressured by the age-old imperative to produce legitimate heirs, instead he married Elizabeth Wrottesley, who bore him thirteen children in sixteen years.

Anne Horton turned her attentions to another aristocratic suitor, the Duke of Dorset. It was these two famous associations that led Horace Walpole to remark acidly: 'The Duke of Grafton's Mrs Horton, the Duke of Dorset's Mrs Horton, everybody's Mrs

Horton.' Anne was forty; the duke was twenty-four. The duke, who had just succeeded to his title on the death of his uncle, had a reputation as a womaniser, a gambler and a sportsman. Anne must have known she could never keep him: for one thing, he became besotted with the ballerina Giovanna Zanerini, who became all but mistress of Knole House, his family seat. By 1776, Anne's relationship with him was over but she was forty-seven and not ready to be put out to pasture just yet. She set her sights on Charles, the Second Viscount Maynard, and they were married – with what must have been considerable relief on Anne's part – that same year. Although she and the viscount did eventually separate, Anne lived to a ripe old age, dying just outside Paris in her eightieth year.

A much adored, much envied woman: was Anne Horton Donellan's lover? She, more than anyone else, fits the description given in the *Nottinghamshire Gazette* of a lady with a house, table, servants and carriages. Such a woman had wealth and status – carriages alone were notoriously expensive to run, not just the vehicles themselves but the grooms, stables, liveried footmen and drivers that went with them. Hers were emblazoned with a noble lord's coat-of-arms – the ultimate status symbol. The woman who stepped out of such a carriage either ruled her lover's heart, his bed or his house – and sometimes all three. The famous, well-kept mistress of a still more famous aristocrat whose attentions were often elsewhere – either in Parliament or with his other women – would have suited Donellan perfectly. Unlike Elizabeth Hartley, Anne Horton had a high-society profile but not a reputation that could be damaged by having a personal favourite. And lastly, Viscount Maynard and his new wife lived at No. 36 Soho Square – which fits the description of 'in the vicinity of Rathbone Place' – the two were a minute's walk apart.

(Anne Horton *née* Parsons is often confused with another Mrs Horton, born Anne Lutrell, who married the Duke of Cumberland. She was the widow of Christopher Horton and married the Duke in Calais in 1771 in what was popularly viewed as a very clever romantic campaign by her to become 'Her Royal Highness' – the duke was the uncle of the Prince of Wales. But the marriage enraged the king, resulting in the Royal Marriages Act of 1772, which forbad any member of royalty from marrying a commoner. This Anne Horton died in Trieste in 1808 aged sixty-six. Although a beautiful woman with many admirers, and with a father who had a shameful reputation of his own, she is often erroneously and unfairly labelled 'anybody's Mrs Horton'.)

Whoever the elusive 'Mrs H' was, Donellan would have known the geography of Rathbone Place well. It was just a few minutes' stroll from the Pantheon. A map of 1840 shows the houses on its eastern side set back in gardens. An account by Edward Walford shines a light upon this lost semi-rural part of London. Built by a Captain Rathbone in 1718, Rathbone Place had previously been pasture; at its northern end was a windmill (now commemorated in Windmill Place). Walford quotes an old resident of the street, Mr Smith, as saying: 'at the top of that street was a long pond with a windmill … a halfpenny was paid by every person at the hatch to the miller for the privilege of walking in his grounds … another halfpenny hatch was between Oxford Street and Grosvenor Square.'[11]

For Donellan, it would have been a leisurely walk back from here to the Pantheon. From Rathbone Place, which still had its windmill in 1770, he would have walked down to Oxford Street, with Soho Square directly in front of him. To his left was Hanover Yard and slightly beyond that the crossroads at Tottenham Court Road and Oxford Street, an area known for its coaching inns and which still today retains its Georgian facades and the remnants of large curved arches to admit horse-drawn coaches. One of the inns was the Boar and Castle Hostelry and Posting House, which dated back to 1620; another was called the Blue Posts.

At this point, where Rathbone Place meets Oxford Street, small shops and pastry houses would have edged the street. Turning right and crossing the unpaved road, Donellan would have been able to see the roof of the Pantheon ahead of him, occupying a large plot between Oxford Street and Great Marlborough Street, which runs parallel with it on the other side. Philip Turst had owned the land on which the Pantheon was built, and he had at first tried to interest Teresa Cornelys, owner of Carlisle House, in his venture, but the negotiations broke down. This is where a Miss Ellice, who knew Cornelys, stepped in. She had 'conversations with some of the Nobility' as to whether a winter evening entertainment venue would be popular, and Turst asked her to be a shareholder with him. The estimated cost of the building was £15,000 (£955,000 in today's money), which was to be raised by the sale of shares at £300 each. Ellice – who may have entertained hopes of marrying Turst after the death of his wife, although if so she was to be disappointed – bought thirty, and building began on 5 June 1769. When rumours started circulating that the project was over-ambitious, Ellice lost her nerve (or possibly her hopes of marriage) and sold back nineteen of her shares to Turst.

The building costs now rose to £25,000 and Turst proceeded to sell fifty more shares at £500 each. It is recorded that John Donellan paid £600 (£38,000 in today's money) for his share, and the list of his fellow shareholders both in 1771 and again in 1774 reveals the tradesmen, artisans and minor nobility who threw in their lot with this brash new venture. The Pantheon might have been built to entertain the upper classes, but its finances were solidly rooted in trade and the professions, the rising middle class.

Among Donellan's fellow shareholders were Albany Wallis, David Garrick's executor and a prominent London lawyer; another lawyer, Henry Dagge, who had a quarter share in the new Covent Garden Theatre and Royal Opera House; Paul Valliant, a prominent bookseller and printer; and John Cleland, the author of *Fanny Hill*. Other shareholders who took on the 61-year lease in August 1774 were William Franks, who was responsible for building houses at the upper end of Rathbone Place; Sir Thomas Robinson, who had built Prospect Place next to the party-loving Ranelagh Gardens; and one William Hamilton. This could have been the man who had painted Elizabeth Hartley (but aged only nineteen in 1770, he was too young to have sustained a wife or mistress in Rathbone Place, thus excluding him from being the 'cuckold' referred to in local newspapers).

Alternatively, this shareholder could have been the far more famous Sir William Hamilton (1730–1803), who joined the Society of Dilettanti before it transformed into the Hellfire Club. Other founder members of the society included the painter Joshua Reynolds and Charles Greville, who was the lover of Emma Lyon, later Emma Hart, later Hamilton's wife. In 1743 Horace Walpole said of the society, 'the nominal qualification is having been in Italy, and the real one, being drunk'. The Hellfire Club, with the lecherous and violent Francis Dashwood at its helm, was the Bad Boys Club of Georgian England. In his younger days William Hamilton may well have raised hell with the worst of them, but by now he was far more interested in the geology of real-life fire and brimstone, in particular Vesuvius. He returned to Italy to study it and there married the one-time whore Emma. Educated, wry, forgiving and sociable, he may well have invested in the Pantheon during his brief years in London. His wives do not fit the profile for 'Mr H', however: he was devoted to his sickly first wife Catherine Barlow, and he did not marry the lascivious Emma until 1791.

There is one final traceable 'Mr H' from the list of shareholders: Edward Hoare, Second Baronet and MP for Carlow 1768–9; but, newly married in 1771, it is unlikely that his wife Clothilda, from Ballycrenan Castle, Ireland, would have taken a lover like Donellan, even if he were a fellow countryman. Therefore it would seem that Donellan's lover's husband, if a shareholder as the newspaper suggested, is not on the surviving shareholders list.

Donellan was a member of the committee, convened in August 1771, that supervised the building and running of the Pantheon, along with Henry Dagge, Tomkyns Drew, William Franks, Robert Ireland, Thomas Moore, Edmund Pepys, Sir Thomas Robinson, Paul Valliant, John Wyatt and Turst himself. John Wyatt (according to the *Monthly Magazine* of October 1813) had encouraged the scheme from the beginning and his brother James was the designer. Another brother, Samuel, was the builder, while yet another brother, William, was the treasurer in both 1771 and 1772.

Johann Von Archenholz describes the building thus: 'The construction of the Pantheon, which in grandeur and extent exceeds that of Rome, proves that Mrs Cornelys' lessons were not thrown away on the English … everything is great, majestic and magnificent ...' The entrance was through a sheltered portico with four columns to the front, which in turn opened out into a hall 50 feet wide and 15 feet deep. Doorways opened into card rooms and then on to the grand staircases and corridors which gave access to the rotunda. This large assembly room was inspired by the church of Santa Sophia in Istanbul, with its enormous circular dome, some 60 feet in diameter, occupying the centre. The famous architect Robert Adam called it 'the most beautiful edifice in England'.

A print from 1810 included in Ackerman's *Microcosm of London* shows the main assembly room painted pale green, with colonnaded upper walkways, a lavishly painted ceiling, large chandeliers and a huge crush of people engaged in what looks to be a frenetic dance, with more than one ankle being flashed among the ladies. At the back of the vast hall are an elevated stage with an orchestra and six private boxes overlooking the throng.

Despite rumours emanating from Horace Walpole that the Pantheon had cost £60,000 (£3.8 million), the actual cost was much lower. Turst continued to clash with some of his shareholders, and in the 1770s filed a suit in Chancery which listed the bills: the building itself had cost £27,407 2s. 11d.; there was £2,500 for expenses connecting it to Poland Street; and the furnishings, paintings, statues, the organ, and James Wyatt's 5 per cent fee for designing the furnishings came to £7,058 16s. 6d. The total for the whole building was therefore £36,965 19s. 5d. – or £2.354 million in today's money.

Donellan, still manager despite the debacle with Sophia Baddeley, must have felt that he was at the centre of the social universe. Not bad for a bastard son who had found it necessary only a year before to plead for a half-pension from the army. He now had an obliging mistress and a share in a wealthy venture; so perhaps the figure lounging casually against the column in the Lewis Walpole library print really is him – master of all he surveyed. But he was living on his wits and a slightly dubious reputation; to be truly secure in society, he needed respectability.

The stage was set for the next part of his story: the seduction of Theodosia Boughton.

6

The Major Players
John and Theodosia

'Wilt thou go with me, sweet maid,
Say, maiden, wilt thou go with me
Through the valley-depths of shade'

John Clare, 'An Invite, to Eternity' (1847)

IN THE MAGAZINE *All Year Round* which Charles Dickens owned and edited, an anonymous contributor recounted the John and Theodosia story in 1871, over ninety years later, in an article entitled 'Old Stories Re-Told. An Old Rugby Story. The Little Bottle of Laurel Water'. In it, John Donellan and Theodosia Boughton's first meeting is described. Anna Maria and her daughter were travelling to Bath and stopped at a roadside inn for the night, only to find that every room had been taken. 'There he was in all his glory,' it continues. 'Smooth, graceful, stealthy as a snake ... butterfly King of all that sham world ... young, handsome, soft of speech he came, he saw, he conquered.' The captain insinuated himself into the ladies' lives by offering them his own room. A kind gesture, but one which is given the melodramatic overtones of a premeditated plot.

A more objective version of the story was given by Arthur Griffiths and John Howard in *Mysteries of Police and Crime* in 1899, by which time the account of the lovers' meeting seems to have been accepted, even if the 'roadside inn' has been transmogrified into the finest hotel in Bath:

> Lady Boughton was unable to find accommodation in the best hotel, and Donellan, who was there, promptly gave up his rooms. The acquaintance thus pleasantly begun grew into intimacy, and ended in his marrying Miss Boughton.
>
> To haunt fashionable society in London and the chief pleasure resorts in search of a rich partie was a common enough proceeding, and implied self-seeking, but not necessarily criminal tendencies.

In fact, despite these two seemingly authoritative versions, there is no reliable account of John and Theodosia's first meeting. These two were written around a century after the event; contemporary newspapers cast a differing light. The consensus seems to be that the Boughtons were in some fashionable social setting when they crossed Donellan's path. Whether it was by happy accident, or by design by John Donellan, is impossible to know.

On the face of it, Donellan was an attractive suitor. He was an ex-military man whose courage had been confirmed by none less than Clive of India. As Master of Ceremonies at the Pantheon, he would have known everyone who mattered. He was charming and sociable – a fact never denied. He had no wife in tow, no bastard children to support. He did not, however, have a title or an annual income. Anna Maria would probably have seen him as an entertainingly acceptable acquaintance, but not in any way an equal. A man one could speak to or acknowledge, and a man who might well introduce one to a true nobleman, but not marriage material.

Theodosia evidently thought differently.

What young woman, flattered and amused by the kind of attention she never received in the depths of the country, excited by being at parties and balls, exhibited freely by her mother as wanting a husband, would really care about his exact status if a handsome military man seemed to adore her? Every girl yearned to be feted by an officer. In *Pride and Prejudice* (1813), when the frivolous, headstrong Lydia Bennet (who was eventually to elope with an ex-soldier) visited Brighton: 'She saw the streets of that gay bathing place covered with officers, saw herself the object of attention to tens and scores of them at present unknown.'

Donellan was so different from the country squires Theodosia had previously encountered, or even the titled folk of Warwickshire like the Denbighs. He had, after all, seen the world; he could speak of his adventures in India. In addition to his military service Donellan knew everyone in London. Even the aristocracy recognised him.

The first meeting escalated into an affair. For Donellan's part, the lure was not only money: Theodosia was ravishingly pretty. A miniature portrait of her, painted in 1774 when she was seventeen,[1] shows a dark-eyed girl with an abundance of long dark hair and a sweet expression; Edward Allesley Boughton Ward-Boughton-Leigh, her grandson, described her in 1882 as a 'good-looking young woman'. To meet such a girl from a wealthy family would have been attractive indeed to the increasingly impoverished Donellan.

The relationship with Donellan was, however, fatal to Theodosia's reputation. Even four years later, when she was the mother of two young children and respectably married, the *Nottinghamshire Gazette* of Saturday 14 April 1781 felt fit to dredge up the scandalous circumstances of her marriage, contending that the couple met at the Pantheon and within a very short space of time they had eloped and were secretly married in June 1777. This has a ring of truth.

Elopement was a word that struck cold terror into the hearts of aristocratic parents: centuries of tradition and money, not just their daughter's honour, were at stake. That was why girls were so tightly chaperoned, a task at which Anna Maria had somehow failed. Either married or single, elopement was never forgotten in the women who succumbed. Lady Sarah Bunbury eloped with Lord William Gordon in 1769; Lord Sussex's daughter did so in 1771; Admiral Millbanke's daughter eloped with a Mr Tilman in 1786; and Lord Southampton's son with Miss Keppell in 1784.

The whole extended Boughton tribe rose up to condemn Theodosia's marriage. 'The resentment of the lady's relations were too violent to be soothed by apologies,' claimed the *Nottinghamshire Gazette*. 'The rage continued for some time unabated and the delinquents were abandoned to the world.'

'Abandoned to the world.' This was serious stuff: if the Boughton clan had abandoned Theodosia, it would have followed that she would have been left without a penny and Donellan would have been forced to look after her. For a rake who had only been interested in deflowering a virgin, that would have been that – Theodosia would have been left in some seaside watering hole while her seducer high-tailed it back to London (and his accommodating mistress). For a man who had eyes only on Theodosia's money, there might even have been a headlong dash to Warwickshire to persuade his new wife's family to settle an amount on the now-ruined girl. Interestingly, Donellan did neither of these things. The couple stayed away from Warwickshire and fended for themselves, which could not have been easy. It would have been impossible to be accepted even within the walls of the Pantheon if the union were considered to be a seduction. It seems that Donellan was in it for the long game, and his protection of Theodosia at this time points to a relationship based on something a lot more meaningful than money alone.

If Donellan was condemned later as a conniving money-grabbing scoundrel and seducer, he certainly did not behave like one now. He acted like a man in love.

How was it possible for Donellan to marry a minor without her family's consent?

Two legal options would have been open to John and Theodosia: marriage in church after banns had been published, or marriage by special licence (the preferred option for the aristocracy). The Clandestine Marriage Act of 1753 established whose consent was needed: firstly, the minor's father (in Theodosia's case, no longer living), or a guardian specifically appointed by the father (which had been done for her brother, but not Theodosia). Only if neither father nor guardian existed would consent be the mother's responsibility, and then only if she had not remarried. (Control over her children might have been one of the very logical reasons that Anna Maria had not chosen another husband.)

However, the consent issue could be bypassed. The Act said that if the couple had had their banns read in church, the marriage could go ahead only if there were no objections; positive consent was not needed as it was with a licence – only a lack of opposition. Nor could the marriage be invalidated if the couple did not live in the parish where the marriage had taken place, or where the banns had been called: the direction was only for guidance, not mandatory. So, the marriage could be legal even without positive parental consent. However, this would mean that John and Theodosia would have to escape somewhere distant, somewhere they would not be recognised or their names were not known, and to live there for a month without being found out.

The quicker alternative was marriage by licence. Before the Act of 1753, those who married by licence had to swear under canon law either that they were both over twenty-one, or that they had parental consent, and two witnesses were needed to swear that the parents did indeed approve. However, this was canon law, which could be – and regularly was – circumvented, not least by obliging Anglican ministers who for the right fee were prepared to risk being suspended for three years.

Half of all those women who married by licence were daughters of gentlemen or wealthy farmers; only 5 per cent of those who were married by the calling of banns in church were in the same class. And so the expectation would have been that, rather than waiting a month to take the lower-class option, John and Theodosia would have married by licence.

There was a problem with that option, though. Although John and Theodosia could have been legally married by banns without Anna Maria's consent, they needed her approval to marry by licence. However, the Act stated that such positive parental consent could be sought 'even retrospectively'.

So, even though they could marry without Anna Maria's consent at the time, they would need it eventually.

Anna Maria could have opposed the marriage by going to court, but there were hurdles there for her. In order for litigation to proceed, certain circumstances had to be in place. Firstly, the marriage had to contravene the clauses of a will (which it did not). Secondly, consent had to be refused (it was). Thirdly, the marriage had to have gone ahead without consent (it had). But lastly Anna Maria had to have enough money to contest the case (she did not).

Once Anna Maria found out that Theodosia was married, what could she do? She did not approve, but there was no word in Theodosia's father's will setting out conditions for her marriage. The cost of a court case was frightening: a lot of the Boughton estate was already mortgaged, and court cases had been known to cost upwards of £1,000 (£64,000). On top of this would have been the public disgrace, the picking-over of family problems in public. While Anna Maria hesitated, John Donellan attempted to win her round.

The 1781 *Nottinghamshire Gazette* piece reported that John's attitude towards his wife was always respectful and that 'he used every means to facilitate esteem'. Presumably he wrote to Anna Maria pleading his cause, and possibly also to Sir William Wheler and Sir Francis Skipwith, Theodosius's legal guardians. He may well have told them what he told the court in his own trial later, that he had seen a lawyer before he married Theodosia and had drawn up a will showing that he was not interested in her money. On 7 May 1781, the *Northampton Mercury* said that John Donellan made a will in August 1777 'by which he disposes of his property to Sir Theodosius after the death of Mrs Donellan in case she should die without issue from him'. This will was, apparently, drawn up by a Mr White of Castle Yard, Holborn, and was supposedly concrete proof of Donellan's lack of financial motive.

However, this is not quite as selfless as it sounds: what John Donellan was actually saying was that if both he and Theodosia died before Theodosius, and they did not have any children, Theodosius would get all John Donellan's money. Which was not actually much of a promise: Donellan had very little money to leave, and the will presupposed that either he or Theodosia were infertile, or that their children all died, and that Theodosia died, and that *he* died before Theodosius. Not exactly probable, and so not a hugely generous gesture.

Whatever John pleaded or promised, it did not seem to affect

Anna Maria's resolve, at least not at first. But a change was on the way. The *Nottinghamshire Gazette* went on: 'during a visit to a sea coast a reconciliation took place between the parties.'

What caused this change of heart?

The most probable reason was that Theodosia was pregnant (at the time of her brother's death three years later, she already had two children). After several months of separation, either an accidental or an arranged meeting would have presented Anna Maria with visible evidence that she was going to be a grandmother. Living alone at Lawford Hall, worried by her son's behaviour, she may well have decided to welcome her daughter back into the fold. If she had not done so, and given her consent to the marriage, it would have remained technically illegal until Theodosia reached the age of twenty-one.

The couple were not quite ready to return to Lawford yet, though. It is known that they were living in Bath in 1777, and the likeliest contender for the 'sea coast' where the reconciliation took place is Brighton.

Although Weymouth, which was closer to Bath, would become the favourite seaside resort of the ailing king in 1777, Brighton was still the resort of choice for the rakish Prince of Wales and the fast young set. The Prince of Wales was only sixteen, but he was already famous for a wild lifestyle that at various points of his life was to make him ill (he was treated for venereal disease as well as many other complaints). From 1750, when the physician Richard Russell moved to Brighton, he had upheld the town and its sea bathing as a cure-all. Brighton therefore fulfilled a dual purpose for the Prince: he could indulge himself well out of sight of his ailing father and the interfering House of Commons (who had an annoying habit of trying to make him accountable for his spending), and he could give himself a rest cure when his exhausting life took its inevitable toll.

In 1760, Russell published 'A Dissertation on the Use of Sea Water', quoting Euripides, in which he claimed that 'sea water washes away the evils of mankind'. His claims for the efficacy of Brighton water in particular were responsible for its transformation from a modest little town with a population of 3,600 in 1786 to a thriving metropolis of 40,000 by 1830. Russell's book claimed cures and treatments for all kinds of ailments, from 'scrofulous tumours of the ear' and 'scirrhus of the liver' to 'dry leprosy' and 'obstructions of the rectum'. Some of the claims for sea water were pure fantasy – in one case, Russell declared that 'two girls who could not speak and every time they drew in their breath they made a noise not unlike the crowing of a cock' were perfectly restored by sea bathing, an unusual remedy for what sounds like whooping cough.

His prescriptions for some other poor benighted patients were equally challenging: 'An old woman had been afflicted with a violent Itch for some four or five years,' he wrote. 'She was sent to drink the sea water and likewise bathed in it. The sea water made her stomach very uneasy ... she returned home quite free of the disease.' And more unpleasantly still: 'A man of illustrious family had his body and all his joints covered with white leprous scabs. The disease was hereditary and he had taken mercury, antimony, Viper's Flesh in vain. After he began to bathe in sea water the disease would give way and the scales fall off ... ' Russell also claimed that those who had been bitten by a mad dog should be 'dipt' as soon as possible, but added helpfully that this would be of no use if the patient had already been 'affected by the Dread of Water'.

Bathers climbed into a sea-bathing machine which was rolled out into the waves. Steps were lowered into the water and the patients – nude in the case of men, and usually dressed in a modest linen or woollen costume in the case of women – climbed down the steps and into the arms of the 'dippers', who helped them submerge in the water or swim.

In this sporting and lively atmosphere, in a town favoured by the Prince of Wales, Anna Maria decided to reconcile herself to John and Theodosia's marriage. The union was apparently strong, and Theodosia was undoubtedly pregnant. Pragmatism took the place of outrage, and John Donellan was welcomed into the family fold.

It was June 1778 when John and Theodosia came to live at Lawford at Anna Maria's invitation.

A letter from Edward Allesley Boughton Ward-Boughton-Leigh to Sir Charles Rouse-Boughton of 1882 discusses at length the couple and their relationship with Theodosius. 'Sir Theodosius had been staying at Bath with Mr & Mrs Donellan for five or six months,' he wrote, 'and I have Lady Boughton's diary which shows that she paid Donellan a considerable sum for the keep of Sir Theodosius and his house and probably a servant.'

This has a significant bearing on later events. Anna Maria trusted Donellan to look after her son, enough that, when Theodosius left Eton, she sent him to live with the newly married couple. This would indicate the rift was securely healed, and Anna Maria evidently felt that Donellan was a man who could advise Theodosius and steer him away from 'particular complaints'. In this Donellan was not successful – Theodosius's range of treatments testify that the boy could not keep his hands off prostitutes – but Anna Maria's actions show that in her mind it was preferable for Theodosius to stay with the Donellans than at either Eton or, indeed, Lawford Hall. During these months, Edward Allesley Boughton Ward-Boughton-Leigh claims that Theodosius even put his name down for Magdalen College, Oxford, a family tradition which not all the Boughton men had taken up.

When the Donellans moved to Lawford Hall in June 1778, Theodosius went to Rugby to be privately tutored – probably to cram for Oxford entry.

John and Theodosia's daughter Maria Boughton Beauchamp Donellan was born that year, but her birth is not registered at Newbold, so presumably she was born before June. Another girl was born the following year, but sadly Theodocia King Donellan (registrar's spelling) was buried on 9 December 1779 at Newbold. John Boughton Beauchamp Donellan, their son, was born in July 1780 and was therefore just a babe in arms when Theodosia visited Donellan in Warwick Gaol in the autumn of 1780.[2]

When Theodosius returned from Rugby to live at Lawford Hall in November 1778 it was a changed place. When he had gone up to Eton, he had left behind a widowed mother and his 18-year-old sister; now, just four years later, his sister was a married woman with a child and John Donellan was the man of the household. Donellan, by every account, was very much in charge, and Anna Maria deferred to him on most household matters, a fact which reputedly annoyed Theodosius intensely – so much so that at one point he rallied his drunken friends to try and have Donellan thrown out at the point of a sword. The attempt inevitably failed and frayed tempers were subsequently smoothed over.

Evidence is scant as to what was going on in the family at this time, but Anna Maria did draw up a new will dated 28 September 1778, just three months after John and Theodosia took up residence.[3] In it, she gives 'the whole moiety of my estate ... to Esquire William Beauchamp Rye of Bath and Doctor in Physick and his son Robert'. What Anna Maria was effectively doing here was returning to her own family – her brother and her nephew – the estates worth £1,400 (£89,000 today) which she had inherited from her sister Elizabeth Shipton.

However, the next clause is more perplexing. In this Anna Maria states that if Theodosius were to die or 'forfeited' the estate, the whole was to be divided between Sir William Wheler and her brother William and nephew Robert. It is doubtful that this had legal credence, as Theodosius's father had left the estate to his son, and thereafter to Theodosia, so technically it was not Anna Maria's to bestow. Perhaps she saw the impossibility of this, because she later voided the will. But why, three months after her daughter and new son-in-law came to live with her, did she try to exclude Theodosia from her inheritance if Theodosius died? And what did she mean by Theodosius 'forfeiting' his inheritance?

The answer as regards her daughter may be simply that Theodosia had come of age the year before, and was now married. Anna Maria may have thought – wrongly – that she could overrule her own husband's will now that Theodosia was an independent person. But it is Anna Maria's change towards Theodosius which is more interesting. The wording of the will indicates that she had reservations about either her son's physical or mental health. The estate could only be 'forfeited' if he were declared insane or so desperately ill that he had no control or understanding over his affairs. Perhaps the incident of the rowdy teenagers trying to drag Donellan out of the house had preyed on her mind; perhaps Theodosius's bar-room brawls were becoming notorious. Perhaps she was simply a mother at her wits' end. Whatever the reason, Anna Maria in late 1778 was making plans to hand over the estate to Sir William Wheler and her own family members. Moreover, she was trying to overturn her husband's will by keeping the inheritance from her daughter – and, thereby, her son-in-law.

What was Anna Maria's state of mind in drawing up such a document? Did she feel so threatened by Theodosius's behaviour that she thought the Boughton estate was at risk? Did she not trust Theodosia and John to handle their financial affairs?

Whatever her reasons in September 1778, the will was not acted upon. (Anna Maria was to draw up another will after Theodosius's death, however, which points to a definite lack of confidence in Theodosia.)

Meanwhile, little record remains of Theodosius's feelings and actions. Only one of his letters survives, dated 9 March 1780, some eighteen months later, in which he writes to George Harris, the solicitor:

Sir –

In answer to yours of 28 February last wrote to me by the desire of Mr Lister. I must beg you to inform him that I will discharge the small debt at the time promised and not before. Had he wrote to me since the death of my grandmother he would have had no occasion to have troubled you upon this Business, which was not according to promise, to have settled prior to my coming of age.

I am Sir, your most obedient, T. Boughton[4]

The Listers were still about. The parents had spent a great deal of time and money pursuing Theodosius's father for rights to land taken from Grace Shukburgh by Theodosius's grandfather

Edward; now evidently one of their numerous children was trying to settle another debt.

Theodosius's tone is rather petulant. 'Had he wrote to me since the death of my grandmother ... ' Mr Lister had not. Grace Shukburgh Lister, Theodosius's grandmother, had died in February 1779, a year before, and so twelve months had passed without any communication between the two families except for this attempt to reclaim money through the lawyers. Theodosius is brief: Mr Lister can have the money once Theodosius turns twenty-one, and not before.

The only other surviving document of Theodosius's is a small calfskin-covered notebook. An inscription on the cover reads: 'Sir Theodosius Boughton: His Account Book 1777.'[6] This would have been given to him to record his outgoings, expenses and income once he had returned from Eton; but apparently Theodosius had little use for it. Inside, half a dozen pages have been torn out; the rest of the book is completely empty.

However, there was another notebook belonging to Theodosius which would have proved useful after his death. The *Northampton Mercury* of 23 April 1781 records a 'written paper in the handwriting of Sir Theodosius found in his Bedroom after his death' which lists the time and place where he believed he had contracted his last infection, together with a list of the medicines that Mr Powell had give him and their effects. This list never came to light at the trial: the newspaper states that it was 'in Lady Boughton's custody'.

By August 1780, Lawford Hall was home to four adults and two children. Anna Maria was fifty-two years old and had been a widow for eight years; Theodosia was twenty-three, married for three years and the mother of two young children, one of whom had been born only the month before. John Donellan, transplanted from a lifetime in military service and more latterly the hothouse atmosphere of London society, was forty-three. Sir Theodosius Edward Allesley Boughton was twenty, and within a year of inheriting everything the family owned and becoming lord and master of Lawford Hall.

7

'Wonderful News ...'

'Suspicion is to be distinguished from proof – a thousand suspicions do not form one proof. Suspicion may form a proper ground of accusation, but never of conviction'

S. M. Phillips, *Famous Cases of Circumstantial Evidence* (1873)

A HUNDRED MILES FROM LAWFORD HALL, the news of Theodosius's death was received not with horror but with elation. Poston Hall, now known as Poston House, is a Palladian mansion set in glorious rural Herefordshire midway between the county town of Hereford and the Welsh border; in 1780 it was the home of Theodosius's second cousin, Edward Boughton, the son of Shukburgh Boughton and the grandson of Catherine Shukburgh.

Edward was the family black sheep, though as the elder boy was fond of giving advice to his vastly more responsible younger brother, Charles. Edward, who was living openly with his serving maid Sally, was a passionate man at odds with his family, who variously described him as 'an odd animal' and a 'damned prig'. A portrait of Edward shows a mild-looking, handsome young man who seems wistful rather than disagreeable. He was, however, constantly in debt to Charles, who worked in a government post in which he had rapidly gained promotion. The uncomfortable debt between the two might explain Edward's excitement as expressed in the following letter.

On 1 September, two days after Theodosius's death, Edward wrote to Charles: 'I have just received from Caldecott the wonderful news of Sir Theodosius Boughton's death and shall set out immediately for Warwickshire.'[1]

The satisfaction was shared by Edward's mother Mary. On 24 September she also wrote to Charles: 'I shall sincerely rejoice at any acquisition of Fortune yr Brother may now have gain'd ...' – evidently thinking better of Edward now that he seemed to be richer.

In addition to the baronetcy, the Shukburgh descendants were convinced that Theodosius's entire estate, including Lawford Hall, would also become the property of Edward.

It is not known exactly when Edward arrived in Warwickshire. Like Sir William Wheler, Theodosius's guardian, Edward's presence at the funeral is not recorded. Nor is it known if he attended the autopsy in the churchyard on 9 September.

A coroner's inquest was begun on the same day as the autopsy, in the house of the parish clerk of Newbold-on-Avon, John Parker. It was Saturday afternoon when the coroner, Robert Fox, took ten depositions.

The first deposition was from a 23-year-old miller from Rugby called Thomas Hewitt, who swore that he had known Theodosius for 'upwards 3 months'. A friendship between a tradesman and a baronet was unlikely; the exact nature of the relationship and its origins are unknown. One thing is certain, however: Theodosius gave Thomas Hewitt a task that he did not entrust to any member of his family or servant at Lawford Hall. Hewitt swore on oath that in mid August Theodosius had asked him to buy some '*Occuli Indicus* Berries'. And the person who had sold him them was none other than Mr Bucknill, 'a surgeon from Rugby'. Hewitt had then boiled the berries in water, mixed them with spirits of wine and put them into a small phial and delivered them to Theodosius, who had 'put them into his pocket, from which time the examinant knows not what is become thereof'.

'*Occuli Indicus* Berries' are now more commonly known as *Cocculus indicus*. The fruit of a climbing shrub indigenous to eastern India and the Malay archipelago, if boiled and distilled, the berries produce picrotoxin, a powerful convulsive poison.

Cocculus indicus is prescribed in homeopathic medicine today as a stimulant and convulsant to help cure motion sickness and general weakness; but in 1780 it was a known remedy for the effects of not only TB but also mercury poisoning – a feeling of stiffness or paralysis in the back and legs; sleeplessness; night sweats; nausea and vomiting. Theodosius did not ask Powell or indeed any medical man to distil the mixture; the logical conclusion to be drawn from this is that he did not want his family or the family apothecary to know how much his self-medicated mercury had affected him.

It was later quoted in the prosecution brief at the trial that the mixture had been ordered by Theodosius to 'kill fish'. However, quite why a deadly poison like this was necessary in addition to the arsenic that Theodosius already used to lace fish in order to kill rats was not explained. Thomas Hewitt was not called to give evidence at the subsequent trial.

The next coroner's deposition was taken from Anna Maria Boughton. In it she testified that Theodosius had 'for a considerable time preceding ... his death' taken various medicines sent by Powell. She said that she had gone into Theodosius's bedroom at 7 a.m. on 30 August and given him Powell's medicine, which she had, she said, poured into a basin. There had been a large quantity of sediment at the bottom of the phial and the mixture had a 'very offensive and nauseous smell'. Her son had complained that he would not keep it down, but then he appeared to go back to sleep, and so she went out of the room and left him. Five minutes later she came back to find Theodosius 'with his eyes fixed, his teeth set, and the froth running out of his mouth ... He expired a few minutes afterwards.' She said that she called John Donellan to the room. He asked her for the phial, put some water into it, swilled it and poured the whole lot, including the sediment, into a basin; then he put his finger into the liquid and tasted it, saying that it had a nauseous taste.

Her final remark was that Mr Powell had shown her a bottle

of the same mixture which he had prescribed to Theodosius, but that the smell of the mixture that Theodosius actually took that morning was 'very different'.

The third deposition was from Thomas Powell, the apothecary, who testified that on 29 August he had sent to Theodosius a mixture of fifteen grains of jalop, fifteen grains of rhubarb, twenty drops of spirits of lavender, two drams of simple syrup and two drams of nutmeg water mixed together with an ounce and a half of pump water.

The next deposition was from Sarah Steane of Long Lawford, who simply stated that she had been sent for to lay out Theodosius and that 'He seem'd and appeared in every respect the same as other corps'; next was William Frost (the coachman), who said that Theodosius appeared to be in good health on the evening preceding his death.

The sixth deposition was by Bradford Wilmer, the surgeon, who gave an account of his and Dr Rattray's visit to Lawford Hall to examine Theodosius's body. He explained that, owing to the body's putrid state, they had decided that no cause of death would be ascertained by opening it up. Wilmer testified that he had also attended the open-air autopsy, and gave a detailed account of the appearance of the internal organs. The stomach contained less than an ounce of a thick brown fluid which they had taken out and put into a basin, but this fluid contained 'no grittiness or any metallic particles'. The lungs were very inflamed and putrid and in some parts black; and on each side of the lungs there was 'about a pint of extravasated blood in a fluid state'. Wilmer concluded his deposition by saying that Powell's mixture would not have caused Theodosius's death, and that, significantly, 'it was impossible to tell what occasioned the deceased's death.'

The seventh deposition was by David Rattray, a 'doctor in physic' from Coventry who concurred with Wilmer, saying that they had decided on 4 September that 'nothing conclusive could be acquired from the dissection of the body, being so putrefied.' He agreed with Wilmer's account of the open-air autopsy, but added that 'the stomach a good deal inflamed, but the bowels immediately surrounding, more particularly to the kidneys, black, full of blood, and in a soft state'. His deposition differed from Wilmer's in one crucial respect. He testified that Powell's prescribed medicine could not have caused death but that, having heard Lady Boughton's account, 'it seemed to him that from such account and the symptoms of the deceased after taking the medicine, that the same was probably the cause of his death' – meaning, presumably, that poison had been substituted for Powell's draught.

Bernard Geary Snow, a 'surgeon of Southam, Warwick', made the eighth deposition, in which he said that he had been present at the autopsy and agreed with Rattray and Wilmer's accounts. He gave no opinion as to whether the mixture in the phial was the cause of Theodosius's death. The ninth deposition was by Samuel Bucknill, 'surgeon'. As the depositions were drawn up following a series of questions posed by the coroner, it is extraordinary that Bucknill was not questioned about Hewitt's account that he had prescribed a substance that could be distilled into a powerful poison. Consequently, there is no record of why Bucknill gave the berries to Hewitt; why he thought such a substance appropriate; nor whether a distillation of the berries could produce the effects described on Theodosius on the morning of his death. Bucknill said that he had opened the body that day, and that he agreed with the description of the body provided by Wilmer, Rattray and Snow. He went on to say that the deposition of Lady Boughton had been read to him and that the medicine prescribed by Powell could not have caused the death, but he agreed with Rattray that 'the medicine administered by [Lady Boughton] to the deceased was the probable cause of his death'.

Of the four doctors and surgeons who gave evidence to the coroner, therefore, Bucknill and Rattray agreed that whatever had been given to Theodosius by Anna Maria had *probably* caused his death; Snow did not comment; and Wilmer – by far the most experienced of them – stated that it was *impossible* to say what had caused the death.

The tenth deposition was by Samuel Frost, 'late servant to the deceased', who testified that on the morning of 30 August Theodosius had given him directions for the day, and that at that time 'the deceased seemed in his usual state of health and in perfect good spirits'. There is, of course, a difference between 'his usual state of health' and 'good health'.

Donellan did not give a deposition on 9 September, but he did write to the Reverend Newsam, whom he knew would be attending both the autopsy and the inquest afterwards with Lord Denbigh. The prosecution brief kept a copy of his letter, which was not referred to in court or in Donellan's own *Defence*.

Saturday 9 September, Lawford Hall.

As I hold myself duty bound before God and the world to vindicate the reputation of my family and self in particular respecting the death of Sir Theodosius ... I confess I am anxiety itself ... Therefore I beg you will request of Lord Denbigh with the friends of his Lordship that I understand are to be with you today, to be as near the corpse as safety will permit at Newbold ... we are perfectly innocent of any unfair intentions towards him ... my wife and self very rarely visited Sir Theodosius's side of the house and were as strangers to his proceedings as the Pope was. When Sir Theodosius took his physic I was at Newnham Wells; Lady Boughton and myself were to ride out early but she told me from her window it would be some time before she could be ready to ride out ... upon my coming back the coachman told me he was going to the Doctors and I gave him the mare I had ... when I entered the house Lady Boughton told me Sir Theodosius had been extremely ill since she gave him the physic that morning ... I found Sir Theodosius in bed very ill; I called to him but he made no answer to me (my wife all this time was in bed) ...

Donellan then explained that he rinsed out one bottle and put its contents in a basin to taste it but 'I could not tell what it tasted of'. He then said that Samuel Frost had the bottle which contained the physic: 'He tells me that one that was left in the kitchen is it, which he has.' (In his later *Defence* Donellan said that he himself had the bottle, and had taken it from the kitchen to the parlour.)

After the last deposition, the coroner closed business for the day and adjourned the inquest until the following day at three o'clock. No follow-up was recorded the next day, however. In 1781 the *Scots Magazine* reported that the coroner had dismissed the jury at 5 p.m. and ordered them to attend the next day at 3 p.m., but that he himself did not turn up and at 8 p.m. he sent a message that he would fix the hearing for some date in the future. The jurymen went to their local JP, Lord Denbigh, who, with a Reverend Blomfield, 'appeared in the vindication of the rights of society thus violated' (presumably this means that Lord Denbigh leaned heavily on the coroner) and the next hearing was promptly fixed for 14 September.

Captain Murphy's *Life of Captain John Donellan*, published in 1781, gives a more detailed version of events. According to Murphy, the jury were utterly mystified by the delay on 10 September; although he suggests that perhaps the coroner was 'confused by the novelty of the business' or 'by his delicacy for the honour of a respectable family'. He notes, however, that the delay simply fanned the flames of the rumours that something was badly awry at Lawford Hall.

The prosecution brief at the trial gives another, more detailed and altogether more revealing explanation. This claims that 'when the Jury were attending to hear the evidence, Captain Donellan was present the whole time, even against the desire of the Jury, so that he in great measure kept Lady Boughton and such of the servants as were witnesses in awe ... when she mentioned the circumstance of the rinsing of the bottles he immediately pulled her by the sleeve ...'

By the time that the inquest was next convened on 14 September, Lord Denbigh had stepped in to take control: 'At the meeting,' the prosecution brief continues, 'Lord Denbigh and the Reverend Bromfield (another Justice of the Peace) [presumably the same person as the Reverend *Blomfield* referred to by the magazine] thinking before the Coroner had not done his duty, attended to see that the

Inquest was properly held. In consequence of their attendance, Lady Boughton and the other witnesses were all separately examined in their presence; Lord Denbigh strongly objecting to Captain Donellan being present ... to prevent the restraint the witnesses seemed to be under before ...'

Denbigh's presence helped Anna Maria Boughton to see Donellan's actions in a significantly altered light.

On 14 September, Anna Maria Boughton testified a second time. This version of events was markedly different from her first. The time of administering the medicine, the time of Donellan's entering the room, and of Anna Maria's leaving the room, and the approximate time of Theodosius's death – all of which had been referred to in her first deposition – were not now mentioned. This second statement centred completely on Donellan's actions. Anna Maria explained as follows:

> ... the circumstance of John Donellan swilling the bottle led her to suppose that some unfair dealings had been carried on respecting her son, and that he had died by the medicine she had given him; and that she herself was so much alarmed at it, that she declared she should like to be opened when she died.

In other words, Anna Maria was afraid that 'unfair dealings' could extend to her – so much so that she mentioned her own death and her request for an autopsy as if it might be imminent. An intriguing detail was revealed the following year in a commentary written in April 1781 in 'A Gentleman's Reply'.[2]

It claimed that 'Lord D' – presumably the Earl of Denbigh – 'had a private interview for upwards of half an hour with Lady Boughton before she went into the room to be again examined; there does not remain a doubt that his Lordship had something which very much terrified her, for every time that something was said which was thought to mitigate against Mr Donellan, she looked at his Lordship, who never failed in return a nod of approbation.'

This seems proof that, while Denbigh ensured that Donellan was not there to oversee proceedings, he *was*.

In her first deposition of 9 September, Anna Maria had said that John Donellan had rinsed out the phial with water into a bowl and that he had tasted the mixture and said it was 'nauseous'. In her second deposition Anna Maria says that Donellan took the bottle off the chimney piece, swilled it out and 'threw the water and the medicine which was left at the bottom of the bottle away together upon the ground.' Donellan then took a second bottle from the chimney piece and also threw its contents to the ground. Next he instructed Sarah Blundell, who was in the room, to take the bottles away. Anna Maria stated that she objected, but that Donellan insisted and the bottles were removed.

Then came another damning indictment. Anna Maria testified that when she and Donellan had returned to Lawford Hall after her first deposition, he had expressed 'surprise and disapprobation' at her previously volunteering information about his swilling-out the bottles. She then said that it had been Donellan's idea to keep Theodosius's medicines in an outer, unlocked room.

After Anna Maria's new statement, the servant girl Sarah Blundell was called again. She swore that Donellan had instructed her to take away the used medicine bottles (plural) just as Anna Maria had said.

Meanwhile, John Donellan wrote a letter dated Thursday 14 September to 'The Coroner and Gentlemen of the Jury at Newbold'. He evidently felt it wise to add more detail to the account he had already given to the Reverend Newsam. He wrote:

Gentlemen:
I hold it my duty to give you every information …

During the time Sir Theodosius was here, great part of it was spent in procuring things to kill rats, with which this house swarms remarkably. He used to have arsenic by the pound weight at a time, and laid the same in and about the house, in various places and in as many forms.

We often expostulated with him about the extreme careless manner in which he acted, respecting himself and the family in general; his answer to us was, that the men servants knew where he had laid the arsenic, and for us we had no business with it.

At table we have not eaten anything for many months past which we perceived him to touch, as we well knew his extreme inattention to the bad effects of the various things he frequently used to send for, for the above purposes, as well as for making up horse medicines; he used to make up vast quantities of Gulard, from a receipt which he had from Mrs Newsam; she will give you a copy of it, if you please, and it will speak for itself.

Since Sir Theodosius's death, the gardener collected several fish which Sir Theodosius laid: he used to split them and rub the stuff upon them; the gardener was ordered to bury the fish ...

Lady Boughton, my wife and self have showed the utmost willingness to satisfy the public respecting Sir Theodosius's death, by every act within the limits of our power ... every one that came to the house should see the corpse before it was put into the coffin on the fourth day; and the eighth day the corpse was sent to the vault at Newbold.

I am, gentlemen, your most obedient servant,
John Donellan.

Five days had passed since both John Donellan and Anna Maria Boughton had attended the first coroner's hearing on 9 September. In that time, Anna Maria had decided that 'unfair dealings' had occurred, while John Donellan centred his account on the poisons freely available in the house, brought there by Theodosius himself without any apparent regard for the safety of the rest of the family – the implication being that, if Theodosius died by poison, it was through some accident or design of his own. Why Thomas Hewitt's testimony as to a possible source of poison is not mentioned by Donellan is confusing, as ingestion of picrotoxin would have produced a very quick death such as that experienced by Theodosius.

What is so curious about Anna Maria's depositions, though, is not only the change in her evidence – in the first, Donellan tastes the residue from a basin; in the second he throws it, untasted, on the floor – but that if she had suspected Donellan from that very first morning of poisoning her son, why had she allowed him to supervise the visits by the doctors? Why had she not written to or visited Sir William to express her fears? Why had she not prevented the funeral? Anna Maria had power; she had influence; if she had the slightest misgivings, would it not have been natural to express them to Sir William or the family solicitor at the earliest opportunity? Why had she waited until public disquiet had forced an autopsy?

The explanation that Anna Maria gives in her second deposition is that she had been disturbed by Donellan's irritation at her mentioning the bottles at all in the first deposition. Consequently, she had thought over the events in the light of his bad humour and concluded that 'unfair dealings had been carried on'. Her renewed examination of the events of the morning had, apparently, resulted in her deciding that Donellan had acted quite differently to her first account. But this version is not simply an addition to or expansion on the first version. It is a completely *different* account of his actions and, by implication, his motives and mood.

Sir William, in the later trial, makes no mention of having been approached by Theodosius's mother. He deposited with the court a full and complete set of the letters that had passed between himself and John Donellan, but made no mention of any correspondence with Anna Maria.

If Anna Maria had really seen Donellan throw the contents of the bottle on the ground, would that not have *immediately* struck her as suspicious? Yet if Donellan had, as per her original deposition, simply rinsed out the bottle, tasted its contents and pronounced them 'nauseous', that would not necessarily have aroused any suspicion at all, and so her silence after her son's death is more understandable.

At what point in the intervening five days had Anna Maria decided to change her evidence, and why? And, aware of the difference between the two depositions, what gave her the confidence to do so?

The decision now lay with the coroner and a jury which he had summoned from the neighbourhood. In 1780, a coroner was a substitute for the High Sheriff of the County. There was no concept of the Crown bringing a case to court; the Director of Public Prosecutions was not instituted until a century later. Nor were there any police or public prosecutors. The prosecution of almost all criminal offences was private; it was up to the victim to pursue the perceived offender. Charges had to be filed with a local magistrate, evidence presented to a jury and then subsequently provided for the trial. There was no overriding concept of 'the people' protecting society; it was one person against another. Anna Maria filed her charges against Donellan.

The *Coventry Mercury* newspaper reported on Monday 18 September that 'on Friday last' – that is, on 15 September, the day after Anna Maria Boughton's second deposition – John Donellan was arrested and brought under guard to Warwick Gaol, 'where he is now confined, charged with the wilful murder of Theodosius Boughton'.

8

A Very Long Winter

'Isolation is the sum total of wretchedness to a man.'

Thomas Carlyle

THE FULL IMPACT OF THEODOSIUS'S DEATH slowly began to
filter through to the Shukburgh side of the family. On 28 September, Lucy Wright, Edward Boughton's sister, wrote to their brother
Charles:

> I am now most impatient to receive some further account than
> the newspaper gives of the horrible affair in Warwickshire …
> I have written two letters to my brother and rec'd no answers
> to them … my brother's business at Lawford Hall [was] occa-
> sioned I find by a most base and infamous poisoning. Pray tell
> me who it was who first detected the fact and occasion'd the
> Grave to be opened?

On 6 October, her mother Mary also wrote to Charles, but the
matriarch's mind was still on money:

> I very sincerely rejoice in yr Brother's acquisition tho the cause
> is shocking to a dreadful degree … I've never been able til now

by yr Letter to know what Estate yr Brother got, whether an old family mansion came with it ...

By 12 October, however, Edward was back at Poston Hall and writing to Charles with news of Anna Maria, and an exasperated complaint about the locals:

My good Aunt fears that poor Sir Theo was ill prepared for so early and sudden summons into Eternity. I have had a letter from Caldecott, in which he mentions that Donellan had retain'd almost all the Counsel who come to that Circuit. I found when I came there that a strong idea prevailed among the Country people that I was the person committed to Warwick Gaol. I wonder most at their extreme stupidity.[1]

Edward's letter shows how much gossip was still circulating even after Donellan's arrest – and its capacity to get the facts dramatically wrong.

As for Anna Maria – Edward's 'good Aunt' – the *Scots Magazine* of 1781 later reported that Lady Boughton had been 'distracted' and 'frantic' since Donellan's arrest, 'and to add to the calamities of the family, the daughter is far advanced in pregnancy'. Although edited by the redoubtable James Boswell, the magazine had its facts wrong here. Anna Maria may or may not have been 'frantic', but it is very unlikely that Theodosia had a 'far advanced' pregnancy. It was only just over two months since her last child had been born.

It was going to be a very long winter for John Donellan.

The County Assizes were over for that year; he would have to remain in prison until they reconvened in April of 1781.

Donellan was arrested at Lawford Hall and taken via the outskirts of Coventry and Rugby to Warwick. He was, according to the chronicler of Rugby School, Matthew Bloxam, at first conducted on foot by two constables from Long Lawford to Rugby. Bloxam paints a humiliating picture:

As [Donellan] approached the town, many of its inhabitants ...

went out on to the Lawford Road to meet him; amongst them were several members of the School, for there existed a feud between him and the School on account of his having prohibited them from fishing in the Avon near Lawford Hall and with them he was no favourite ... among those was a poor idiot lad who had been much tormented in the town and was well known in Rugby by the taunting name of Taffy White. As Donellan approached, walking between his guards, the poor idiot with apparent glee ran and danced before him exclaiming, 'Who's Taffy now? Who's Taffy now?' [2]

It is debatable whether this is an accurate account of Donellan's journey, as someone of his social rank would have been expected to ride in a cart or a carriage; but perhaps Anna Maria had forbidden the use of one from Lawford. Constables were not paid by the county, so in this instance they probably saw the progression of Donellan through the various villages as an opportunity to allow the public to gawp at the man that the county had been gossiping about so freely. It would have been a fraught journey for Donellan, to say the least.

And what of the gaol where Donellan was to spend the winter? The centre of Warwick had suffered a large fire in September 1694; 450 buildings had been destroyed. The cost of rebuilding it had virtually crippled the town corporation, and the Shire Hall in Northgate Street was only begun in 1753, with the adjoining gaol still in the process of reconstruction when Donellan arrived there.

An undated plan of the gaol now in Warwick Records Office shows a lodge and main entrance on Barrack Street (then Bridewell Lane) with buildings marked 'Debtors' to the east and 'Misdemeanours' to the west. Running alongside Northgate Street was a building marked 'Clerk of the Peace'; next to the Governor's House were a series of courtyards, and below these to the east and west were the 'Women's Prison', a 'Day Room' and a 'Felons' Prison'. South of the Felons' Prison was a small courtyard with a treadmill building in its centre.

An account of 1815 also describes a 'bridewell' – probably a house of correction where beggars and vagrants were set to work – at the north-west end of Barrack Street: 'a strong and handsome building with a good stone front and a garden before it'.[3]

Gaols at this time were primarily places where people were held for only a short while before trial, not the six months that were in prospect for Donellan. Those who did languish for years were normally debtors.

As it was later reported that Donellan shared a cell with the debtor John Derbyshire, it is probable that he was taken to the Debtors' Prison on the east end of Barrack Street, which would have offered more comfortable accommodation than the Felons'. Here Donellan would have been able to pay for extra luxuries such as bedding, food and alcohol, as a prison warden then counted the payments for such things as part of his salary; nevertheless, Warwick Gaol provided a rather stark contrast to his home for the last two years.

Fourteen miles away, at Lawford, Anna Maria Boughton had much to occupy her mind. Most pressing was who had the authority to administer Theodosius's estate and collect the rents that formed the majority of their income.

On 21 October, Theodosia independently sought counsel's opinion on her legal position, asking whether her husband's arrest would affect her inheritance of her brother's estate; in the same month, Anna Maria applied to the Archbishop of Canterbury for 'letters of administration' covering Theodosius's affairs.[4] Permission was granted on 31 October, making Theodosia an heiress, as Theodosius's income from his estates was released.[5]

Theodosia visited her husband in Warwick Gaol at the beginning of October, taking their son John, then aged only three months, with her. (She would visit John four times in all, according to the *Nottinghamshire Gazette*.) Accompanying her was her maid, Susannah Sparrow (referred to later as Sukey).

In his *Defence* Donellan reported a conversation which the gaoler Mr Roe had had with Susannah. The girl was in the kitchen belonging to Roe, which was 'adjoining the gaol', with three others: John Derbyshire, the debtor who knew Donellan; a Thomas Bayly, also a debtor; and Mary Douglas, a servant girl of Mr Roe's.

Derbyshire asked Susannah if the rumour he had heard was true: that she had said 'something against Mr Donellan at a country wake'. She replied that she had said nothing against him, and that she believed that Donellan was as innocent of the charge brought against him 'as the child she then had in her arms' – Donellan's son. She then added that she had been sent for several times by the local JPs, 'and threatened by them unless she disclosed what she said at the country wake; and she told them she said nothing against Mr Donellan there, nor knew anything against him'.

Bayly was also reported to have heard this conversation and added that, once Susannah was seated in the garden outside, she had said, 'She was sure her master was innocent, and wondered much at Lady Boughton's conduct towards him.' Mary Douglas also reported a conversation with Susannah: 'She was sorry to her soul for her master, and was surprised at Lady Boughton's cruel and inhuman behaviour.'

Neither Roe nor Susannah nor Bayly nor Mary Douglas were ever called to testify at the trial. It was thought by Webb, Donellan's barrister, that they would 'not be favourable witnesses'.

John Derbyshire, however, was called. His evidence would work against Donellan.

Meanwhile, October saw the publication of various letters in local newspapers about the conduct of the coroner's court. The *Coventry Mercury* published an article on 16 October purporting to be by a friend of Donellan. In it, the author denounced various pieces that had already been published, saying that they were designed to 'deprive him of that candour and impartiality characteristic of an English jury'. The reports, it said, were untrue; especially the rumour that Dr Wilmer had been to see Donellan after Theodosius died and was 'closeted up' with him for some time.

But more significantly, it absolutely blasted the coroner's jury, claiming that they were tenant farmers who had been annoyed at Donellan for persuading Lady Boughton to raise their rents. The countryside was 'prejudiced' and that prejudice had extended to Warwick Gaol, it claimed, where Donellan had been 'refused comforts' and 'deprived of the assistance of his lawyers' and where all his personal papers were being read by the gaoler. The article was signed 'A Friend to Justice'. It drew an immediate reply from the members of the coroner's jury.

On 21 October, a letter was published which rebuffed the 'scandalous libel' that had been levelled against them. The article of 16 October was 'uncharitable, cruel, impious, false and rash', the letter stormed. None of the jurymen were Lady Boughton's tenants, except one; the coroner had given them no reason why he could not meet with them the day after the depositions were taken except to say he was busy, and they had later found out that he was busy 'stopping at Lady Boughton's that evening'. It was, the letter said, strange conduct – and the reason was that the coroner had wanted to see John Donellan. While the members of the jury had been kept waiting, the coroner had called Donellan into the garden and talked with him for fifteen minutes. Worse still, one of the jurors, William Crofts, claimed that he had seen Donellan pull on Lady Boughton's sleeve during the depositions 'in a very unbecoming passion'. The letter flatly asserted that Donellan and Wilmer *had* met several times, and that the coroner knew this to be true. The jurors signed their names: Edward Boddington, John Alebone, William Robbins, William Cave, Joseph Richardson, William Cornish, Samuel Pace, Edward Greenaway, John Norman, William Norman, William Liggins, William Crofts, William Townsend, Richard Pell, Robert Line, Richard Webb and Robert Onely.

Both John Donellan's *Defence* and legal documents from these months demonstrate an unbearable tension that had arisen between Theodosia and Anna Maria. In Warwick, Donellan regularly received letters from his wife, so he said, in which she complained about the 'cruel behaviour of her mother'. Responding to them, he told her to quit Lawford Hall 'lest she should fall a sacrifice to the fate of her brother'.

Unknown to him at this time, however, his letters were being intercepted and read by the gaoler; Roe admits as much in his statement for the prosecution brief. Donellan would later use this in a desperate ploy to bring public opinion around to support him, but for now he wrote what he thought was a private appeal: 'In a letter sent by Captain Donellan when he first came to Warwick,' Roe reveals, 'before he suspected I would examine his letters, he desired Mrs Donellan to speak to Lady Boughton to say nothing about the phial and then all would be well.' The prosecution notes that the letter was given to Theodosia, and that before the trial she was asked to produce the original – but she never did.

Presumably Donellan is talking about the washing of the bottle here. He seems to be suggesting that if Anna Maria kept quiet about it, he would be acquitted. When he received no such assurance, his attitude changed dramatically.

Only a matter of weeks into his incarceration, Donellan felt free to express his opinion that Anna Maria was a dangerous, even lethal, opponent. He wrote of his fears for his wife's safety, and referred to the fact of 'sudden deaths having happened in the family ... the late Sir Edward Boughton died suddenly'. He spoke of the 'neighbourhood knowing Lady Boughton's cruel disposition' and finally revealed that Anna Maria had once admitted to poisoning all her husband's pack of hounds, 'which she confessed to Mr Donellan as a fact, but told him at the same time that nobody ever knew who did it, and begged him not to mention it to his wife'.

The gloves were off. Whether Donellan had suspected Anna Maria of poisoning her own son while he was still at Lawford, or whether it was a conclusion he had come to after she delivered her altered depositions to the coroner, which cast such a suspicious light on him, is hard to say. Sir Edward Boughton, who had ridden post-haste from Herefordshire on Theodosius's death, was now jointly paying for Donellan's prosecution with Anna Maria. Nor could Donellan count on the support of the local aristocracy – the Whelers, the Denbighs, the Shukburghs. The ranks had closed, and he was alone.

On 8 December, Donellan wrote a letter to Theodosia. It was addressed to her at 'Lawford Hall – or elsewhere'.

My Dear,
I am now informed that [her solicitor] Mr Harris's clerk is here

and hope by this time you have removed to the friendly roof I last recommended to you; and no longer remain where you are likely to undergo the fate of those who are gone already by sudden means ... [Donellan seems to allude to both Theodosia's brother and father here.]

In my first letter to you from Rugby 14th Sept. last I mentioned a removal, I had my reasons, which will appear in an honest light in March next, to the eternal confusion of an unnatural being,

I am, dear Wife, your affectionate Husband, John Donellan.

The letter was delivered into the hands of the gaoler, Roe, unsealed. In Donellan's *Defence* this is referred to by his solicitors, Inge and Webb, as an oversight due to 'his hurry and confusion'. They note that 'his adversaries had obtained a copy of it'. In the same paragraph, they claim that Donellan was misrepresented in his accusations about Anna Maria; he had merely stated facts – sudden deaths *were* a feature of the Boughton family. Lady Boughton had once told him, he maintained, that she had poisoned a pack of hounds belonging to her husband (presumably after she found him in bed with the maid, or after hearing of his mistress); her conduct on the morning of Theodosius's death 'did induce him to believe that she was the perpetrator of it'. However, they make the point that Donellan had never accused Anna Maria in so many words of being a murderess. The distinction is a rather fine one, presumably made because of the horror with which such an accusation might be greeted. And it was indeed seized upon by the prosecuting counsel at the trial.

According to the prosecution brief, however, Donellan left the letter unsealed deliberately. They claimed that he had told the gaoler that he had 'left it open so that it might be read and made public'. They said that the solicitor's clerk had copied it, and then sent it to Theodosia; the original was not available because Theodosia had burned it.

Within a few days, Anna Maria had fallen dangerously ill. Whether because of the publication of Donellan's letter is a matter for conjecture.

It was just before Christmas, and soon Donellan received the news that was to spur him into action. He was, he wrote in his *Defence*, told by the gaoler Mr Roe and 'others' that 'she [Anna Maria] had taken poison and was then upon point of death from its effects'.

Donellan dashed a letter to Theodosia, telling her to beg Anna Maria to confess to poisoning her son, and to bring Sir William Wheler to hear the confession 'as the most respectable person in the neighbourhood'. Donellan's lawyers noted, when publishing his *Defence*, that this desperate letter implied a consciousness of his own innocence and 'a natural desire of having his character justified to the world by the only positive and expiring opportunity'.

It is indeed a good moment at which to take stock of Donellan's reactions. Anna Maria was a religious woman who had already told Theodosius's cousin Edward Boughton that she feared that 'poor Sir Theo was ill prepared for so early and sudden a summons into Eternity'. Her son's death without the benefit of confession of his sins and the absolution of the Church would have weighed on her mind. Donellan knew her and her beliefs; he had, after all, lived at Lawford Hall for two years and had been – in his words – privy to at least one of her secrets, the poisoning of the dogs. And if she was about to die, then Donellan believed that she would confess her own crimes, and he wanted Sir William Wheler to be there to hear them. So if he had committed the crime, he would have known there was no hope of Anna Maria confessing to something she had not done. However, if *she* had committed the crime, he would have believed that she would confess it now rather than be damned for eternity.

It was his great chance at reprieve, and he acted with the absolute conviction of an innocent man. Unless, of course, he was so utterly in command of the situation that he had worked out how to throw the blame on to Anna Maria at the very moment of her death. It is conceivable that his letter to Theodosia and the request to bring Sir William Wheler to Lawford Hall were part of a coldly calculating smokescreen – a double bluff.

However, Anna Maria Boughton did not die. She was very ill, but it is not known whether this was as a result of an unsuccessful poisoning, an unsuccessful suicide attempt or an unsuccessful murder attempt by someone at the Hall. Indeed, it is not even known whether she ingested poison. Poison, illness, fever – whatever the cause of her illness, Anna Maria survived.

The family lawyer, Caldecott, who was fond of adding a paragraph of gossip as a postscript to his business letters to the Shukburgh branch of the family, wrote to Edward Boughton on 22 December 1780 that Lady Boughton had had a fever and been 'considerably ill' for several days. He added cryptically: 'The loss of her would have been a fortunate circumstance for Donellan as it would probably prevent his conviction.'[6]

But Caldecott's brief note gives another piece of news which is utterly revealing about the situation between mother and daughter: 'Mrs Donellan is gone to live in Northampton.' Theodosia had evidently believed everything Donellan had told her, and obeyed his instructions. Despite her mother's dangerous illness, and although she had two small children to look after, Theodosia had moved out of Lawford Hall.

Soon after her recovery, Anna Maria made her will on 10 February 1781. It is an astonishing document, seething with bitterness towards her daughter.

'I, Dame Anna Maria Boughton of Lawford Hall,' it begins, 'seriously contemplating the frailty and uncertainty of human life …'

Her bequests were as follows.

To her 'cousin Hannah King of Northampton', and to the daughters of two local vicars, she left £100 (£6,200 in today's money). To the churchwardens and minister of Newbold church she left £60 (£3,770) for the poorest inhabitants of the parish 'on St Thomas Day annually and forever'. She also left £40 (£2,500) to the poor of Adstone in Northamptonshire 'annually and forever'. To Hannah Rye (her brother's daughter) she left £648 (£41,000) – the only part of her estate inherited from her mother, and part of her 'jointure' which she was free to dispose of. Hannah was also left all of Anna Maria's furniture, jewellery, porcelain, books, paintings, clothes and household linens, and indeed 'all my goods, chattels, effects and Personal Effects whatsoever'. By contrast, Theodosia received 'the sum of one shilling only' and her two children, Anna Maria's own grandchildren, nothing at all.

At some point in the future – the alteration is undated – Anna Maria thought better of this vengeful and humiliating document. Without recourse to a solicitor, in private, she wrote across the bottom next to her original signature:

'This will I canceld myself, Anna Boughton.'

But she did not destroy it. She kept a copy; and in due course the will, in all its latent fury, passed into the Boughton archives.[7]

The date of the trial was set for 30 March.

But Donellan was not always calm and reasonable during the remainder of his imprisonment. The *Northampton Mercury* of 9 April 1781 reported that he had become drunk on several occasions, and when the gaoler had tried to take him back to his room, Donellan had told him, 'In fifteen months I will be High Sheriff of the County, and then I will turn you out of office.' In the same article, the gaoler (not named, but presumably Roe) had also maintained that Donellan was so convinced that he would be found innocent that he had made an arrangement to meet a friend in London the day after his trial.

One other very telling incident was reported only years later, in 1883, by James Fitzjames Stephen, in an article he wrote about his grandfather James Stephen, one of the leading members of the Anti-Slavery Society, who as a young man of twenty-two had written a very lengthy article condemning the unfairness of Donellan's trial and the way in which it had been conducted. We will return to James Stephen's account later; but his grandson wrote:

My grandfather was introduced to Donellan's attorney, who professed to Donellan to retain Mr Dunning; he referred the attorney to Mrs Donellan for authority to incur the necessary expense. Mrs Donellan said she thought it needless to pay so high a fee. When the attorney reported this to Donellan, he burst into a rage and cried passionately, 'And who got it for her!' Then, seeing that he had committed himself, he suddenly stopped … the story itself is hearsay and more than a hundred years old.

If reported correctly – and the writer admits that the account is unsubstantiated – was this simply a petulant outburst that Donellan had been denied the best? (Dunning was the best that money could buy.) Or did this speak of something more?

Donellan had 'got it for her' – in other words, he got the fortune for his wife. But by accident, design, or on command?

Before the trial began, John Donellan wrote a very detailed and lengthy account of his relationship with the Boughton family for his solicitors, Inge and Webb, for the use of his defending team in court. It was published in April 1781 at Donellan's request, together with additions he had made the day after the trial. In its published form it was entitled *A Defence and Substance of the Trial of John Donellan, Esq. … Founded on the case solemnly attested by the Sufferer after his Conviction*. In it he also covered events prior to Theodosius's death, the morning of the death, and what happened in the following days and while he was in prison.

The information which he provided, if true, was to a large extent ignored by his counsels. The explanation they gave after the trial for doing this was that Donellan's witnesses – servants and tradesmen – were not reliable or impressive enough to bring to court.

The counsels' blatant misuse or lack of use of pertinent information, however – especially where it contradicted Anna Maria's version of events – is extraordinary.

There is some evidence that, to his friends, Donellan was more pessimistic about the local people, although still hoping for a positive outcome to the trial. Captain Murphy's *Life of Captain Donellan* printed a letter supposedly from Donellan to a friend, dated Saturday 24 March. It reads:

I expected you down here yesterday as you promised; but not seeing you I have been very uneasy. Let nothing prevent you from setting off immediately, if this letter reaches you in London, and pray bring — with you. The people here are as violent as ever: their cruelty to me is not to be accounted for, as I never injured a single person in the country since I first came into it. However, their malice will be of no avail. As soon as the trial is over, I will open your eyes on the whole of the unhappy business, and which will satisfy you on the particular matter you mentioned in your last.
Assuredly yours,
John Donellan.

The day before the trial, Edward Boughton returned to Warwick and wrote to his brother Charles:

Donellan's trial comes on tomorrow and tis general opinion that he will be found guilty. The Grand Jury found the bill on hearing but a small part of the evidence, and the Judge in his Charge express'd himself concerning circumstantial evidence in a manner which was thought unfavourable to Donellan … I really think that the whole forms such a mass of evidence as leaves in my mind little doubt of his conviction.

He then went on to reveal some compelling new evidence:

Some additional discoveries have of late been made and one in particular of great importance which has hitherto been kept secret to prevent Donellan getting intelligence of it. Lady Boughton's description of the Dose that it smelt like the Taste of Bitter Almonds suggested to the Surgeon that it must have been prepared from a Distillation of Laurel.[8]

He went on to describe a still which had been found in John Donellan's bedroom; its discovery would play a telling role in the hours to come.

Although not revealed at the trial itself, a further report on Donellan's interest in the poison distilled from laurel leaves would surface some time later. In *The Lives of Twelve Eminent Judges* (1846) William Townsend reported that 'In Donnellan's [*sic*] library there happened to be a single number of "Philosophical Transaction" and of this single number the leaves had been cut in only one place, and this place happened to contain an account of the making of laurel water by distillation.'

However, all this lay in the future.

As Donellan prepared himself for the trial the next day his mood and confidence were, reported the gaoler, buoyant. He was, after all, planning to go to London the day after the trial. Spectators would say how calm he was in court. As far as he was concerned, of course, he had given a complete refutation of Anna Maria's evidence in his prepared notes for counsel; he would have expected that they would use them to rapidly secure his release.

Donellan knew of various rumours that he had tried to kill Theodosius before – the *Nottinghamshire Gazette* of 14 April confirmed that it was 'publicly said in the very week of the trial that Captain Donellan had made repeated attempts on Sir Theodosius's life'; and that 'the popular odium was excited against him to an unprecedented degree'.[9] But he also knew that there was nothing concrete to support the accusation held against him. Every piece of evidence was circumstantial.

The case crucially, and tenuously, rested on Anna Maria Boughton's account; in fact, as S. M. Phillips wrote nearly a century later in *Famous Cases of Circumstantial Evidence*: 'the argument turned upon the breath, the smell of a woman, distracted at that moment with the loss of her son, and ready to ascribe that evil to the first thing that came her way.'[10]

9

The Trial Begins

'I do not care to speak ill of any man behind his back; but I believe the gentleman was an attorney.'

Dr Johnson

30 MARCH 1781, the date of John Donellan's trial at Warwick Assizes, was exactly seven months to the day after Theodosius Boughton had died. The accused was brought the few yards from the gaol into one of the two imposing courtrooms that still stand today: octagonal rooms that had been completed just thirteen years before, in 1758.[1]

One of Donellan's friends from London, William Walsh, accompanied him into the court and proceeded to advise him on court procedure. Not that Donellan would have welcomed it. Walsh, who had begun life as a valet to Philip Stanhope, the illegitimate son of Lord Chesterfield, and finished it as a commissioner in the Custom House, was described by the publisher Henry Colburn in 1828 as 'a ready-made joke'. However, Colburn went on to comment: 'Walsh had been well acquainted with Donellan and attended him with great kindness from the gaol to the Court House.' Once in the court, however, Walsh's kindness wore thin; he pointed out the jurors, the lawyers and the crowds, and finished with the judge, adding jauntily, 'The judge will put on a black cap and sentence you to be hanged.' The story of Walsh's cheerful tactlessness was to be told in his dining club for years afterwards.

Most criminal prosecutions at this time were by jury trial. Jurymen were just that – men; no women were allowed. Ownership of property was considered a good qualification for a juror, although members of the aristocracy were never chosen. Farmers, artisans and tradesmen were typical jurors, their register compiled annually by the county under the supervision of the Justices of the Peace. Not that owning property in itself automatically entitled a man to be a juror; in neighbouring Northamptonshire in the 1770s, only about ten people per thousand head of population were eligible to be jurors. Three-quarters of adult males were deemed too poor to qualify, whether they owned land or not.

Consequently, John Donellan would have faced a jury of local men who had made a considerable amount of money from their own land, tenant farms or businesses. As the Boughtons and their friends owned much of the local land on which the tenant farmers flourished, and as local tradesmen were to an extent dependent on aristocratic patronage, it is likely that most of the jurors either had the Boughtons and their contacts as landlords, or were at least anxious not to offend them (despite any protests to the contrary).[2]

It was also well known that the selection of jurors could be tampered with by neglecting to keep up a current list of freeholders; judges like Baptist Nunn in the 1720s regularly scrutinised and altered lists of jurors with the connivance of the under-sheriffs. The seven-month gap between Theodosius's death and Donellan's trial allowed ample time for the jurors selected to be approved by local JPs. The Justices of the Peace were also landed gentlemen; from 1732 JPs had to have an estate of £100 (£8,500) a year.

Standing in the dock, Donellan would also have been uncomfortably aware of the punitive nature of English law; despite the reforming politician William Eden arguing for fewer capital crimes in his *Principles of Penal Punishment* in 1771, no less than 240 offences carried the death penalty. This had been enforced by the Waltham Black Act of 1723, which had added fifty new capital offences; and in 1781 a man, woman or child could be hanged for offences ranging from murder and highway robbery to the seemingly absurd 'being in the company of gypsies for more than a month', writing a threatening letter, or, in the cases of children aged seven to fourteen, simply having 'evidence of malice'.

Not all death sentences, however, were carried out – less than 30 per cent – yet being condemned to the pillory could be equally bad. Less than a week after Donellan's trial, it was reported in the *Morning Chronicle* and *London Advertiser* that 20,000 people attacked two men put in the pillory for homosexual acts.[3] It was only a year since branding had been abolished; it would be another ten before the execution of women by burning would be outlawed, and not until 1817 was the public flogging of women stopped. The court at Warwick did not flinch from imposing the severest penalties. In the 1780s, those hanged there included 'Elizabeth Green, for stealing 2 guineas, aged 24', 'Sam Smith for house-breaking, aged 17' and 'Sam Packwood, for shop-lifting'.

Such was the state of English law at this time that the role of defence counsel was not clearly defined. In 1781, cross-examination of witnesses was not consistent practice, and defence counsel could not address the jury or give a summing-up. However, perhaps most damaging of all to a defendant's case was that he or she was not allowed to speak in court. A defendant could only have a statement read out in court, a statement which had been prepared before the witnesses had been heard. So-called expert witnesses could also give opinions on the defendant's guilt: a point that was to prove crucial for Donellan.

The events as shown in the opening chapters of this book were portrayed from Anna Maria Boughton's point of view. Now her testimony, taken from the original trial transcript, will be compared with the version Donellan prepared for his lawyers and as he annotated it after the trial.

The contrasts both between Anna Maria's and Donellan's accounts, and between the case that Donellan had prepared and what little of that case was used, are remarkable.

If the odds were not already heavily stacked against him, the presiding judge, Sir Justice Buller, presented the final insurmountable obstacle to Donellan. Not only had Buller opined in Warwick the week before that he thought Donellan was guilty, but he had an aggressively punitive reputation.

Francis Buller had been only thirty-two when he had been appointed to the bench in 1778 – the youngest judge ever to sit in British courts: Donellan now faced a man of his own age who had risen rapidly to high office and who was at the height of his intellectual powers. Buller was to preside over many high-profile trials in his illustrious career. However, a year after Donellan's trial he made a ruling that earned him a nickname for life which echoes down the centuries even now: Justice Thumb. In 1782, he ruled that it was permissible for a man to beat his wife providing that the stick used was no thicker than the man's thumb. A Gillray cartoon of November 1782 shows Buller selling conveniently sized sticks and saying, 'Here's your nice family amusement for winter evenings', while in the background a husband beats his wife with the words 'Murder, hey? It is Law, you Bitch! It is not bigger than my thumb.' Nor was Buller hesitant in handing out the death sentence: having himself had several sheep stolen from the flock on his Devonshire estates, he invariably hanged anyone found guilty of sheep stealing.

Buller was not physically imposing; an engraving by Francesco Bartolozzi shows a short man, with small hands of which the left fist is clenched. He looks to his left with a piercing, steady gaze – the same expression shown in the Gillray cartoon – and a rather weak, feminine mouth is offset by an aquiline nose and heavy, dominating eyebrows. Above a lavishly trimmed set of scarlet robes, a double chin is clearly visible.

Buller was born into a wealthy family in Crediton, Devon, in March 1746, and married the heiress to the nearby Churston estate, Susanna Yarde, in 1763, when he was only seventeen and his wife was twenty-three. Educated at Christ's Hospital, he was admitted to the Inner Temple in the same year as his marriage: he would remain passionately attached to the law – and, to all outward show, to his wife – all his life. Although he had married into money, Buller's own family was already well off. Downes House, where he was born, owned over 5,000 acres of land in Devon and Cornwall which by the mid-1800s was generating an income of over £14,000 (more than £800,000 today) per annum; added to this, documents in the Cornwall Record Office show that Buller owned further property in London.

Despite all his wealth and reputation, however, Buller was uncomfortable with his life. 'He was unhappy,' wrote the playwright Joseph Cradock.[4] 'He resorted too frequently to whist to divert himself from uneasy thoughts.' In *The Lives of Twelve Eminent Judges* Townsend commented: 'Buller's life was disfigured by an appetency for political intrigue, and his somewhat unscrupulous use of borough influence for purposes of party ... his many virtues were tarnished by an inordinate love of money and passion for high play.' Buller himself readily admitted his addiction to gambling; he claimed that his idea of paradise was to spend all day in court and all night at the gaming tables. (His sedentary existence was to be his ultimate downfall; after years of poor health, in June 1800 he suffered a catastrophic heart attack while playing a game of piquet, fell from his chair and died instantaneously, aged fifty-four).

In a contemporaneous set of memoirs, Buller was described as having 'great quickness of perception ... although perhaps his perception is sometimes too quick'. 'It has exposed him to the charge of impatience and petulance very indecorous in a judge ... Buller seems to possess the greatest inflexibility of opinion.'[5]

But Cradock's *Memoirs* revealed something even more disturbing and pertinent to the coming trial. In them he writes of a meeting he had with Buller just a week before: 'One of the last times I ever met him was on the day of his coming to Leicester at the house of an eminent physician there.' (There were not many 'eminent' physicians in the area, aside from those who were to testify later against Donellan.) 'At the Assizes, on the Sunday, we all dined at Nework's Leicester, and some gentlemen who were all to meet again next week at Warwick; the general conversation was Donellan, and his guilt was asserted by all.'

By *all*? One wonders at the identity of the 'gentlemen'. Were some of them court officers? Was the 'eminent physician' any of those who had refused to examine Theodosius's body? Buller would not have sat down to dinner with tradesmen, but with men of property, his equals. Is it possible that the Earl of Denbigh shared the same table, or some of Anna Maria's richer tenant farmers?

It would be reasonable to assume that around the table sat the local Justices of the Peace: no JP would miss the opportunity to meet the famous Justice Buller. They would undoubtedly be the same men who had schooled Anna Maria Boughton in her evidence just days before. Her private tuition by the JPs was to become a scandal after the trial, but for now it was a secret only for the few. Cradock picks up on this. 'The only doubt seemed to be,' he says, 'that as Lady Boughton, the mother, was all but a fool, her evidence, which was necessary, might not be effective.' This would have been a terrible anxiety for the prosecution, whose case rested almost entirely on Anna Maria's testimony. A later commentary, *Celebrated Trials Connected with the Aristocracy* by the barrister Peter Burke, written in 1849, confirms, if not the stupidity, then at least the dullness of the leading witness. 'Lady Boughton was not a very intellectual woman,' it notes kindly, so she had to be helped to give evidence in a coherent manner. Or, alternatively, in a way that would not incriminate her. Cradock adds, 'I am sorry to say it, that Judge Buller's charge was imprudent, for it prejudged Donellan.'

It would have been a very unusual juryman indeed who would have been able to approach the trial now with anything like objectivity.

Proceedings began early, at seven thirty in the morning.

The indictment was read out: 'poisoning by arsenic ... two grams of arsenic ... that he did put, infuse in and mix together with water into and in a certain glass phial bottle of the value of one penny ... did put and in the place and stead of a certain medicine lately prescribed ...' it droned on, at last coming to the point. '... Sir Theodosius Boughton did take, drink and swallow down into his body ... and did die.'[6]

John Donellan was asked how he pleaded.

'Not guilty,' he replied.

An interesting legal point occurs here. Over and over again Donellan was accused of substituting laurel water for Theodosius's medicine. Indeed, great pains were taken to show that he might have distilled the laurel water himself, with the gardener testifying that laurel grew in the garden of Lawford Hall. But laurel water is not arsenic; it is prussic acid.

After Donellan's plea of not guilty, the jury was sworn in.

The indictment was opened by one of the counsel for the Crown, Mr Digby, who then passed the main drama over to his colleague, Mr Howarth.

Howarth spoke for over an hour.

Beginning with a description of how vile and underhand the use of poison was, he rapidly moved into a description of Theodosius, 'possessed of a good constitution, affected by no indisposition that could endanger his life'. Donellan's motive was clear: the Boughton fortune had 'induced the prisoner to plan and execute the abominable crime'. And he had to be quick, because Theodosius was planning, in the week of his death, to go and stay with his friend Fonnereau 'til he came of age', that is, for eleven months.

Powell's treatment of Theodosius for 'slight' venereal disease was described. Howarth stated correctly that the medicine was brought to Lawford Hall on the evening of 29 August, and that Theodosius went fishing at five o'clock. This leaves open the issue of who had access to, or took delivery of, that medicine. Howarth reported that 'most of the menservants' were out with their master, while 'Lady Boughton and Mrs Donellan were out walking for some hours in the garden'. Howarth then went on to say that in order to explain his 'absence' all evening, Donellan claimed he had been fishing with Theodosius.

Howarth described Theodosius's death in detail: how the medicine was on the chimney shelf and not under lock and key; how Theodosius complained to his mother that the draught was 'nauseous'; how Anna Maria smelled it herself, thinking it smelled like bitter almonds, and then gave Theodosius the cup again. Almost as soon as the medicine was finished, Theodosius 'appeared to be in a very considerable degree of agony; his stomach heaved violently;

his eyes seemed much affected'. Lady Boughton 'takes no further notice of him at that time'; she left the room and returned again in ten minutes to find her son 'in the very agonies of death'. He died half an hour later.

As Anna Maria testified that she went into Theodosius's room at 7 a.m., that puts Theodosius's death at approximately 7.50 a.m. – according to Howarth.

Howarth now took the opportunity to say that poison was to blame. Theodosius was 'a young man, having a good constitution, labouring under no disorder' and he fell ill immediately after taking the draught. 'No man,' Howarth declared, 'hearing these circumstances related, can for a moment doubt that poison produced these effects,' going on to say that learned men would demonstrate that the poison 'certainly was laurel water'. However, a few sentences later he corrected himself. It was no longer a certainty but 'a strong *probability* that the poison used was a distillation of laurel water'.

'I shall show,' he continued, 'that the prisoner at the bar was skilled at distillation; he was possessed of a still; he worked this still … I shall show that the prisoner was frequently in private locked up in his own room using a still.'

Next Howarth outlined Donellan's behaviour on the morning of Theodosius's death. He entered the room, he said, and demanded at once to see the medicine bottle. 'The prisoner took the bottle down; he immediately poured water into the bottle, he shook it, he rinsed it; he then threw the contents of it into a basin of dirty water.' (This was not the version that Anna Maria had given in her second deposition to the coroner, the deposition that had forced Donellan's arrest.) Lady Boughton had objected, Howarth continued, saying, 'For God's sake, don't touch the bottle!' This phrase was not in either of Anna Maria's depositions nor in her testimony in court.

Donellan, according to Howarth, took no notice. 'The prisoner,' Howarth continued, 'fearing lest by accident he might have taken up the wrong bottle, reaches down another from the shelf, pours water also into the second bottle, rinses it well, throws the contents of that also into the basin of dirty water.' Worse yet, Donellan instructed the maid Sarah Blundell, 'whilst the young man was lying in the agonies of death', to take away the bottles. Lady Boughton objected, and Donellan 'was warm upon the subject; he insisted upon it; he pressed the woman to take them down.'

In neither of her depositions nor her testimony at the trial did Anna Maria say that Donellan was 'warm upon the subject', or indeed that he had insisted with any amount of firmness. Howarth portrayed a man whose temper was raised; Donellan's account flatly denied this; Anna Maria's does not stress it. Here, however, Howarth was presumably referring to his own prosecution brief, which noted that 'Donellan was angry with the maid that she did not make more haste'.

Howarth then moved on to Donellan's attitude once the apothecary Powell arrived. Already described as impatient, bullying and surly, Donellan apparently tried to impress on Powell that Theodosius had taken cold when he went fishing the night before, 'and that cold occasioned his death'. Powell was then 'suffered to depart' without being given the opportunity to explain the effects of the medicine or to inspect the bottles. He left the house 'without having the bottle shown him'. This, Howarth declared emphatically, 'is a circumstance which ought alone to decide the fate of the prisoner'. In fact, Powell did not testify that he was 'suffered' to leave. He left of his own accord, and he had simply not asked to see the medicine bottle.

Donellan was then described going about Lawford Hall trying to persuade the servants that Theodosius had not been poisoned. The boy caught cold, he was supposed to have said; he had wet his feet while fishing; he had died of a venereal disorder. And as soon as Donellan had finished doing that, he had written to Sir William Wheler to tell him that the boy had died, in words 'calculated to impress with the idea that the death was a natural one, and the result of a long illness'. Sir William's remarkable inactivity is skimmed over; but it was stated that it was not until Monday that he communicated 'suspicions of poison' and asked for named doctors to inspect the body. Great play was then made by Howarth that Donellan did not show the doctors the letter in which Wheler had mentioned poison. 'Doctor Rattray and Mr Wilmer had no idea at all of the occasion of their being sent for.' In fact, when they asked Donellan why they had been sent for he replied, 'For the satisfaction of all.'

Shown into a room to see the corpse, the doctors 'declined doing any such thing' (i.e. opening the body) because it was in such a state of putrefaction. There would be 'danger to themselves if they attempted to open it'. They left the house without Donellan asking them about the cause of death, and once again Howarth makes a great show of the men being 'suffered to depart'. There is no suggestion that the doctors had failed in the duty that had been asked of them. Howarth himself, however, had already said that the doctors had seen a letter from Sir William expressing 'his satisfaction that the family were disposed to have the body opened'. So there was no doubt of what they were expected to do, and no doubt that a failure to open the body was their own decision, not Donellan's.

Howarth grew a little heated about the doctors and the letters. He claimed that Donellan only showed the second letter to Sir William, the one in which he said of the doctors that 'they fully satisfied us'. 'Good God!' Howarth declaimed. 'In what does this satisfaction consist? In my apprehension, were there no other fact in this case but that single letter, it speaks as strongly as a thousand witnesses testifying to the actual commission of the crime.' In other words, this one letter was more convincing than a thousand witnesses claiming to have seen Donellan put poison into a bottle and make Theodosius drink the contents.

A reminder of this letter's contents:

Dear Sir,
Give me leave to express the heartfelt satisfaction … observing your advice in all respects. I sent for Dr Rattray and Dr Wilmer; they brought another gentleman with them; Mr Powell gave them the meeting, and upon receipt of your last letter, I gave it to them to peruse and act as it directed.

In the letter that Donellan refers to here Sir William had said that he wished to have the body opened and that it would be 'very improper' to have himself or any other person present while it was being inspected. Poison was not mentioned. Donellan goes on:

The four gentlemen proceeded accordingly and I am happy to inform you that they fully satisfied us; and I would wish that you hear from them the state they found the body in, as it will be an additional satisfaction for me that you should hear this account from themselves. Sir Theodosius made a very free use of an ointment and other things to repel a large boil which he had in his groin. So he used to do at Eaton, and Mr Jones told me often. I repeatedly advised him to consult Dr Rattray or Mr Carr; but as you know Sir Theodosius, you will not wonder at his going his own way, which he would not be put out of. I cannot help thinking but that Mr Powell acted to the best of his judgement for Sir Theodosius in this and the last case, which was but a short time finished before the latter appeared. Lady Boughton expressed her wishes to Sir Theodosius that he would take proper advice for his complaint; but he treated hers as he did mine.

She and my wife join in best respects,
John Donellan.

The defence counsel, Mr Newnham, asked that this letter be read to the court. He must have been convinced that there was nothing in it that could harm his client.

Howarth maintained that the letter was designed to mislead Sir William and make him believe that an autopsy had been carried out, despite the fact that Donellan had asked Rattray and Wilmer to give their findings directly to Sir William. By the time that this letter had reached its addressee, though, it would have been reasonable to assume that the doctors had told Sir William that this had not been done, and that this was entirely their own decision.

By now, the jurors would have been cross-eyed trying to work out who wrote what and when. They certainly were not given the impression that Wheler was curiously slow to act in the first place, or in any way to blame for not turning up at Lawford Hall himself to see what was going on. Nor was any blame for not establishing the cause of death attached to the doctors who could not bear to touch the body, or even turn down the shroud so that they could see below the neck, despite knowing that their instructions were to carry out an autopsy. The accusation from Howarth, instead, was crystal clear: Donellan had managed events so that no one but himself had the full story.

Howarth then explained the to-ings and fro-ings of Dr Bucknill and the events of the day of the funeral, although he did not say that Bucknill and Snow missed each other, or that it was Snow who gave the order for the body to be buried and that Bucknill decided to visit a dying patient instead of waiting at the Hall.

Howarth laboured on for some time about the fact that Donellan made 'a specious show' of offering to defer the funeral. Why? he demanded. So that Rattray and Wilmer, 'who could give no information upon the subject', could come back. He did not mention that Donellan sent servants to find Rattray and Wilmer, or that Sir William himself, who should have made the final decision, had chosen not to attend the funeral.

Howarth continued by describing the 'wonderful alarm in the minds of all the people' that Theodosius had been buried, the 'gentlemen' who had called in the coroner, and the open-air dissection of Theodosius.

Finally, he turned to describing the coroner's court itself, in which Donellan had been seen tugging on Lady Boughton's sleeve to prevent her saying something. He claimed that, when Lady Boughton and Donellan returned to Lawford Hall, he chided her 'for meddling in it' and told her to answer just the questions put to her. Most significantly, though, he changed his story. Theodosius had no longer died of cold or a disease; he had been poisoned. And in prison Donellan had confided to Derbyshire that this was the case, and that Powell, or the servants, or Anna Maria herself were to blame.

Howarth became quite inflamed in his closing sentences. 'For the purpose of removing suspicion from himself, he now dares to lay a charge where suspicion has never fallen!' he exclaimed with high drama. The transcript does not relate whether he chose to point to Anna Maria at this juncture, or if indeed she was sitting in court, but the outrage is clear. A mother was being accused of killing her own son; an aristocratic woman, a lonely and respected widow whose only son represented the sole chance her branch of the family had of retaining the baronetcy. It would have sent a ripple of horror around the court. With a flourish Howarth concluded: 'Justice demands the punishment of the murderer; it remains only for your verdict to determine the guilt, and to consign the criminal to his fate.'

Of course, that was not precisely accurate.

It was not the jury's verdict that would determine guilt. The jury was certainly capable of consigning Donellan to his fate, but the determination of guilt lay in the veracity – or not – of the evidence that was to come.

The first witness to be called was Thomas Powell, the apothecary. It was Powell, more than anyone else, who had the means and opportunity to carry out the crime of poisoning; yet never a hint of suspicion was cast on him other than Sir William Wheler's oblique reference in his letter of 4 September to John Donellan, in which he stresses that Powell needs to 'clear his name'.

Powell was questioned by Mr Wheeler.

After establishing Powell's identity and residence and the date of Theodosius's death, Wheeler moved on to the victim's health.

Q: In what state of health was he when you first attended him?
A: He had got a venereal complaint upon him.
Q: To what degree?
A: Not very high; rather slight. A fresh complaint ... I gave him a cooling physic for about three weeks ... and an embrocation to wash himself with.
Q: Did you then cease to give him physic?

A: Yes ... for about a fortnight. [I repeated] the medicines
    because he had a swelling in his groin.

Q: How long before you sent Sir Theodosius this last
    draught?

A: On Tuesday afternoon, the same day I sent the last
    draught, I saw him ... he told that [these draughts] he
    took on the Saturday last made him sick.

Q: In what state of health did he then appear?

A: In great spirits and good health.

Powell was then asked to produce a phial of the same mixture
that he sent to Theodosius. He did so, and described it: rhubarb
and jalop, spirits of lavender, nutmeg water and simple syrup. He
also produced another mixture, exactly the same, but with laurel
water substituted for the syrup. (These had been brought to help
Anna Maria when she gave her evidence later.)

He was then asked to describe the events of 30 August.

Q: Was you then sent for to Lawford Hall?

A: I was.

Q: At what time?

A: About eight or nine o'clock ... [William Frost] said that
    Sir Theodosius was very ill, and that he was sent by Lady
    Boughton to fetch me; I went immediately ... I met
    Captain Donellan in the courtyard; he went along with
    me into the room ... some servant was there, I cannot tell
    which ...

Q: In what situation did you find Sir Theodosius Boughton?

A: I saw no distortion.

Q: What did you see?

A: Nothing particular.

Q: Was he alive or dead?

A: He had been dead near an hour.

This puts the death at shortly after eight o'clock. But it raises
another question. Powell lived in Rugby, about four miles away.

Anna Maria said that she rushed downstairs and sent for Powell at about 7.20 a.m. Powell testified that he set out as soon as the servant arrived from Lawford Hall. Even taking the lowest speed of a cantering horse (about 10 m.p.h.), the servant would have arrived at Powell's by 7.50 a.m. at the latest. And even allowing Powell ten minutes to get ready, and to take a slower pace back, the latest time for his arrival would have been about 8.40 a.m.

Twenty minutes – and in all probability more – are missing. In reality, taking an average speed between a cantering and a galloping horse (and the servant was a young man who would have pressed the horse hard, having been told there was an emergency), more like forty-five minutes or an hour are missing.

There is only one conclusion.

Anna Maria did not send for Powell at 7.20 a.m.

Q: Did Mr Donellan ask you any question?
A: He asked me no question.
Q: Did you say anything to him?
A: I asked him how he died; Captain Donellan told me in convulsions.
Q: Did you see anything of the bottles you had sent?
A: I saw nothing of them; they were never mentioned.
Q: Do you remember having any other conversation with Mr Donellan about Sir Theodosius?
A: His general intent was to make me believe that Sir Theodosius Boughton had taken cold.

Aside from Powell being allowed to speculate on Donellan's 'intent', which he could not have known for sure, it is what has been left out of the questioning that is so striking. Why did Powell not ask to see the bottle? Would he not have wanted to check that Theodosius had drunk from the bottle that he had sent, rather than another one? Didn't his reputation rest on this bottle? Would he not have wanted to reassure himself that Theodosius had not drunk from some other source? Some time later, one of the doctors would testify that the supposed poison, laurel water, had an acrid smell. Why did Powell not notice such a smell so soon after the death? If he did notice the smell, why did he not remark on it to Donellan or Anna Maria?

Powell was then cross-examined by Donellan's lawyer, Newnham. But instead of asking Powell any of the above questions, he simply requested the exact measurements of the ingredients. During his brief replies Powell began to say that he saw Lady Boughton soon after he saw Donellan, and that she confirmed that her son 'was convulsed soon after he took the medicine'. At this point, after a cross-examination of less than five minutes, Newnham sat down, and Powell left the stand.

Powell was not asked about why Theodosius would have been sick after taking his prescription of the previous Saturday; he was not asked his opinion of the 'swelling in the groin' and whether that tallied with 'a slight complaint'. Nor was he asked if the embrocation he prescribed contained mercury, and how often Powell had prescribed mercury, or what Theodosius's history of venereal disease was. Indeed, he was not asked any question that might establish a long-running illness: how many times Theodosius had been infected, for instance; or what Lady Boughton had said to him about Theodosius's health when she first consulted him. Nothing at all, in fact, to establish that this was not a young man 'in great spirits and good health'.

A shocking omission on the part of the defence, but it was understandable that the prosecution would not ask. Because the prosecution brief itself revealed just how sick Theodosius had really been, and how much medication Powell had given him.

Under the heading 'Evidence' in the prosecution brief, Powell had told the prosecution team that in June he had prescribed Theodosius 'three mercurial bolus' (pills) for a new venereal infection, along with 'electuaries' (laxatives) and doses of 'cooling physic'. These appeared to have cured Theodosius by the beginning of August. A fortnight afterwards, the boy discovered a swelling in his groin, and for this Powell prescribed potassium bitartrate, another electuary, rhubarb and jalop and an embrocation of 'strong Gulard wash'. Powell also told the team that Theodosius had admitted to using mercurial ointment.

Therefore, in the eight weeks before his death, Theodosius had been given three mercury pills (a bolus was usually a fairly large size), a great deal of laxative and a Gulard wash. Gulard was a very expensive treatment made from an aromatic wood; less toxic than mercury, it was used to treat skin inflammations. But taken in excess, Gulard could cause seizures and heart failure. In addition, Theodosius had used a mercurial ointment of his own. The prosecution team also had a letter from Theodosius to Powell dated 29 August, the day before he died. The letter was never produced in court, and Donellan's team did not know of its existence. In it, Theodosius complained that the swelling in his groin had not gone down: 'The swelling is nearly the same as it was before,' he complains. 'I have used the greatest part of the embrocation. If it is possible for me to have any more you will please send it ... I have taken the electuary according to your order every night and morning.'

This is not a patient in recovery or good health.

A swelling in the lymph nodes of the groin is a sign of the secondary stage of syphilis, and no amount of laxative would cure it.

10

'No Such Thing'

'Weigh not so much what men assert, as what they prove.'

Philip Sidney

HOWARTH OPENED THE QUESTIONING of Anna Maria Boughton in a simple manner: what was Theodosius's age, and his expected fortune? Who would inherit the money if he died before he reached his majority? How long had Donellan lived at Lawford Hall, and for how much of that time had Theodosius also lived there?

Anna Maria answered the questions accurately, although she did not say that Donellan and Theodosia had come to live at Lawford at her invitation. She estimated Theodosius's fortune at £2,000 (£125,000) a year. What she omitted to add – and was not asked about – was that there was a mortgage on the estate of some £7,000 (£440,000). This is footnoted in Donellan's published *Defence* by his solicitors. They added that John Donellan was in full expectation of the livings of Newbold and Great Harborough, for which he had been studying theology for the past two years, and which were worth £500 (£31,400) a year, and were in the gift of Theodosius. They added, 'the estate ... was not actually worth as much as the livings.'

A letter from Theodosia's grandson, Edward Allesley Boughton

Ward-Boughton-Leigh, to Sir Charles Rouse-Boughton in 1882 confirms this picture. Having described the estate, he concludes: 'I have mentioned this subject to show that there was not more than trifling pecuniary inducements to commit murder on Donellan's part as Donellan might – and probably would have been – very comfortably circumstanced on the death of Lady Boughton.' Edward was not, however, in court to speak up for Donellan. His defence came a hundred years too late.

Anna Maria was not asked about the exact nature of the estate in cross-examination by Donellan's lawyers. This information would have removed the primary motive attributed to Donellan by Howarth in his opening statement – that he had committed the crime to obtain his share in an 'opulent' and 'considerable' fortune. And it would have drawn attention to the point that, if Donellan had killed Theodosius, he would have murdered the very person who could have provided him with a comfortable income once he came of age.

Anna Maria was then asked if she had spoken to Donellan about her son's health; she replied that she had, and that Donellan had warned her against leaving Lawford Hall because 'something or other may happen; he is in a very bad state of health'.

Questioning then passed on to the visit of Fonnereau, Theodosius's friend. Anna Maria confirmed that he had arrived at Lawford after Theodosius died, but that the original plan had been for him to stay for a week and then for him and Theodosius to go back to Northampton.

Q: Was he going to stay a long or short time there?
A: He did not say how long.

This answer contradicts Howarth's opening speech, in which he suggested that Donellan had to poison Theodosius quickly before the boy went to stay with Fonnereau, because he was going to be away for eleven months: 'Sir Theodosius ... proposing to stay with him until he came of age called for immediate execution of the prisoner's plan.'

In his *Defence*, Donellan has something to say about this misrepresentation of time:

> It has been said, and spread about the country, that Sir Theo-
> dosius wanted no more than a month or two of being of age,
> and that Mr Donellan had suspicions of his marrying a Miss
> Fonnereau, and that as he, Sir Theodosius, had invited the
> young lady's brother to Lawford the week of Sir Theodosius's
> death, and was to return with him when he went back, he per-
> petrated the horrid deed ascribed to him under the idea that he
> should have no opportunity of doing it while Mr Fonnereau
> was at Lawford and that if Sir Theodosius returned with him,
> he would be of age, and would marry Miss Fonnereau before he
> came back, and then that the chance of his possessing his estate
> would be quite gone … The fact was, that he wanted eleven
> months [of being of age]; and in regard to the other matter of
> his marrying Miss Fonnereau, no one except Lady Boughton
> ever entertained the least suspicion of the kind.

And he could not resist adding:

> Her ladyship indeed frequently expressed apprehensions of it
> (as she did of almost every young lady he had the least acquaint-
> ance with).

The prosecution brief notes that 'Fonnereau had a sister who
Captain Donellan seemed apprehensive Sir Theodosius should
think of marrying.' So both sides wanted to bring this unnamed
woman into the frame as a motive, but neither could furnish
direct proof of Fonnereau's sister being any kind of real marriage
prospect.

Next Anna Maria explained that Powell had supplied a bottle
of physic, that Donellan knew of this, and that he had encouraged
Theodosius to keep it in an unlocked outer room.

She was then asked how many menservants had accompanied
Theodosius fishing on the night before he died, to which she

replied, 'Samuel Frost was the only one.' Again this is a direct contradiction of her own lawyer's opening speech: Howarth had said that 'About five o'clock that evening, Sir Theodosius, taking with him most of the menservants, went to the river fishing.' It is also a contradiction of the notes in the prosecution brief, which claimed, 'Sir Theodosius had two or three servants with him at the time.'

Howarth added, 'Where the prisoner was at that time I believe cannot be explained to you.'

In fact, Donellan did provide a very detailed explanation of where he had been that evening, but had not put it in his prepared statement for the court: it only came to light later in the *Defence*. That afternoon, Donellan claimed to have walked for some time in the fields beyond the garden with his daughter and then returned to see Anna Maria in the garden, where he helped her pick fruit. At about five o'clock, they saw Theodosius ride past to go fishing. Donellan left the garden only briefly to ask Samuel Frost to bring a ladder to help them reach the higher fruit on the trees; he was gone a very short space of time, during which the servants had sight of his movements.

Afterwards Donellan said that he walked to Hewitt's mill to discuss repair work with a carpenter called Matthews. He arranged for Anna Maria to meet Matthews, with himself, at the Hall at six o'clock; Sarah Blundell had come into the garden to say that the visitors, Matthew and a Mr Dand, were there; and both Donellan and Anna Maria had walked into the Hall and discussed various business with them for about ten minutes. Afterwards, Donellan went to the mill with Matthews and walked to the flood gates with him, and did not return until just after nine o'clock in the evening.

Donellan's lawyers did not call either Dand or Matthews to give evidence. A footnote in Donellan's posthumous account says: 'Dand and Matthews were subpoenaed; but Mr Newnham thought it would be impossible to account for Mr Donellan's time' - surely a most peculiar decision by a defending lawyer? It was left open for Anna Maria's team to be able to say, 'Where the prisoner was I believe cannot be explained to you' - the implication being that Donellan was in Theodosius's bedroom pouring laurel water into his physic. It should be noted that it was never proved that the bottle of physic was actually in the bedroom at this time, however. Samuel Frost testified that he had given the medicine directly into Theodosius's hands in the company of Mrs Donellan, and that Theodosius had put it into his pocket.

In her replies to the next few questions, Anna Maria denied seeing Donellan for over two hours after about five o'clock. She said that Donellan had come back to the house at about seven and told her that he had seen Theodosius fishing, and had tried to persuade him to come home in case he caught cold. (The prosecution brief said that 'after walking in the garden some time they all came in together'.) Anna Maria then testified that her son came back about nine o'clock, 'seemed very well', asked if he could use a servant to go on an errand for him the next day and went straight to bed.

This contradicts the notes in the prosecution brief gleaned from Anna Maria previously, which state: 'He went fishing about 4 o'clock and returned about 8.'

In her cross-examination by Mr Newnham, Anna Maria said that Donellan had already gone to bed by the time Theodosius returned at about nine o'clock. In his *Defence* Donellan emphasises the crucial nature of the timing and the geography of the house to show that he could not have had access to Theodosius's room to tamper with the medicine. He accounted for his time until 9 p.m. He then said that he went into the parlour and spoke to Anna Maria. She said that she was angry with her son for staying out so late because it meant that she would have to light candles, but 'expressed no other concern'.

Donellan's and Theodosia's bedrooms were directly above the parlour; Theodosius's and his mother's were in the other wing of the house. Donellan made the case that if he had returned downstairs Anna Maria would have seen or heard him from the parlour; he would then have walked down an 80-yard passage and up another staircase to Theodosius's bedroom. In order to do this, he would have needed a candle; the light would have been seen.

This ended Anna Maria's evidence on the events of 29 August.

The next questions concerned the following morning, the morning of Theodosius's death.

Q: At what time did you see him [your son] the next morning?

A: About seven o'clock.

Q: At that time of the morning, how did he appear in his health?

A: He appeared then to be very well. [Anna Maria had been asked this three times out of the last seven questions. She answered each question in exactly the same words, as if by rote.]

Q: Did you go into his room at that time?

A: He had desired me … to give him his physic … I asked him where the bottle was; he said, 'It stood there upon the shelf.' First of all, he desired me to get him a bit of cheese in order to take the taste out of his mouth … he desired me to read the label … there was written upon it, 'Purging draught for Sir Theodosius Boughton' … as he was taking it, he observed that it smelt and tasted very nauseous, upon which I said, 'I think it smells very strongly like bitter almonds' … he laid down.

Anna Maria here omits what she had told her lawyers for their brief: that the bottle had stood next to an empty bottle that contained the medicine which Theodosius had taken on Monday.

An absolutely vital difference that the prosecution did not reveal here was that, for the brief, Anna Maria had said that the mixture had the colour and smell of rhubarb as well as bitter almonds. The conclusion is that, if laurel water had been given, it had been added to the rhubarb medicine. Therefore it was not a neat mixture. Testimonies in court implied that Anna Maria unwittingly handed her son a phial of laurel water, nothing else; whereas, in fact, it had enough of the original mixture in it both to colour it and give it a rhubarb taste.

In court now, Anna Maria was given two bottles to smell: the first contained a draught of the mixture which Powell said he had prepared; the second contained laurel water. She identified the smell of the second as 'very like the smell of the medicine which I gave him'.

In the prosecution brief, but not mentioned at the trial, great attention was paid to the fact that Powell had said that 'he pushed in the cork very tight' of the medicine bottle, but Anna Maria had said that she 'took out the cork, which came out very loose'. Perhaps this omission at the trial was because it could be argued that Theodosius himself had opened the bottle already.

Q: What was the first observation your ladyship made of any appearance upon Sir Theodosius after taking the medicine?

A: In two minutes he struggled very much; it appeared to me as if it was to keep it down, and made a prodigious rattling in his stomach, and guggling; and he appeared to me to make very great efforts to keep it down.

It is at this point, interestingly, that the court transcript notes that the following questions were asked not by Anna Maria's lawyer, but by 'Court' – presumably Sir Justice Buller. (Such an interruption, sometimes stopping or manipulating evidence, would have been accepted practice at that time; fifty years beforehand, a judge would have asked *every* question, as lawyers did not routinely come to court.)

COURT: How long did you observe these symptoms continue?

A: About ten minutes; he then seemed as if he was going to sleep, or inclined to doze. Perceiving him composed, I went out of the room.

This places Anna Maria's departure from the room at about 7.15 a.m. or 7.20 a.m.

I returned in about five minutes after … I found him with his

eyes fixed upwards, his teeth clenched, and froth running out
of each corner of his mouth ... I ran downstairs, and told the
servant to take the first horse he could get, and go immediately
for Mr Powell.

The timings are a little awry compared to the prosecution brief,
which said that the convulsions ceased after six or seven minutes
and that Anna Maria returned after six or eight minutes. This
differs from the trial evidence by five to eight minutes.

On cross-examination, the defence counsel Newnham asked
Anna Maria if she had planned to go riding with Donellan that
morning. She agreed that she had; they were to go to 'the wells'
that is, Newnham Wells, approximately three-quarters of a mile
away. Newnham then asked if she had seen Donellan before he
came up to Theodosius's bedroom. She said that she had: he had
been standing waiting in the yard –she had seen him from a window
– and she had called down to him that she was going to put her
riding things on and would be ready in fifteen minutes.

Q: This was after you left your son's room, when you thought
   he was going to sleep?
A: Yes.
Q: How happened it, after your son had had these convulsive
   appearances, and had frightened your ladyship so much,
   that you did not disclose to Mr Donellan that he was in
   that condition, and you could not ride out?
A: I thought he appeared as if he was going to sleep ...

We therefore have Anna Maria returning to Theodosius's room
at about 7.20 a.m. in her first testimony and calling for Powell to
be brought at the same time; under cross-examination she says
that she was getting ready to ride. Did she return, then, after five
minutes or fifteen minutes, or later still? Donellan was standing
in the courtyard with the horses ready; but had anyone else gone
into Theodosius's room while Anna Maria was getting ready or,
alternatively, in the five minutes' absence that she first testified to?

Neither question was asked.

We return to Anna Maria's questioning by the 'Court'.

> COURT: When did you first see Mr Donellan after that
> [i.e. after she had run downstairs and sent a servant for
> Powell]?
> A: I saw him in less than five minutes [that is, about 7.25
> a.m.]. He came up to the bedchamber and asked me,
> 'What do you want?'

Here, Donellan's posthumous account and Anna Maria's differ enormously, particularly as regards timing.

Donellan wrote that he had risen at 6 a.m., because Anna Maria had wanted to ride out to visit 'a person's house to make some enquiries respecting a servant girl'. He waited 'a considerable time', walking about the yard and the garden, but when his mother-in-law did not appear he stood under her window and called her. For a while she did not reply; then she appeared at 'a window at the stair-head between Sir Theodosius's room and her Ladyship's' and told him that she would not be ready for some time. So far this agrees with Anna Maria's version: the conversation was the one she reported to have happened at 7.20 a.m., although in her evidence she had said that she would be ready in fifteen minutes.

Donellan then wrote that, growing impatient, he:

> ... thought he might take a ride to Newnham Wells, distant
> about three-quarters of a mile from Lawford Hall, to take the
> waters there [which he usually did] ... observing William Frost,
> the coachman, standing in the yard with the horses, he went to
> him, and, taking the little bay mare out of his hand, bade him
> put Lady Boughton's horse in the stable ... William Frost swears
> that he desired him to pull out his watch, which is a matter so
> absurd ... Mr Donellan returned in less than three-quarters of an
> hour and was met by William Frost ... Sir Theodosius was taken
> ill and he was going for Mr Powell, and said that Lady Boughton
> desired him to take the mare as she would go fastest ...

So, if we are to take Anna Maria's testimony and Donellan's word together, Donellan returned at about *eight* o'clock from Newnham Wells, not 7.20, when he met the servant who had just been told to fetch Powell. This also ties in with Powell's testimony: if William Frost left at 8 a.m., he would have returned with Powell about 9 a.m. – the timing is much more believable.

This either means that Anna Maria gave Theodosius his medicine at about 7.45 a.m., not 7 a.m.; or that she did indeed give him his medicine at seven, but had been absent from his room from 7.15 a.m. until just before eight o'clock. If the first is correct, why did she swear that it was earlier? If the second is correct, she had left her son for far longer than 'five minutes'. The only logical explanation, if what Donellan says is true, is that Anna Maria gave Theodosius the medicine at 7.15 a.m., left the room, saw Donellan and told him that she would be some time, and only went back to the room just before eight, having got ready for her morning ride.

In that case, she checked on Theodosius after three-quarters of an hour, not the five minutes she testified to. Why did she not say so? Did it seem careless to leave the boy for so long after he had complained at the medicine? Was she trying to show how stringently she had looked after him, by checking again after only five minutes? How could she be so sure that Powell's testified timescale would not contradict her?

This subject is returned to later in Anna Maria's testimony by her own counsel.

When asked by Howarth what happened after Theodosius died, she says that some time afterwards she was in the downstairs parlour and Donellan returned to the subject of the bottles.

Q: What passed further on that?
A: I turned away from him to the window and made no answer upon it; upon which he repeated the same.
Q: What happened then?
A: He desir'd his wife to ring the bell to call up a servant. When the servant came, he ordered the servant to send in Will, the coachman.

Q: Relate what happened between Mr Donellan and the
   coachman.
A: When the coachman came, Mr Donellan said, 'Will, don't
   you remember that I set out this morning about seven
   o'clock?' 'Yes sir,' said he. 'You remember that, don't
   you?' 'Yes sir.' 'And that was the first time of my going
   out. I have never been on the other side of the house
   this morning. You remember that I set out there at seven
   o'clock this morning, and asked for a horse to go to the
   Wells?' 'Yes sir.' Mr Donellan said, 'Then you are my
   evidence.'

Donellan was already anxious about Anna Maria's attitude: the
significance of her objecting to his washing out the bottles had not
been lost on him. He asked for 'evidence' that he was out of the
house when Theodosius took his physic.

But it is to be noted that Donellan rode away at, or near to,
seven o'clock. If he did so, then he had already had his conversation with Anna Maria at the open window. Yet Anna Maria testified that this was *after* she had given Theodosius his medicine. So if
Donellan is correct, and William Frost is correct, and we compare
their versions to Anna Maria's testimony that she gave the physic
to her son before speaking to Donellan, then Anna Maria administered the medicine fifteen minutes before 7 a.m., at 6.45 a.m.
However, just to complicate matters, Donellan's account contradicts this. He wrote that 'Lady Boughton hastily told him that soon
after she spoke to him out of the window, she gave Sir Theodosius
his physic.'

Why did Anna Maria say this if she had in fact, as she testified
in court, given the physic *before* speaking to Donellan? (A: I said,
'I shall be ready in about a quarter of an hour, I am going to put
my things on ...' Q: That is after you left your son's room, when
you thought he was going to sleep? A: Yes.) Did Donellan get it
wrong? Was Anna Maria simply confused as to which came first?
Or was she trying to obscure the fact that a whole hour had passed
when Theodosius had been left alone, dying on his bed?

1. Believed to be the original Boughton family vault in the churchyard of St Botolph's, Newbold-on-Avon. It stands opposite the 'Long Lawford entrance'. The tomb bears a faint coat-of-arms. On the opposite side of the church is an elaborate pink memorial to later generations.

2. The Rysbrack memorial to William Boughton and Catherine Shukburgh in St Botolph's, Newbold-on-Avon.

3. The only known image of Lawford Hall; the anonymous engraving clearly shows the curving wall described as being close to the river. Though reputedly a building of great merit, the Hall was demolished in the last decade of the eighteenth century, probably on the instruction of Edward Boughton.

4. The exterior of Little Lawford Hall, thought to be the original stable block of Lawford Hall itself.

5. Boughton family armour of great age in Newbold-on-Avon church: the chevron-patterned bird – the crest on the helmet – holds a serpent in its mouth.

6. Believed to be a painting of Theodosius's parents, Edward Boughton (1719-72) and Anna Maria Beauchamp.

7. William Boughton (1663-1716), the Fourth Baronet. William was the patriarch of two family lines descending from his two wives.

8. Shukburgh Boughton (1703-63), the adored son of William and his second wife Catherine Shukburgh. In a court case, Catherine was accused of plying her stepson with alcohol so that Shukburgh would inherit the title. Shukburgh's son, Edward, did eventually come into the baronetcy when Theodosius died.

9. The only known image – and probably not a very accurate one – of Theodosius, published in the *Hibernian Magazine* at the time of Donellan's court case. It seems hardly representative of the dissolute, wayward baronet.

10. Eton schoolyard, *c.* 1820. 'Lady Boughton allowed her son 18 pence a week when first there and half a crown thereafter ... an allowance not suitable to his birth and fortune' noted John Donellan in his *Defence*.

11. The Pump Room in Bath with traders selling their wares, *c.* 1800. Donellan is reputed to have met Theodosia Boughton at Bath in the 1770s.

12. Edward Boughton (1742–94), who inherited the baronetcy on Theodosius's death. Although he never married, he had five children by a serving maid, Sally Davis. He left his fortune to his daughters, his sons having died as infants.

13. John Donellan, his kindly expression here is in contrast to images published in newspapers at the time.

14. The Pantheon, London. It has been conjectured that Donellan is the figure on the far left; but in this print the figure on the far right, slight in stature and with a profile similar to other Donellan images, seems just as likely to be Donellan.

15. Exterior of the London Pantheon, c.1780. The building has long since been demolished and a large retail store now stands on the site.

16. The ravishingly pretty Theodosia – Theodosius's sister – aged seventeen.

17. Mrs Elizabeth Hartley, a possible contender as Donellan's mistress, who was described by Garrick as having a 'slovenly good nature that renders her prodigiously vulgar'.

18. Nancy Parsons, perhaps a more likely contender as Donellan's mistress; this career companion of famous men eventually married the Second Viscount Maynard. She died near Paris in her eightieth year.

19. View along Northgate Street in Warwick. The court building is to the right and St Mary's Church is in the distance.

20. The interior of Warwick Crown Court, a new building in Donellan's day. (Court business moved to new premises in 2011.)

21. John Hunter (1728-93), the famous anatomist, was the only medical witness in John Donellan's defence. 'A poor devil was lately hanged at Warwick,' he told his students later, 'upon no other testimony than that of physical men whose first experiments were made upon this occasion.'

JUDGE THUMB.

or — Patent Sticks for Family Correction: Warranted Lawful!

22. 'Judge Thumb', or 'Patent Sticks for Family Correction', cartoon showing Sir Francis Buller (1746–1800). The sobriquet pursued the illustrious judge for the remainder of his life.

Now came the really damning part of Anna Maria's testimony. She was asked what happened when Donellan came into Theodosius's bedroom.

A: I said, I wanted to inform him what a terrible thing had happened; that it was an unaccountable thing in the doctor to send such a medicine, for, if it had been taken by a dog, it would have killed him; and I did not think my son would live. Then he asked me where the physic bottle was. I showed him the two draughts. He took up one of the bottles ... poured some water out of the water bottle, which was just by, into the phial, shook it, and then emptied it out into some dirty water which was in a wash-hand basin.

Q: Did you make any observation upon that conduct?

A: After he had thrown the contents of the first bottle into the wash-hand basin of dirty water, I observed that he ought not to do that. I said, 'What are you at? You should not meddle with the bottle.' Upon that, he snatched up the other bottle, and poured water into it, and shook it; then he put his finger to it and tasted it ...

Q: Had he tasted the first bottle?

A: No.

Compare this to Anna Maria's depositions to the coroner. In her first deposition, she had said that Donellan had put water into the bottle and poured the contents out and tasted it. In her second deposition, she said that he put water into the bottle, swilled it around and *threw it on the ground*; he then did the same with another bottle.

Donellan's counsel took up the theme in his cross-examination.

Q: Did your ladyship ever mention, when examined by the Coroner, this fact, that Mr Donellan said, 'I should not have known what I should have done, if I had not thought of saying that I did it to put my finger in to taste?'

A: I did mention this before the Coroner ...

Q: I asked your ladyship whether you disclosed before the Coroner that Mr Donellan told Mrs Donellan in your hearing that if he had not thought of saying that he did it to put his finger in to taste, he should not have known what to have done. Did you mention that circumstance before the Coroner?

A: Yes.

Q: And swear it?

A: Yes.

Q: I believe you was examined a second time; was it upon the first or second examination?

A: I am not certain.

Q: Was your examination read over to you before you signed it?

A: Yes.

Q: I wish to ask your ladyship again whether this circumstance was disclosed in your evidence?

A: I said he told me that he did it to taste.

Q: Your examination was read. There is *no such thing* as that contained in it.

Newnham was right. There was no such thing in Anna Maria's second deposition. But he failed to follow this up. He also failed to emphasise that, as well as Donellan's tasting the mixture not being mentioned, an extra damning piece of information was added – that Donellan 'threw the medicine and water upon the ground'. Tasting the mixture is the action of an innocent man who does not know what it contains. Throwing the mixture on the ground is the action of a guilty man who knows very well what it contains and is anxious to dispose of it.

But Newnham did not make this point to the jury. Instead, he went on to question Anna Maria about which horse was taken to Powell – but again without picking up on the disparity of reported timings.

Anna Maria was also asked if a servant was in Theodosius's bedroom when Donellan was there. Yes, she replied, Sarah

Blundell, and added that Donellan had told Sarah to take away 'the basin, the dirty things, and the bottles' and that he put the bottles into her hand. However, Anna Maria had objected, and taken the bottles from Sarah and told her to leave everything alone.

Sarah Blundell had died in the winter of 1780–81, within a fortnight of giving birth to an illegitimate child, so the following evidence was based on the word of Anna Maria alone (as indeed it was for everything that occurred when Theodosius took the physic).

> A: He then desired that the room be cleaned and the clothes thrown into an inner room. I opened the door of the inner room … while my back was turned [he] put the bottles into her hand again, and bid her take them down; and was angry she had not done it at first.

The questioning determines that Anna Maria did not see the bottles actually being taken out; in fact, she was not certain if they had been taken out before she herself left the room after Theodosius died.

It is extraordinary to note that, according to his mother, all this conversation was going on while Theodosius was dying. Anna Maria was not at his bedside comforting him; she testifies that a maid was wiping the froth from his mouth. Catharine Amos later testified that she was the maid in question; that Theodosius was 'motionless' but that 'the stomach heaved very much' and 'he gurgled at the throat'; and that after she had wiped Theodosius's mouth four or five times she left the room because 'my work lay below stairs'. As Catharine was giving evidence, Mr Newnham, Donellan's counsel, suddenly asked Anna Maria a question. Did Sir Theodosius speak after he had taken the medicine? 'Not at all,' she replied.

It was an inappropriate moment: Catharine Amos was answering on another topic at the time. Why did he interrupt her? Did Newnham think that Theodosius had spoken? If so, was it on the subject that Catharine was being questioned about: which still was Donellan supposed to have distilled the laurel water in? Was this something that Theodosius had, in fact, known something about? Did he refer to it as he lay dying? Had he used it himself to distil something? Did he confess as much? Anna Maria's reply was short – 'No, not at all' – but Newnham's interruption is so unusual that it should be noted.

But let us return to Anna Maria's contention that Theodosius was still alive when the argument about the bottles took place. To recap:

> Q: When all this happened, the washing the bottles and
> removing the clothes, was Sir Theodosius dead?
> A: He was nearly dead.

Compare this to Donellan's account:

> On entering his room he found Sir Theodosius in the agonies
> of death, his eyes being fix'd, his teeth set, and foaming at the
> mouth. He looked upon the sad spectacle with horror and amaze-
> ment for some little time, and then Sir Theodosius went off.

Presumably, this means that Theodosius died; and he died, according to Donellan, *before* the bottles were washed.

Donellan's account of what happened directly after is as follows:

> Mr Donellan took the bottle from the chimney-piece, and held
> it up to the window in order to see more fully whether there were
> any dregs or not, and which he found then to be quite clean and
> dry; but thinking that it was perhaps probable, by putting a
> little water into the bottle, he might be able to get something
> off the sides and by that means discover what the medicine was,
> he put about a teaspoon of water into the first phial bottle and
> after rinsing it well poured the same out into a small white basin
> on the table, and dipping his finger in it, tasted the same several
> times, after which he told Lady Boughton that he could not
> ... taste exactly what the medicine was, but that what little he
> could taste of it, was, he thought, rather nauseous.

He also addressed the issue of the bottles being cleared away. Contradicting Anna Maria, Donellan said that she began to clear the room, putting Theodosius's belongings into an adjoining one. 'He thought it was intended that there would be a general clearing of the room,' he went on, 'and therefore desired Sarah Blundell to help her ladyship ... seeing Sarah coming to take away the bottles, he put some of them into her apron, which was all the assistance he gave ...'

As for the bottle itself, in contrast to Anna Maria's evidence that the bottle was not seen again, and that she did not know when it was removed or where to, Donellan writes:

> Mr Caldecott, the solicitor, enquired for it ... Mr Donellan immediately enquired of Sarah Blundell, who showed where she had put the bottles away (into a hole in the kitchen sometimes used for stewing) upon which he found one he thought might be it ... shewed the same to Samuel Frost ... took the bottle into the parlour, and put it upon the harpsichord ready to be produced when required.

But Donellan's lawyer never asked Samuel Frost to testify to this; the bottle was thought, after Anna Maria's testimony, to be lost. And so the burden of doubt fell on Donellan that he had somehow disposed of or destroyed it.

The prosecution brief was quite clear as to the fate of the bottles, however: it noted that Sarah Blundell had said that 'the basin was soon after washed and the two bottles flung into the stove hole, where they were seen the next day broken and the labels torn off'. However, this was not referred to at the trial.

One further poignant story remains concerning Sarah Blundell. In her testimony, Anna Maria was asked by her own counsel what had become of the girl. Anna Maria replied shortly, 'She is dead.' Donellan himself had little positive to say about the servant, either, writing in his *Defence*:

> Sarah Blundell is since dead ... she was a woman of known bad

character, and died in childbirth of a bastard; a matter which she so artfully concealed that nobody suspected anything of the kind till she was taken in labour, and even then did not confess what was the matter with her …

However, he went on:

During the time this woman was in labour, she was so extremely ill, that it was expected she should die before a delivery; and, as Mrs Donellan was particularly humane to her, she told her, in the presence of Sukey Sparrow, Mrs Donellan's maid, that she knew no harm of her husband, and that she told Mr B— [Balguy, one of the prosecuting counsel?] every time he sent for her, she knew nothing against him. This was spoke at a time when she thought of dying every moment, but she lingered upwards of a fortnight afterwards, and, during that time, every unfair advantage was taken to extort things from her, and Mr Caldecott, the solicitor in this prosecution, was with her the day of her death, but she was speechless that day and the day preceeding … notwithstanding, Lady Boughton had a coach and chaise, she sent this woman away from Lawford, at the time she was so ill, in a cart.

If Theodosia was still at Lawford, showing humanity to Sarah Blundell while the girl was in labour, then this puts Sarah's delivery of her child and her subsequent illness some time before Christmas 1780, as Theodosia had left, according to Caldecott, by December.

Anna Maria was evidently not disposed to show Sarah Blundell – who after all had supported her second deposition to the coroner – any such humanity. One wonders at her callousness in sending Sarah away in an open cart in the depths of winter.

Who was the father of the 'bastard child'? The prosecution brief notes that Sarah Blundell's 'sweetheart' was the footman John Yateman; but Yateman, despite being in the house at the time and having some relevant details about Donellan, was never called. In fact, all that we know about him is taken from a few sketchy references in the brief. Anna Maria never talks of him.

Why did Yateman not come forward at the trial to support Anna Maria's case? Did he bear her a grudge about Sarah's treatment? Or was his lack of support because he had realised that Sarah's child was not his?

The later questions to Anna Maria by her own lawyer concerned a comment that Sir Theodosius's stockings, which he had worn the night before, were wet; and that perhaps he had caught a cold and it was this which had occasioned his death. She said that the stockings were dry.

We return to the closing questions of Anna Maria's own lawyers.

Q: Do you remember Mr Donellan receiving a letter from Sir William Wheler, and when was the first letter he received from Sir William?

A: He received a letter from Sir William Wheler desiring that the body might be opened.

Q: Do you remember being shown the answer to that letter?

A: Yes, I do.

Q: Who showed it you?

A: Mr Donellan.

Q: Do you recollect having made any observation upon his answer which he sent Sir William Wheler after Dr Rattray and Mr Wilmer had been there?

A: I remember he read the letter; I thought it of no use; that it would be unnecessary to send it.

Q: Did you state any reason why the letter was to be objected to?

A: I did not; I said, 'He had better let it alone, and not send such a letter as that.'

Q: You disliked the letter, but the reason of your dislike you did not explain to him?

A: No; but he said it was necessary to send an answer, and he would send it.

Howarth refers here to 'the first letter he received' and its answer. The first letter that Donellan received from Sir William, dated 2 September, was merely an acknowledgement of the news. Presumably Howarth is referring here to Wheler's second letter, in which he asked for an autopsy because he had heard rumours of poison. Donellan's reply was that 'we most cheerfully wish to have the body of Sir Theodosius opened'. Howarth is establishing that Lady Boughton knew an autopsy would be carried out.

The letter which Anna Maria says Donellan read out to her after Rattray and Wilmer's visit was dated 5 September; in this, he confirmed that they had been to Lawford ('they proceeded accordingly') and then went on to describe the seriousness of Theodosius's venereal infection. Howarth did not pursue specifically why Anna Maria objected to the letter. Why he raised it, with its references to Theodosius's repeated infections and lack of regard for his mother's wishes, is a puzzle. Perhaps he wished to show that Donellan did not care for Anna Maria's feelings in the matter.

Newnham, in his cross-examination, however, took up the issue of Theodosius's health.

Q: When did you hear Captain Donellan say that your son was in a bad state of health, how long before his death?

A: He often talked about it for three weeks or a month before his time of death.

Q: That was only after he had been attended by Mr Powell for a recent complaint, but before that you was pleased to say Mr Donellan often expressed to you that Sir Theo was in a bad state of health?

A: I had said that my son had been ill of a particular disorder.

Q: Had you not written to Bath in the year 1777 and 1778 that his fine complexion was gone and he was in a very bad way?

A: I said I was afraid he was in a bad way, for his complexion was altered.

Q: I quote your words, 'His fine complexion was gone'?

A: Yes.

At least Newnham took the opportunity this time to follow up on a crucial issue. Theodosius was not 'possessed of a good constitution, affected by no indisposition that could at all endanger his life', as Howarth had described in his opening speech. Nor indeed did he have 'a slight venereal disorder'. But Howarth had compounded the misinformation in his opening speech by adding that when Samuel Frost saw Theodosius on the morning of his death, 'he appeared in perfect good health, that he leaped out of bed for the purpose of getting something'.

Newnham's cross-examination attempted to show that Anna Maria knew very well that Theodosius had been unwell for some time; the loss of his 'complexion' was a telling side-effect of prolonged illness – contemporary drawings and cartoons show the drained appearance and the rotted skin of prostitutes and their customers. As early as 1667 the notorious Earl of Rochester had written a pamphlet describing the 'Shankers (chancres, venereal ulcers) or Cordes or Buboes dire' of what was called 'the great pox' and which was traditionally treated with mercury. 'A night with Venus, a lifetime with Mercury' was a popular saying.

It is to be presumed that the men of the jury knew all too well what both Howarth and Newnham were referring to, and perhaps the subject was not pursued out of deference to the delicacy of Anna Maria's feelings. But a little more detail from Newnham would have given credence to Donellan's contention that Theodosius's illness was well established and he was in far from 'perfect health'.

Newnham also covered the issue of Theodosius regularly buying poison, which he used to lay in dead fish in order to poison rats:

Q: Whether you don't know that Sir Theodosius did amuse himself in laying poison for fish?

A: Sir Theodosius did sometimes amuse himself in laying poison for fish.

Q: Where did he put those things that he used to amuse himself with?

A: I won't mince the matter.

Q: Don't you know of his buying large quantities of arsenic?

A: He went for a pound, and after his death a quantity of arsenic was found in his closet.

Q: Where did he use to keep that?

A: In his inner closet.

Q: Which was sometimes locked?

A: Mostly.

Newnham next tried to show that Donellan had on several occasions tried to prevent or resolve various quarrels and fights in which Theodosius was involved:

Q: Do you recollect a quarrel that happened between Sir Theodosius and a gentleman at Bath?

A: Yes, and Mr Donellan interfered to prevent anything happening.

Q: Does not your ladyship recollect a quarrel your son had at Rugby?

A: Yes.

Q: Pray, who was sent for on that occasion?

A: Mr Donellan.

Q: Did not your ladyship go to Mr Donellan's room door and early in the morning press him to go over immediately?

A: Yes.

Q: Did not you put the letter under the door?

A: I wrote a letter, and had it put under the door, desiring him to go to Rugby, on account of a quarrel that happened there.

Q: Did Mr Donellan interfere and prevent any mischief happening there?

A: He told me that he did.

Q: Now, as to a third quarrel; whether he had another quarrel with a gentleman at Daventry?

A: They were both at Rugby.

Q: With a Mr Wildgoose of Daventry, at Rugby?

A: Yes.

Q: Was there a quarrel with Mr Chartres?

A: Yes, at that time I believe, but I am not certain.

But Anna Maria began to resist 'recollecting' any more about Theodosius's continually bad behaviour and Donellan's role in rescuing him from harm. When the subject of Donellan preventing serious injury to Theodosius when the boy insisted on climbing the church tower at Newbold came up, Anna Maria answered that she did not remember any danger or accident; and that Theodosius did not mention the matter in the coach as they returned home.

Towards the end of the cross-examination, the prosecuting counsel, Howarth, interrupted:

Q: You have been asked of instances of friendship shown by Mr Donellan to your son; what was Mr Donellan's general behaviour for some months before he died? Did he treat Sir Theodosius with respect, friendship, and tenderness, or otherwise?

A: About a fortnight before my son's death I heard –

At this point Anna Maria was stopped by Justice Buller.

COURT: Have you heard your son say anything about Mr Donellan's behaviour when he gave you the relation mentioned by Mr Newnham [i.e. the instances of Donellan resolving quarrels]?

A: They used to have words, to be angry with each other; they did not in general live in friendship and intimacy.

Newnham regained the questioning.

Q: I presume that they had the sort of words that occasionally happen in all families, more or less?

A: I paid no great attention to it.

Buller interrupted again. He asked about the conversation in the parlour after Theodosius's death about the washing of the bottles, but the questioning ended on Donellan's mood.

COURT: Was that spoken in a passion or resentment, or how?
A: Rather in a way of resentment.

The above exchange, coming as it did right at the end of Anna Maria's testimony, was a case of outright manipulation. Prosecuting counsel, evidently to Buller's disapproval, mentioned 'respect, friendship and tenderness'; as Anna Maria answered, Buller stopped her, framing his question in a way that encouraged her to say that Theodosius resented Donellan's interference. Newnham tried to repair the damage – 'the sort of words that occasionally happen in all families …?'. But directly after Anna Maria's non-committal reply, Buller interrupted again.

And, with his prompting, Anna Maria's evidence ended with one word summing up Donellan's behaviour: resentment.

But there was one last issue not touched upon in court.

It was an accusation made by Donellan, and, as such, was purely Donellan's word against Anna Maria's. In his *Defence*, Donellan described the morning that Theodosius died and Anna Maria's behaviour just minutes – and hours – later:

In about an hour after Sir Theodosius died, Lady Boughton sent for different people from Rugby, to give them directions about his funeral; and before ten o'clock that morning, being Wednesday the 30th of August last, they all of them attended and received their instructions from Lady Boughton while she was at breakfast.

This is quite astonishing, if true. Less than two hours after her son has died, Anna Maria was, supposedly, eating breakfast and instructing the funeral directors; an unenviable task which anyone closely related to the deceased would have found harrowing enough even the next day. The funeral directors were there by ten o'clock; Rugby, as noted, was about four miles away. The journey would not have been as excruciatingly urgent as it had been when William Frost rode out to fetch Powell, and therefore would have taken longer. To ride four miles at an orderly pace might have taken half an hour – with the return journey, an hour; therefore Anna Maria's instructions were sent within an hour of Theodosius dying.

Her son died; she argued with her son-in-law; she sent servants for the funeral directors (the names of which presumably took some research and discussion, unless she had a pre-prepared list to hand); and she sat down to breakfast. All within two hours. Also 'some time that morning' she disputed the issue of the bottles again with Donellan in front of Theodosia.

This does not read like a woman prostrated by grief.

According to Donellan, there was more to come, however. Anna Maria took the time after breakfast to consider another matter:

She also, some time the same morning, unlocked the great parlour door, and calling Mr Donellan into the same, said, that as Sir Theodosius was then dead, he (Mr Donellan) might consent to let her (Lady Boughton) have a particular farm, rented by one Thomas Parsons, which Mr Donellan's wife came into possession of on Sir Theodosius's death, adding at the same time, that his wife would consent to anything he might agree to. She also told him, that he might consent to let her relation, Mr Rye, a young clergyman, have the reversion of the living of Newbold, if he pleased; and further said, that if he would consent to those things, she would have his life put into his Marriage Settlement. She also said, that she had proposed these things long before Sir Theodosius's death, and that she had absolutely spoken to a Mr Smith, an attorney of Northampton, about altering the settlement, and that he had drawn a draft of deed for the purpose; and also that she had mentioned it to Sir William Wheler.

This account shows extraordinary calm on Anna Maria's part. With her son lying dead in his bedroom, within three hours she had not only organised a funeral and eaten breakfast but had turned her mind to the family fortune. Whether she wanted Parsons' farm for its income, or to live in herself, is not clear; but she was certainly trying to obtain something for her brother's son, Robert Rye, from the estate.

Sitting in the great parlour, she must have considered her options. If her later testimony is to be believed, then less than three hours after she had remonstrated with her son-in-law over washing out a bottle which she suspected to contain the poison that had caused her son's death, she was negotiating with him for financial favours. What was her state of mind or motive to negotiate with someone who had acted so suspiciously? Had she considered the events, and thought she had overreacted? Or, despite reservations about Donellan's role, had she decided that murder could never be proved, and so she was prepared to wrestle more than she might ordinarily be expected to receive from Theodosius's estate?

Alternatively, perhaps she was demonstrating an unnatural calm at this stage because Theodosius's death had not been a shock to her. If Donellan is to be believed, Anna Maria had been considering the topic for some time, and had been talking to an attorney about it. Had she already envisaged Theodosius's death and made plans to safeguard her financial future should Theodosia inherit? Why would this be necessary if Theodosius was in the state of 'perfect health' that her own lawyers described?

Donellan claimed not to have responded to Anna Maria's suggestions. 'Mr Donellan was astonished at these suggestions,' his *Defence* continues, 'and making no other reply than that of telling her Ladyship he was no more than guardian to his children, and therefore would never do anything to their prejudice, left her.'

The prosecution had noted down something even more amazing, however, when they talked to John Derbyshire in Warwick Gaol: 'Captain Donellan had said that Lady Boughton proposed that, if he would give up his interest in Sir Theodosius's property, and a farm of about £200 a year, she would ask no more and all should be well.'

Not surprisingly, the prosecution thought it best not to trespass too far into this territory. Anna Maria's supposed attempt at black-mailing Donellan was never mentioned.

Whatever Anna Maria's reasons for discussing the estate at this unusual moment, Donellan himself said that he was not prepared to engage in such a conversation. Stressing that his only concern was for his children – his *Defence* adopted something of a morally offended tone – he left the room.

Perhaps this refusal to consider Anna Maria's financial future was far more damaging than Donellan ever imagined.

11

'Not Particularly Intended for Anatomical Pursuits'

'All that belongs to human understanding, in this deep ignorance and obscurity, is to be sceptical, or at least cautious; and not to admit to any hypothesis, whatsoever ...'
'A wise man proportions his belief to the evidence.'

David Hume, *An Enquiry concerning Human Understanding* (1748)

CATHARINE AMOS, the cook-maid at Lawford, was called to the stand directly after Anna Maria Boughton. She confirmed Theodosius's symptoms on the morning of his death but only after laboured prompting did she admit to Donellan owning a still:

Q: Did Mr Donellan bring anything to you at or about the time of Sir Theodosius's death?

A: No.

Q: At any time before his death?

A: No.

Q: Was anything brought to you by Mr Donellan within a fortnight or three weeks before the death of Sir Theodosius Boughton?

A : No.

Q: You said you was cook-maid?

A: Yes.

Q: Was the oven under your direction?

A: Yes.

Q: Was anything brought to you at that time?

A: Yes, a still.

Q: Who brought it?

A: Mr Donellan ... .he desired me to put it into the oven to dry it.

The rumour that Donellan was distilling laurel leaves for poison was rife locally. ('It has also been propagated about the country that Mr Donellan made use of a still and that he distilled poisons in it,' noted his *Defence*.) The fact that he brought the still down to the kitchen to dry it out after Theodosius died was never disputed by Donellan. His case was, however, that he had used it to distil roses and lavender for his wife. It was never proved that laurel leaves had been used in the still, only that laurel grew in Lawford Hall's garden (the gardener was called at the trial to confirm this, and this alone). No one had ever seen Donellan picking laurel leaves; nor seen him take any kind of vessel or phial for holding laurel water; nor seen laurel leaves in the still; nor seen a container of laurel water anywhere in the house. (However, it did much later transpire that Donellan had used a laurel-water foot lotion.) The servants who cleaned his rooms never spoke of or testified to the bitter almond smell described by Anna Maria anywhere about the rooms or in his clothing or on his hands – a smell that Rattray maintained in his evidence was so strong that when he tried it out on animals it 'made his gums bleed'.

Donellan wrote in his *Defence* that he had brought the still to the kitchen because he had put lime water in it to destroy fleas in his children's rooms. (Donellan used to wash the bedsteads with lime water 'as the women servants can testify' and he claimed that he had filled the still with that simply because it was the first thing to hand; popular commentaries of the time say that this was a completely ineffectual remedy.) Donellan further made the point that, if the purpose of the lime water was to obliterate the smell of laurel water, then the lime should have been in both parts of the still, whereas it was only in the lower.

The part of his *Defence* prepared before the trial reads as if Donellan took it for granted that the servants would be called to verify this. But they were not. Nor was the gardener cross-examined; 'Counsel were instructed to cross-examine the gardener but did not do it,' his solicitors remark in their footnotes.

Prosecuting counsel Digby next called the Reverend Newsam, the vicar of Great Harborough.

Newsam confirmed that he had seen Theodosius at Lawford Hall on the Saturday before his death and that Donellan had told him that Theodosius:

> … had never got rid of the disorder that he had brought with him from Eaton, but rather, in his opinion, had been adding to it; that he had made such frequent use of mercury, inwardly and outwardly, that his blood was a mass of mercury and corruption; that he had a violent swelling in his groin … that he had frequent swellings in his throat, and his breath was so offensive that they could hardly sit at table to eat with him. My answer was, 'If that was the case, I did not think that his life was worth two years' purchase.' He replied, 'Not one.'

> Q: Perhaps you can tell, from the appearance of Sir Theodosius Boughton, what was the actual state of his health at that time, and for some time before?
> A: He looked like a man to all appearance in health.

While Newsam's description of Theodosius's infection is the most lurid yet, he was not prepared to venture an opinion as to whether Theodosius's life was as short as Donellan predicted. Under cross-examination by Mr Green, he admitted that Theodosius had been under the care of William Kerr, a respected local surgeon and the founder of Northampton Hospital. Kerr was called to the stand to substantiate this. But he was not asked about the extent of Theodosius's illness or the effects on the body of pro-longed treatment with mercury.

A note in Donellan's *Defence* reads:

> Mr Newnham did not think it prudent or necessary to ask for the bills of the different Surgeons, or to cross-examine Mr Powell at all; therefore the court remained ignorant of Sir Theodosius having had any other venereal complaint than the last infection, or of his ever having taken or used mercury at all.

The first of the medical men who had been called to examine Theodosius after his death, and who witnessed the autopsy, now gave evidence: David Rattray. Mr Balguy, named by Sarah Blundell (according to Donellan) as the man who tormented her for proof of Donellan's guilt on her deathbed, asked the questions.

Rattray first testified that he received 'an anonymous note' on 4 September asking him to go to Lawford Hall 'in order to open the body of Sir Theodosius Boughton' and to bring Mr Wilmer with him. However, as Wilmer was out of town that afternoon, it was late in the evening, and dark, by the time the two men arrived at Lawford.

Donellan's account of Rattray's description of 'an anonymous note' is especially critical. 'Some men in the world exult at other men's distress,' his *Defence* concludes, after drawing attention to Rattray's lack of objectivity. 'This gentleman gave evident marks of partiality when he opened his evidence. The letter ... being wrote in a hurry ... did not put his name to it and called Mr Wilmer "Dr Wilmot". This advantage over the unfortunate prisoner pleased Dr Rattray ...'

Rattray told how Donellan was waiting for them in the hallway when they arrived; how he said that he expected Sir William Wheler might come; and that they ate supper while they waited for the coffin to be unsoldered. Then he was shown a letter from Sir William Wheler, taken out of Powell's hands in the hallway, which said that Wheler would not be coming because he thought it improper. Donellan searched his waistcoat for another letter, but

Rattray admitted impatience; he wanted, he said, 'to get over such little matters as these'.

Rattray testified that he and Wilmer went upstairs and saw the body alone but Wilmer thought it would 'answer no purpose to open the body at that time'. Then they went downstairs and asked Donellan what was the reason for an autopsy, to which Donellan replied, 'For the satisfaction of the family.'

> Q: Did he at any time intimate to you the suspicion of
>   poison?
> A: No, nothing of the sort.

Donellan's *Defence* weighs in heavily against Rattray's evidence. Rattray's attitude throughout, Donellan predicted accurately in his notes, 'will give as unfavourable account of this business as he can … being very much connected with Sir William Wheler and from hopes thereby of pleasing him, or from a wish … to gain popularity … or from what other motive is not at present known.'

Rattray was then asked about the autopsy on 9 September. Again he claimed to have been contacted in 'some strange round-about way' but he went to Newbold-on-Avon churchyard and watched the disinterment.

> Q: What were the material appearances that struck you at that
>   time?
> A: The body appeared distended a good deal; the face, of
>   a round figured, extremely black, the teeth black … the
>   tongue protruding beyond the fore teeth and turning
>   upwards towards the nose; the blackness descended upon
>   the throat … there was another circumstance which, for
>   decency, I have omitted, but, if called upon, I am ready to
>   mention.
> Q: That circumstance is not at all material …
> A: We proceeded to open the body … the bowels in the lower
>   belly seemed to put on an appearance of inflammation
>   … the heart appeared to be in a natural state … the lungs

appeared what I call suffused with blood ... the kidneys appeared as black as tinder and the liver in much the same state ...

Q: ... independent of appearances ... what was, in your judgement, the occasion of Sir Theodosius's death?

A: I am of the opinion that the swallowing of the draught ... was poison, and the immediate cause of his death.

The prosecution brief had the full statement from Rattray on the state of the body at the autopsy; it emphasised 'gangrene' – or putrefaction – a little more than Rattray was allowed on the witness stand, and made clear how impossible it was to detect poison at all. It also detailed the 'circumstance' which had 'been omitted for decency':

On 9th September at Newbold, the whole body was very much swollen with universal gangrene, the face appeared greatly enlarged, putrid, extremely black; the lips were so much retracted particularly the upper lip as to show the teeth and gums of the upper jaw distinctly. The tongue protruded a considerable way beyond the teeth appearing much inflated, the point bearing upwards towards the nose. The gums were much swelled, the nose small in proportion and apparently in a decaying state on the outer side of the right nostril.

The breast and throat were of a purple colour deepening as it reached the head. The belly afforded proof of it being in a gangrenous state. No swellings in the groin could be discovered either by the eye or by the finger. The genitals were an extraordinary object; the scrotum was much increased in bulk and the penis was in strong erection. The skin around the anus was very black but the inner part of the rectum seemed a bright red.

On cutting through the skin the fat in the cellular membrane was seeming fluid – when the cavity of the abdomen was laid open its contents appeared generally inflamed and distended with air. The stomach lay quite flat. It was impossible to examine the contents of the stomach and bowels *as the importance of the enquiry deserved* owing to the extreme offensiveness of the excrements … when the lungs were raised up, a considerable quantity of blood quite fluid, not less than a pint in the cavity of the thorax … not a single coagulum of blood … the heart was in its natural state and did not partake in the general inflammation that surrounded it.

Rattray was then asked in court to describe various animal experiments he had performed on the effects of laurel water poisoning. He recounted them with enthusiasm.

A: Our first experiment was with a middle-sized dog; I held his mouth open and nearly two ounces of laurel water poured down his throat … in half a minute he dropped dead to the ground. The next animal was an aged mare; we [he and Wilmer] gave about a pint and a half of laurel water; in about two minutes she was precipitated to the ground with her head under her, and tumbled on her back, kicking violently; seemed convulsed with her eyes rolling about, rearing up her head as if in agonies, gulping at her stomach … heaving in the flanks in the most extraordinary manner; and at the end of fifteen minutes, she expired.

He went on, again in some detail, to describe the death throes of another horse 'violently convulsed, groaning, his tongue lolling out of his mouth'.

Q: In your judgement, is the quantity that one of these bottles contains [he had been shown a bottle of the same size as the one Powell had given Theodosius] of laurel water sufficient to take away life from any human creature?
A: In my opinion, it is.

This was misleading on the prosecution's part. Their own brief showed that, even if laurel water had been in the phial, because – according to Anna Maria – a part of the rhubarb and jalop was still in it, the amount of laurel water would not have been 'the quantity that one of these bottles contains'.

There could have been no one in the court who, on hearing the distressing details of Rattray's 'experiments', and immediately afterwards seeing the bottle, would not have remembered the autopsy description of the blackened tongue and imagined Theodosius 'violently convulsed, groaning, his tongue lolling out of his mouth.'

Newnham took up the cross-examination. Rattray admitted that his inspection of Theodosius's body had taken place some eleven days after his death, and that the effects of laurel water on the animals were seen with the benefit of an immediate – not an eleven-days-later – autopsy. He went on to describe Theodosius's face 'with a maggot crawling over its surface' when he was called to Lawford Hall, and that there was a 'violent stench'. He confirmed that Donellan asked him if he would tell Sir William Wheler of their visit and added that he told Donellan he doubted he would see Sir William because of engagements the following day and evening.

Q: Was anything said to Mr Wilmer in your presence?
A: Not that I know, or at present recollect.

Rattray went on to say that the next time he saw Sir William – in other words, the first time he had a chance to tell him face to face that the body had not been opened – was 6 September. He had had a letter from Donellan that morning 'desiring either me or Mr Wilmer, or both of us, to go to Sir William Wheler and inform him of the circumstances that happened at Lawford on the night of the 4th', so he had gone to meet Sir William 'at the Black Dog'. In other words, Donellan was trying to get both men to tell Sir William what they had done – or not done – on the night of 4 September. Neither had written to Sir William to enlighten him.

Sir William had been visited by the Reverend Newsam on 3 September with a message from the Earl of Denbigh urging Wheler to investigate the cause of death; on 4 September he had written to Donellan to say he was sending Rattray and Wilmer over to do an autopsy; on 5 September Donellan had replied saying, 'I wish you would hear from them the state they found the body in.' However, in his evidence, Rattray does not say if he told Sir William that they had not opened the body as instructed.

Donellan's *Defence* makes a pertinent point here. Throughout Rattray's account of his visit to Lawford Hall, he claims not to have known that there was a suspicion that Theodosius had been poisoned. However, the apothecary Powell had been with Sir William when he had written to Donellan asking for Wilmer and Rattray to perform the autopsy, when he had been anxious to prove that it was not his physic that had poisoned Theodosius ('Mr Powell is now with me, and from his account it does not appear that his medicine could be the cause of death'). He had also been present when two doctors had arrived at the Hall that evening – according to Rattray's own testimony: 'When I came into the hall ... Mr Powell, the apothecary, stood by a great table reading a letter ...' Yet the court was now being asked to believe that Powell did not at any point tell either Wilmer or Rattray that Sir William had said: '[I]t is reported all over the country that he was killed either by medicine or by poison. The country will never be convinced to the contrary unless the body is opened ...'

Even accounting for the fact that doctors and surgeons considered themselves of a higher order than apothecaries, and did not normally discuss their work with them, still the omission – when all the 'country' was talking of poison – is astonishing, especially given that Wilmer and Rattray sat down to supper with Donellan and Powell before they went upstairs. Unless, of course, both Wilmer and Rattray thought that Powell *had* prepared poison, in which case they would have kept judiciously silent.

By 6 September, the day that Rattray met Wheler in the Black Dog, Bucknill had reported to Sir William that he had been refused access to Theodosius's body. Rattray told Wheler that an autopsy had not been safe – Wheler's letter to Donellan of 6 September reporting their conversation says: 'I ... find that they found the body in so putrid a state that they thought it not safe to open it ...'

It is plain from this that Wheler had thought an autopsy had been carried out, and that it was not until Rattray told him that it had not that Wheler wrote again to Donellan. This omission was not Donellan's fault. He had felt it proper that the two medical men should tell Wheler what they had found and done, not him; he tried to ensure that they contacted Wheler. Once the real facts became clear on 6 September, Donellan sent servants looking for Snow and Bucknill – or so he maintained.

There is one more question that neither the prosecuting counsel nor the defence asked Rattray. Why, if he met Sir William in the Black Dog on the day of the funeral, did he not offer to go to Lawford to help Bucknill? The answer becomes blindingly clear under Newnham's further questioning. Rattray claimed that he had other business on the day of the funeral – but in truth he was not qualified on the effects of poisons on the human body; nor was he qualified to speak on the subject of anatomy.

Newnham began by bringing up the subject of Rattray's deposition to the coroner's court. In it, Rattray had said that Powell's mixture could not have caused death but that, after examination of the body in the churchyard, he had concluded that, once he had heard the deposition of Lady Boughton, 'it seemed to him from such account, and the symptoms of the deceased after taking the medicine, that the same was probably the cause of death.'

Rattray began his answers with confidence:

Q: I understand you have set your name to a description of certain appearances when you examined the body?
A: I have, undoubtedly.
Q: You set your name to that examination?
A: I did not set my name to anything but my own examination.
Q: Wherein the appearances are described?
A: They are not particularly described; there is something about the stomach and bowels.

In fact, Rattray had described the stomach, bowels, kidneys, lungs, outward surface of the body, face and genitals (briefly) to the coroner. His confidence was now beginning to falter.

Q: For what purpose did you attend there?

A: I did not know that it was necessary before a Coroner's jury to enter into particulars; I was quite novice in the business.

Q: Do you mean a novice in the mode of dissection?

A: No, in the business before a Coroner.

Q: Did the account set your name to contain a true description of the appearances that met your eye upon that occasion?

A: So far as they went, they did.

Q: Did you ever hear or know of any poison whatever occasioning any immediate external appearance on the human body?

A: No ... they have not fallen under my own knowledge.

Q: I do not mean to give offence, but I beg leave to ask whether you have been much used to anatomical dissection?

A: I have been as far as persons not particularly intended for anatomical pursuits. I am not a professor of anatomy.

Q: Did you ever attend the dissection of a human body that was poisoned, or that was supposed to have been poisoned?

A: Never.

Rattray could not, therefore, reliably ascribe any significance to what he had witnessed at the autopsy because he was not professionally qualified to do so. All he could do was, as a doctor rather than a surgeon, apply generalised observations without being able to draw any conclusion that he could back up with independently verifiable proof.

Newnham persisted with the subject of inflammation, and the contents of the stomach: 'a spoonful and a half of a slimy reddish liquor, which I rubbed between my finger and thumb, and it contained no gritty substance that I could perceive', according to Rattray. Although, on being pressed about the red or inflamed stomach he admitted, 'I perhaps don't know the cause of inflammation,' adding lamely, 'the veins being full of blood put on a red appearance.'

Newnham's next questions centred on why the bowels were not fully examined at the open-air autopsy; Rattray answered that 'the smell was so offensive, I did not choose to enter into that matter ... I did not think it in the power of anyone to examine the contents of the bowels, their contents being so strong and disagreeable ...'

'Are not the bowels the seat of poison?' asked Newnham.

'When it passes there, it no doubt affects the bowels,' Rattray conceded.

Newnham turned next to the subject of arsenic.

Donellan's *Defence* commented: 'He [Rattray] has been absurd enough to say that Sir Theodosius was poison'd with arsenick, but he found it would not produce the symptoms which are said to have been the consequence of the medicine taken by Sir Theodosius. Indeed it is well known to the faculty that arsenick never operates in less than six or seven hours.'

Q: Whether many reasons have occurred ... to induce you to form your judgement he died of arsenic?

Rattray now needed to backpedal at a furious rate.

A: At that time I did think he died of arsenic, but now I am clear that I was then mistaken ... Every man is mistaken now and then in his opinion, and that was my case; I am not ashamed to own a mistake.

It is to be remembered that the offence for which Donellan was being tried was poisoning by arsenic.

However, the prosecution was confident that this distinction did not matter. As Judge Buller said in his statement to the jury at the beginning of the assizes, whatever poison had been used did not matter: 'If the indictment should state that the deceased died by any particular poison, and it should appear upon enquiry that he died of another sort of poison, the difference is immaterial with respect to the law …'[1]

The learned judge had seen the error coming, and headed it off at the pass.

Newnham then turned to the crucial point that the chest cavity had been found to be filled with two pints of blood.

> Q: Would not the rupture of a blood vessel occasion death?
> A: The rupture of a blood vessel would have undoubtedly occasioned death …
> Q: Might not a blood vessel, in an effort to reach [i.e. vomit] be broken?
> A: I should conceive that, if, in an effort to reach, a blood vessel of that magnitude had been ruptured, he must have died immediately without convulsions.

The final issue to be dealt with was the 'offensive smell' which Rattray said he noticed when he was experimenting with the animals. He was asked if Theodosius's stomach had the same offensive smell; he said that it did. However, he did not mention this when he was questioned earlier about the substance from Theodosius's stomach that he had rubbed between his thumb and finger – he was able to do that without the 'particular taste in my mouth, a kind of biting acrimony upon my tongue … I complained to Mr Wilmer, "I have a very odd taste in my mouth."' But he did add that, at the time, he had attributed the smell to the 'volatile salts' leaving the body: the normal smells, in other words, of putrefaction.

Neither Wilmer nor Bucknill commented on this strange smell or taste. Nor did Rattray mention them in the original description of the body he had given when the prosecution brief was prepared.

Rattray went on to describe laurel water as having the power to drive blood 'from the part of the body where it should be' and to 'empty the arteries' and 'push blood into the veins', but concluded, 'that is my opinion at present, as far as I have gone into the matter.'

His was an opinion based on limited research and inconclusive experiments. Yet it stood unchallenged, leaving the impression, unsubstantiated by any other medical source, that laurel water – if laurel water had indeed been used on Theodosius – had the ability to 'empty the arteries' and (in another lurid word picture associated with the autopsy) that the chest cavity apparently filled with blood.

The prosecuting team, in the form of Mr Balguy, resurfaced in the final moments of Rattray's testimony to drive home the point that, when asking Rattray and Wilmer to attend Lawford Hall, Donellan had never mentioned poison, and that Rattray did not know the 'tendency of the inquiry'. If he had, Rattray answered, 'I should have sat there a month, rather than have left the body unopened.'

A great pity, then, that Rattray did not think to ask Powell, who was with them at Lawford Hall. And a great surprise that Powell, having just seen Sir William Wheler, who was in a flat panic over the subject of poison, did not mention the subject at all.

The next four witnesses to be called were all 'gentlemen of the Faculty': Wilmer and Bucknill, who had examined Theodosius's body; and two 'experts', Dr Ashe, a physician who lived in Birmingham, and Dr Parsons, a professor of anatomy at Oxford University.

Wilmer confirmed that the subject of poison was not mentioned on the evening of 4 September – 'I never heard a word of poison.'

Q: Supposing it had been communicated to you that Sir
   Theodosius Boughton had died by poison, should you
   have been satisfied without opening it?
A: I should have then opened the body at all events.

Wilmer was also asked about Rattray's animal experiments, and confirmed them all in detail, reading from notes that he had taken at the time. He stated that the experiments were attended by Sir William Wheler, but he did not explain why the three men were particularly interested in the effects of laurel water, or why Wheler, who was not medically qualified, should be interested in witnessing them. An explanation, however, does appear in an article published after the trial, in the *Hibernian Magazine* ('Compendium of Entertaining Knowledge') for May 1781.

The article explains that the idea of experimenting on animals with laurel water had been the idea of Bradford Wilmer. Anna Maria had told Mr Wilmer that the draught smelled like bitter almonds; Wilmer had then researched the subject of poisons and found that 'laurel water was a poison having the peculiar flavour and smell of apricot kernels, and bitter almonds'.

Having asked 'an ingenious chemist in London' to prepare a mixture of the same, he told Sir William, who then consulted the family solicitor Caldecott. Caldecott made it his business to visit Lawford Hall, and found that 'three days after the death' John Donellan had asked a servant to clean out a still which he had been using. We know from Edward Boughton's letters just before the trial that the discovery of Donellan's possession of the still had been 'kept secret to prevent Donellan getting intelligence of it'; nevertheless Donellan did address the issue in his *Defence*.

Wilmer then proposed trying the laurel water on a horse, to see its effects; and this was the reason why, in March, just a matter of days before the trial, Wheler, Rattray and Wilmer had gathered to see the deadly consequences of the draught.

It must be noted that the experiments, the secrecy, Caldecott's investigation at Lawford Hall and the research by Wilmer all sprang from a single source – Anna Maria Boughton saying that the draught 'smelt like bitter almonds'; a smell not detected in the bedroom after Theodosius's death, or by the servants, or when the body was viewed on 4 September, or at the autopsy except by Rattray.

Wilmer's evidence to the prosecuting counsel ended on a rather significant point: he confirmed that he knew nothing about the effects of laurel water on the human body – 'I do not know it of my own knowledge, but from my reading.'

Mr Green, acting for Donellan, conducted the cross-examination of Wilmer.

His questions centred upon the effects of apoplexy and epilepsy in human beings; Wilmer confirmed that epileptics foam at the mouth, and that sometimes their tongues are blackened. Asked about loss of blood, he stated that 'the loss of blood will evidently occasion convulsions' and confirmed also that two pints of blood (or what he thought was blood) were in Theodosius's chest cavity. His evidence here contradicted that of Rattray, who had said that 'if a blood vessel of that magnitude had been ruptured, he must have died immediately without convulsions.'

Next Wilmer was asked about Donellan's requests after he and Rattray had seen Theodosius's body on the evening of 4 September, and here again he directly contradicted Rattray's testimony. Wilmer claimed that he had not himself been asked to tell Sir William Wheler about their decision not to open the body that night, but said, 'I believe he [Donellan] asked Dr Rattray whether he should see Sir William Wheler. I think Dr Rattray said he believed he should, and would give him an account of the business.'

So, although Rattray disclaimed any responsibility in not advising Sir William, his own colleague – much the senior and more respected man – said this was not true.

If Wilmer was correct, why did Rattray lie about this? Why did he tell Donellan that he would inform Wheler that the body had not been opened, and then not do so? Or did he actually tell Sir William on 5 September, and Wheler did not act on it until the next day, 6 September, when they met at the Black Dog?

Whatever the answer, it lay between Wilmer, Rattray and Wheler. If there was an attempt to obscure the lack of an autopsy on 4 September, it was not Donellan's doing.

Dr Ashe was the next witness called by the prosecution.

On being asked the cause of Theodosius's death, he answered that 'he died in consequence of taking that draught'. He also claimed that Theodosius's appearance at the autopsy was similar to that of animals which had died by poison.

Ashe was only on the stand for a matter of minutes, and was not cross-examined, but in those few minutes he was asked nine questions, of which three were on how Theodosius died, and two of those asked him to confirm that poison was the cause.

It is strange that Ashe was called to the stand at all; he had not been involved in the case. It is possible that he was asked to give testimony because he was well respected locally (he founded the Birmingham General Hospital and was its first physician). He was also a passionate amateur botanist, and therefore it could have been felt that his repeated statements about poison bore some additional weight – although his knowledge of botany was never referred to in court.

The next medical witness was Dr Parsons, professor of anatomy at Oxford University. The prosecution, in the person of Howarth, got straight to the point:

Q: What, in your judgement, occasioned the death of Sir
Theodosius Boughton?
A: From the description of his health … and from the violent
nervous symptoms that immediately followed … he died
in consequence of taking the second dose, which proved to
contain a poison … her ladyship said it smelt like the taste
of bitter almonds which particularly characterises the smell
of laurel water …

This is an extraordinary statement. The dose had *not* been 'proved to contain a poison', unless Anna Maria's sense of smell was proof.

Parsons was then asked to distinguish between epilepsy and apoplexy. (Apoplexy is what nowadays would be referred to as a stroke.)

A: Epilepsy is distinguished by a total absence of sense but
an increase in motion of several of the muscles so that the
patient will appear convulsed … apoplexy is a sudden
privation of all the powers of sense and voluntary motion,
the person affected seeming to be in a profound sleep …
as a part of Sir Theodosius's symptoms, the state in which
he lay seems to have been more of the apoplectic kind
than the epileptic.

Q: Was the heaving of the stomach the effect of apoplexy or epilepsy or of this draught?

A: No doubt, I think, that the draught was the cause ...

Q: And from your knowledge of the effects produced by laurel water, your opinion is that laurel water was the poison thus administered to Sir Theodosius Boughton?

A: It is.

The cross-examination by Newnham continued on the theme of apoplexy versus epilepsy. Parsons conceded that apoplexy could result in the sudden bursting of a blood vessel; he also said that there could be no doubt that apoplexy was a *possible* cause of Theodosius's attack.

It was reported in the magazine *The Mirror of Literature, Amusement and Instruction* in 1833 that 'Donellan said Sir Theodosius had been subject to epileptic fits since infancy', but this is the only reference; it was not said at the trial even by Donellan, and though – if true – would be of vast significance, unfortunately the source is unreliable.

In his next reply, Parsons immediately dismissed apoplexy as a probable cause because 'there is no reason to go so far for a cause ... when this medication, as all the world knows, will effect it'.

Q: That is assuming, as a fact, that he took two ounces of laurel water?

A: A much less quantity would be sufficient for the purpose.

The answer is almost comic. Parsons was not being asked necessarily about the quantity. He was being asked about his *assumption* that laurel water was the cause, and converting this assumption into fact. But Newnham let it pass. He concluded the cross-examination with all the 'assumptions' of the medical witnesses:

Q: You ground your opinion upon the description of its smell by Lady Boughton?

A: Yes; we can ground our opinions upon nothing else but that.

No record remains of the reason why Dr Parsons was called, but a good guess would be that a professor of anatomy from Oxford University would be thought to be an impressive, well-respected medical man whose distance from Warwickshire provided at least some degree of objectivity. As such he fulfilled the same criteria as John Hunter, the anatomist who would be brought for the defence.

The experience and competence of the two men, however, was not comparable. John Hunter was nationally famous; he had conducted over 30,000 dissections in his career; his study and collection of anatomical specimens was second to none. Parsons, in contrast, did not enjoy such a good reputation.

Oxford University in the eighteenth century was not the centre of excellence that it is today. It awarded very few medical degrees and, prior to its reforms of 1833, it was bound by outdated ceremonies and traditions. In 1770, Parsons had become the first professor in the Chair of Clinical Medicine, but the weekly lectures that he was required to give at the Radcliffe Infirmary were not well attended 'on account of the paucity of the students, and the indifference of the Professor', according to the nineteenth-century chronicler of the Royal College of Physicians Arnold Chaplin. Chaplin noted that both professors and students found the lectures and disputations 'irksome', and, although Parsons also held the first Lee Readership in Anatomy from 1767, 'it cannot be said that a single professor contributed to the subject of medicine anything particularly worthy'.

The final medical witness to be called was Samuel Bucknill, who was described as 'professing surgery'. He confirmed that he went to Lawford Hall on 5 September of his own accord and offered to 'take out the stomach', but that Donellan refused to allow him to do so because it would 'not be fair in him or us to do anything after men so eminent in their profession had declined it'.

Bucknill then described the following day, the day of the funeral. He had received a verbal message from Sir William Wheler that he was to meet Mr Snow at Lawford Hall and together they were to perform the autopsy. When he arrived, Donellan told him he was waiting for more orders from Sir William. Donellan's action here is mystifying, in that he already had a letter telling him to let Bucknill proceed. Donellan's hesitation might have been because Mr Snow was not there; but Wheler's postscript to his letter of 6 September says quite plainly: 'If Snow is from home, I do not see any impropriety in Bucknill doing it, if he is willing.' Nevertheless, Donellan was adamant that both men had to be present.

Bucknill described the frantic to-ing and fro-ing around Lawford that day; of his leaving the Hall because he had an urgent case to attend to; of a servant catching up with him to say that Snow had arrived at the Hall; of his own response that he would be back in an hour.

Q: Did you come back in an hour?
A: I came back, I believe, in the hour.
Q: What passed then; was Mr Snow there?
A: I asked Captain Donellan if Mr Snow was gone. He said, 'he was, and he had given them orders what to do, and they were proceeding according to those orders' but, says he, 'I am sorry you should have given yourself all this unnecessary trouble.' I took my horse, and rode away as fast as I could.

There was one witness missing: Sir William's apothecary, Bernard Geary Snow. From 1702, the defence could call witnesses but, unlike the prosecution, could not compel witnesses to attend. Snow, according to Donellan, had given orders that the funeral should go ahead. But why did Donellan take orders from a lowly apothecary and not wait for Bucknill to return to carry out the autopsy? On what authority could Snow give those orders? Donellan protested in his statement to the court that 'the body was buried that evening, but not by my directions or desire'.

Donellan's statement tried to explain the matter by saying that Snow had waited a 'considerable time' for Bucknill, and that when he did not arrive, he had called 'the plumber and others' (the plumber meaning the man who had soldered and re-soldered the coffin) into the parlour. 'After examining them as to the putridity of the body, declared he would not be concerned in opening it for Sir Theodosius's estate; and recommending it to the family to have the same buried that afternoon, immediately left Lawford before Mr Bucknill's return.'

Recommendations are not orders, so why did Donellan tell Bucknill that Snow had 'given them orders what to do'? Was it that Donellan was relieved that an opportunity had at last arisen to bury a body that might reveal his own guilt; or was it simply a case of not wanting to keep a house full of mourners waiting any longer in the oppressive heat? Theodosius's body was laid out on the great hall table all the while; it could only have been a source of distress to his mother and sister. Was Donellan acting out of relief and compassion, or relief and guilt?

Donellan's counsel could not compel Snow to come to the stand and the prosecuting counsel did not call him. In his summing up, even Francis Buller was astonished at the omission. He commented:

> Those, the prisoner says, were his orders. But Mr Snow is not called. You have had no evidence of any thing that passed between the prisoner and Snow. You are told by the prisoner, in his defence, that Snow advised him instantly to bury the body; and if that were the advice given, why in such a case should not the prisoner call Snow to prove what passed between them, and what information he gave to Snow? Or why did he not communicate to Bucknill the reasons given by Snow?

A lawyer examining the case after the end of the trial, James Stephen, decided that Snow 'as agent of Sir William Wheler authorised the funeral'; but the issue of whether Donellan did in fact call Snow to the stand but he refused to come, or whether Donellan did not call Snow at all, is not resolved.

Four vital questions were missed in the examination of the 'Faculty'.

The first was whether Theodosius's venereal infection or his treatment by mercury could have brought about, or contributed to, his death. Despite Donellan's protestations that Theodosius's illness dated back five years, and in that time he had been treated repeatedly with mercury, the court only considered the boy's *current* infection and treatment. This was partly due to a lack of insistence on the defending counsel's part to pursue closer questioning of Anna Maria; partly their failure to produce the bills of the various apothecaries and surgeons. But in greater part it was a general failure, due to medical ignorance at the time, to ascribe lasting damage to either the illness or its treatment.

The second was the history of apoplexy (strokes) in Theodosius's family. Parsons was asked whether apoplexy could be caused by a ruptured blood vessel, and answered yes; but the fact that Theodosius's father, Edward, had died of this condition at the age of fifty-three was not mentioned until Newnham cross-examined Sir William Wheler later in the day. Even then, the prosecution interrupted, enabling Wheler to point out that Edward had been 'short and thick set' whereas Theodosius was 'very thin, and taller than his father'.

It was probably considered that to draw any stronger parallels between father and son would lead nowhere; but if Theodosius's circulatory system had been affected by syphilis and the mercury, then the apoplexy – a circulatory disorder – that caused his father's death becomes more pertinent. No one thought it relevant to take this connection a little further and point out that Theodosius's grandfather had died exceptionally early at only thirty-three; probably because the exact cause of death – whether an apoplexy or not – was unknown. But taking the three deaths together, they do suggest that the Boughton men were prone to either a stroke or early demise; this again casts a shadow over the picture of 'good health' painted by the prosecution.

The third question concerned the use of laurel in most eighteenth-century homes and kitchens, and the use of laurel water itself, in minute quantities, in apothecaries' medicines. Dried laurel leaves, even of the poisonous cherry laurel, were used in flavouring, as were leaves from its sister tree the bay. Laurel water in medicine was prescribed to stop morning sickness and the spasmodic cough of whooping cough. It could also be used to produce increased salivation, as noted by Charles Phillips in his *Materia Medica and Therapeutics* of 1879. Why was the apothecary Powell not asked if he had put laurel water into Theodosius's draught either to increase salivation (which was thought to expel venereal infection) or to inhibit the nausea that he had experienced when taking the first dose the previous Saturday? Had Powell inadvertently added too strong a mixture, or confused its strength?

The fourth issue was the very first deposition that had been put before the coroner in September 1780, that of the miller Thomas Hewitt. Hewitt had testified that he had bought one ounce of '*Occuli Indicus* Berries' from Samuel Bucknill and delivered them to 'the deceased, who put them into his pocket'. Why had Bucknill not been questioned about this? Similarly, why was Anna Maria not questioned in greater detail about the pound of arsenic that she knew Theodosius had in his room for trapping rats? How much of the arsenic was left? Had any of it gone missing? Additionally, what had happened to all the other medicines that Theodosius had been taking? There were various bottles on the chimney shelf; he had confessed to Donellan also to using mercurial ointment. Were any of the other quack remedies that Theodosius was so fond of taking subsequently found and analysed?

The prosecution brief did make a note about the poison supplied to Theodosius by Hewitt: 'It seems Donellan means to prove that the bottle of *coculus indicus* [*sic*] which the miller made for Sir Theodosius to kill fish with is not to be found, and therefore he will presume that Lady Boughton gave that to Sir Theodosius by mistake, whereas we have the bottle to produce.'

This is fascinating stuff. Aside from the bizarre explanation that the mixture was used to 'kill fish' (why, when Theodosius already had arsenic to put in the dead fish to kill rats?), if the prosecution had Hewitt's bottle, what did that prove exactly? It certainly did not prove, as the brief suggested, that it could not have been used to poison Theodosius; only that the bottle was not disposed of. One wonders, too, where the prosecution had found the bottle. Hewitt had already said that he had not seen it since delivering the potion to Theodosius. That presumably meant that it was retrieved from Lawford or its grounds. But where exactly? It could certainly have been in Theodosius's bedroom.

Perhaps the prosecution saw the weaknesses in this argument, for Hewitt's bottle was never mentioned nor produced in court.

If Theodosius was poisoned – and it was certainly the prosecution case that he was – then there was a responsibility to account for several other deadly toxins, and not just laurel water, at Lawford Hall.

A Man of Judgement

'I don't know that the draught was poison …'

John Hunter

IT WAS BY NOW EARLY AFTERNOON, and the court had been sitting for over six hours.

It was the turn of the servants of Lawford Hall to give their testimony: servants which, according to both Donellan and to local newspapers after the event, had been subjected to immense pressure by the prosecuting team. In addition to Sarah Blundell's supposed deathbed questioning by Mr Balguy, the *Northampton Mercury* of 30 April 1781 reported:

Since the Inquest was taken, several gentlemen in the neighbourhood of Lawford Hall have at different times sent for the witnesses against John Donellan to their respective houses and extorted many things from them which are intended to be adduced at the trial. They even went so far as to threaten them with imprisonment and other punishments and, calling their Clerks, have given them absolute orders to make out commitments if they did not say something against Mr Donellan.

If this is true, the effect on the household servants would have been extreme. Not only would testimony in Donellan's favour undoubtedly mean that they would lose their jobs, but possibly also the jobs of any family members employed by Boughton tenant farmers in the area – a penalty that could be easily imposed by Lady Boughton. The extra threat of imprisonment would have been too much to bear. These were not literate, educated people; they would have had no real idea of the powers of lawyers, but they would certainly have known the power of the tight-knit aristocratic community which owned their servants as effectively as they owned their vast estates. Sarah Blundell's example was very recent proof that, once out of favour, a woman could be thrown out of work and accommodation; and without the 'good character' of their past employers, any working person's future was indeterminate, if not lost.

William Frost, the coachman, was the first to testify.

He confirmed that there had been an arrangement for Donellan and Anna Maria to ride to Newnham Wells together on the morning of 30 August. He also said that Donellan came out at seven o'clock, and then went back inside to see where Lady Boughton was. Returning, he said, 'Lady Boughton is not ready yet; I will go to the Wells', and rode away. Frost took Anna Maria's horse back into the stable, and it was only 'a considerable time' later that she rushed downstairs and told him to fetch Powell, saying that her son was 'dangerously ill'.

The prosecuting counsel, Digby, left the subject; which is unsurprising, as Frost – whatever pressure he might have been under – had just confirmed the time lapse as portrayed by Donellan. 'A considerable time' is not the 'five minutes' described by Anna Maria. Frost then confirmed that he was called into the parlour to confirm these times as 'evidence'.

Frost was not cross-examined.

The next servant to be called was Samuel Frost.

(Incidentally, there is no record of whether William Frost and

Samuel Frost were related, although it is possible that they were brothers, as they were both referred to as 'young men'. Similarly, there is no statement of the relationship between Catharine and Francis Amos, the cook-maid and the gardener. However, it is likely that Catharine was Francis's wife, as according to the Newbold parish register a Francis Amos married a Catharine Palmer in February 1781.

To the prosecution, Samuel Frost now testified that he delivered Theodosius's medicine into his hands between five and six o'clock on the evening of 29 August, and that Theodosius took it upstairs. Under cross-examination, Frost said that Donellan joined Anna Maria and Theodosia at seven o'clock in the garden – which ties in with Anna Maria's story. Donellan, however, claimed that he was with Anna Maria all afternoon until Dand and Matthews called at six o'clock. According to Donellan, he was walking to the mill by the time Frost said he saw him in the garden.

The next witness was Mary Lynne, who had been Donellan's own servant.

Mary's answers were strained and nervous:

Q: How long before Sir Theodosius died?
A: I was not there at his death; I had left the place then.
Q: When did you leave it?
A: I cannot justly tell when I did leave it.
Q: Was it a month or six weeks before Sir Theodosius's death?
A: About a month, I believe.
Q: How long had you lived there before you left that place?
A: I cannot justly tell …
Q: Did you live there a twelvemonth, or half a year?
A: No.
Q: Might you have been there three or four months?
A: I might …
Q: Do you know anything about a still?
A: Yes.

Q: Mention what you know about it.

Mary now did something quite remarkable. A nervous country girl, standing in a court of law in a murder trial, subjected to any amount of pressure to reveal that Donellan distilled laurel, she said: 'I will tell the truth, and nothing else. Mr Donellan distilled roses. I do not know that he distilled anything else.'

The prosecution tried to get her to say that the door to the room was always locked, but she denied this.

Q: Do you know anything of his using this still frequently?
A: Yes, distilling roses ...

One can only imagine Donellan's feeling of gratitude to this girl, who went against a popular tide of bad feeling and rumour to defend her former employer.

Francis Amos was the final servant to take the stand.

What Donellan had to say about Francis Amos, the gardener, in his *Defence* is not flattering: 'the poor fellow ... a weak, silly, illiterate man'.

Q: I am asking you if you saw Mr Donellan on the evening after the death of Sir Theodosius Boughton, and whether you had any conversation with him?
A: At night I had.
Q: What did he say to you?
A: He said, 'Now gardener, you shall live at your ease; and work at your ease; it shall not be as it was in Sir Theo's days. I wanted before to be master, but I have got master now, and shall be master.'

Donellan's *Defence* maintained that Amos simply asked Donellan who would be master now, and he was told that it would be Sir Edward Boughton.

Q: Do you know of Mr Donellan using a still for any
purpose?

A: He brought a still for me to clean ... it was full of lime ...

Q: You, as a gardener, know whether he used to gather things
for the purpose of distilling?

A: He might for what I know.

Q: Have you ever got any thing?

A: I have got lavender ...

Q: Have you any laurel trees?

A: Yes.

At this point, defence counsel Newnham made what seems like a bizarre interjection. He asked, 'And celery?' to which Amos answered, 'Yes.'

Celery was in wide use in the eighteenth century for culinary purposes, but it had originally been a medicinal herb. The *New Herbal* of 1551 describes smallage (the ancestor of modern celery) as 'promoting epileptic fits'. But it was also used as a cure for impotence. So perhaps this is what Newnham meant by his interruption – that Theodosius, by resorting to using celery when he was ill, had produced his own epileptic fits. If so, it was a very obtuse enquiry, and one that Newnham did not pursue.

Amos was then asked about Donellan telling him to find pigeons: a curious old-wives'-tale remedy recommended dead pigeons at the feet of an invalid. Amos said that Donellan told him that Sir Theodosius was a 'poor fellow with this damned nasty distemper, the pox' and Amos then added that, when he came back with the birds, Lady Boughton and Theodosia were at the door 'wringing their hands; they said, "It is too late now, he is dead."' He confirmed that this happened at a few minutes after eight.

This is perplexing stuff. Taking Anna Maria's testimony and Donellan's *Defence* together, it would appear that Donellan was in the room when Theodosius died; or, at least, neither account says that he left it. Yet the cook-maid testified that she left Theodosius's room before he died, and about a quarter of an hour later Donellan passed her in the passageway saying that Theodosius had been out very late fishing. Francis Amos says that he came back to the house with the pigeons, but not that Donellan was with him. He met the two women, who told him that Theodosius was dead, but Donellan was not with them.

If we take Donellan's evidence and that of William Frost, Donellan first saw Theodosius between 7.50 and 8 a.m. If we take the servants' evidence, Donellan left the room and was in the passageway and garden; he then returned to the house and, according to his *Defence*, was with Theodosius when he died. His absence, to go downstairs, along the passageway and out into the garden, talking to two servants along the way, and to return then upstairs, could not have been less than five minutes. Allowing that he was in Theodosius's room for five minutes first, and that the boy died within five minutes of his return, the death must have occurred at the earliest just after eight – but most probably around 8.10 a.m. Which was confirmed by Francis Amos.

What was Anna Maria doing while Donellan was gone? Her evidence says nothing at all about his absence. Why, in fact, did Donellan leave the room at all if Theodosius seemed on the brink of death? It seems reasonable to say that he would not do so; but both the gardener *and* Donellan and Catharine Amos agree that he was either in the garden, or on his way to the garden after he saw Theodosius was ill. It can only be presumed that there was an interval when it seemed that he was holding his own; struggling, but not obviously dying. Donellan left at this point, by his own account to try to find an age-old remedy; when he came back, Theodosius was very much worse – on the brink of death, in fact.

What had happened in the room during that time? Was Anna Maria with her son the entire time after Donellan had been called? Was she alone with Theodosius, and at what point did his condition so suddenly worsen?

Anna Maria's testimony does not say that Donellan left the room. Why would she leave out this detail, knowing that the servants could verify it?

The only other person who could reliably say who was present, and what happened during Donellan's absence, was Sarah Blundell. And Sarah Blundell was dead.

There is one other detail of Anna Maria's testimony which does not tally. She said under oath that Theodosius was 'very near dead' when she was remonstrating with Donellan about his washing out of the bottles, and Sarah Blundell was clearing out the room. But there was hardly time, if Donellan left the room and Theodosius died soon after his return, to argue about bottles. It is far more likely that the conversation took place once Theodosius was dead, and the room was being cleared.

It does cast a much worse light on Donellan, however, and gives more sympathy to Anna Maria's story, if Donellan was trying to conceal the evidence while Theodosius lay dying before him.

Francis Amos made one other statement which was not covered in his court testimony. In the prosecution brief, he said that 'He saw Captain Donellan in the garden between 6 and 7 o'clock when he [Amos] called for Samuel Frost and Captain Donellan replied that he was coming.'

Was Donellan or was he not in the garden between 6 and 7 p.m. the previous evening? Anna Maria said no; Donellan said that he left the Hall at about ten past six, walked to the mill and was gone until nine o'clock.

Who was right? Amos and Donellan's stories tally (between 6 and 6.10); Anna Maria's does not.

One servant who was not called to give evidence was the footman John Yateman. In the prosecution brief, however, he gave a statement as follows:

In the afternoon preceeding Sir Theodosius's death, from about 3 in the afternoon until near 7 o'clock, he was in and about the Park and grounds near the house and saw nothing of Captain Donellan. Early in the morning on which Sir Theodosius died he was at the river getting out the net which Sir Theodosius had left there the evening before and he happened to look towards the garden when he saw Captain Donellan leaning over a wall in a private place there next to the river where he had never seen him before, and that as soon as he perceived he was seen he immediately drew back and this witness saw no more of him.

This statement, which came under a section called 'Evidence', misses out one crucial element from an earlier one Yateman made to the prosecution team. In that, he said that he 'saw Donellan swing his hand and throw something into the water' at this time.

Why was there a difference in the statements? It seems that the footman had changed his mind in the later one. And it is curious why Yateman was never brought to the stand to reveal what seems to be good evidence of Donellan trying to conceal something small enough to throw – a bottle, perhaps?

Nothing more was heard of Yateman. It is possible that, after his sweetheart's death, he moved away. Later that year, in November, a John Yateman married a Sarah Nixon in St Michael's Church in Coventry. But it is not known if this is the same man.

Now came the testimony of two men who were not servants.

One was William Crofts, who said that at the coroner's court he had seen John Donellan 'catch [Lady Boughton] by the gown, and give her a twitch' when she mentioned that Donellan had rinsed out the bottles.

Absolutely nothing else was asked of Crofts, nor was he cross-examined; but Donellan explains the incident in his *Defence*:

In the course of Lady Boughton's evidence when she spoke of her daughter's maid, she spoke 'maid' so low that Mr Donellan did not hear it, and thinking she said 'her daughter', he pulled her by the sleeve and told her she had made a mistake, whereupon Lady Boughton recalled her words, and said she meant her daughter's maid.

The next witness was John Derbyshire, the debtor from Warwick Gaol, who had got to know Donellan well during his imprisonment. Derbyshire testified that Donellan talked of Theodosius's death hundreds of times; but one conversation in particular formed his evidence now.

A: We were both in one room together; he had a bed in the same room I had for a month or five weeks, I believe … we had a conversation about Sir Theodosius being poisoned; I asked Captain Donellan whether the body was poisoned or not. He said there was no doubt of it … he said, 'It was done among themselves … himself, Lady Boughton, the footman, and the apothecary.'

Q: Who did he mean by 'himself'?

A: Sir Theodosius Boughton … I said, 'Sure, he could not do it himself'; he said, no, he did not think he did … the apothecary would lose a good patient … it was very unnatural to suppose Lady Boughton could do it. He then spoke of Lady Boughton, how covetous she was; he said she received an anonymous letter the day after Sir Theodosius's death, charging her plump with poisoning Sir Theodosius; that she called him and read it to him, and she trembled; he said she desired he would not let his wife know of that letter; and asked him if he would give up his right to the personal estate, and some estates of about two hundred pounds a year belonging to the family.

Donellan knew that Derbyshire would testify against him. They had quarrelled in prison – Donellan claimed it was because he refused to lend Derbyshire money – and soon after Derbyshire had sent for Caldecott, the Boughtons' solicitor, and told him the story. Donellan knew that it would sound bad that he had said he knew that Theodosius had been poisoned; all he could offer by way of explanation was that he had not poisoned Theodosius himself. Donellan's incarceration had hardened him to the fact that poison was going to be the issue of the trial; but he still instructed his lawyers to find any other explanation they could.

The defence tried to blacken Derbyshire's reputation, showing him to be a bankrupt and having been involved in a contentious

case which had previously been tried by Buller. But Derbyshire
was a placid, even-handed witness: he readily admitted to his
mistakes and added that Donellan had changed his mind several
times about the reasons for Theodosius's death. As a result, he left
an impression of frankness and honesty; but the dramatic speech
about Anna Maria hung ominously in the air.

Sir William Wheler testified next. This was the man who, more
than any other, held the key to the trial. He had been Theodosius's
guardian: as such, he should have been aware of the boy's medical
history, his character, his education and his difficulties at Eton.
He knew Anna Maria Boughton well – a woman described as 'all
but a fool', an heiress who was 'not a very intellectual woman'. No
doubt, when Edward – who was his close friend – had died Wheler
had advised Anna Maria more than once. That was what he was
there for, why he was Theodosius's guardian – as a family friend
and mature older man of wealth and title. His own daughter Lucy
had married within a few months of Theodosia, and it is hard to
believe that the subject of Theodosia's new husband had not come
up in conversation with her.

So this was a person who knew Lawford and the family better than
any of the doctors, better than Powell, better than the servants. He
knew their financial situation, having witnessed several legal documents for Anna Maria and Edward; he knew what drove them, what
interested them, what worried them; he also knew their lands and
estates, as much of them abutted his own. And it is hard to imagine
that he had not visited Lawford at some time during the last three
years to see how Lawford was progressing with Donellan acting as
its master; as Theodosius's guardian he would have been anxious to
know that everything was being conducted responsibly. No record
remains of his slightest disapproval or reservations at that time.

And yet this significant opportunity was lost. Wheler was asked
to read out the letters that had passed between himself and Donellan between the death and the funeral, and to comment very briefly
on Sir Edward Boughton's sudden death. That was all. No answer
as to whether Snow had acted on his authority when the order was

given to bury Theodosius; no explanation of why he himself had not visited Lawford after the death or why he had been slow to respond to the news. The defence counsel did not ask him about the most telling fact of all – that he had trusted Donellan to organise Theodosius's funeral, and that not one of his letters held any hint of accusation on his behalf towards Donellan, and nor had Anna Maria expressed any misgivings.

Yet at some point after the autopsy, Sir William Wheler had become convinced that Theodosius had been poisoned. His attendance at the experiments with laurel water that Rattray had so enthusiastically conducted three weeks before the trial had confirmed his opinion that laurel water had been the cause. From that moment on, Anna Maria had been helped to testify against her son-in-law: in the newspapers after Donellan's trial it was mentioned that the Earl of Denbigh sat in court, nodding approval as Anna Maria turned to him before answering questions. Denbigh and Wheler were close associates.

But it was unthinkable, apparently, that anyone of either Denbigh's or Wheler's rank should be questioned as to their friendships, alliances, knowledge or motives.

Wheler left the stand, no doubt with Donellan's eyes upon him. It was obvious now that, no matter how much Donellan had cared for Theodosia, no matter how well he had managed Lawford, no matter how many times he had saved Theodosius from disgracing himself in tavern brawls (which the next two witnesses, Miller and Loggie, independently verified), these counted for nothing now. There was a social abyss between Donellan and his accusers.

If Theodosius had been poisoned, then a perpetrator must be found; and those who wielded power in society – men like Wheler – had closed their ranks against him.

When Wheler stepped down, Donellan's previous deposition to the coroner, written from Lawford Hall on 14 September – the day that Anna Maria so substantially changed her own testimony – was read out.

Then the Clerk of the Arraigns stood to deliver Donellan's statement for his defence, the only statement of his submissible in court, and which he had had to prepare before the trial began:

> My Lord and Gentlemen of the Jury,
> Permit me in this unfortunate situation, to submit to your con-
> sideration a few particulars and observations relating to this
> horrid charge which has been brought against me.
>
> Although many false, malevolent, and cruel reports have
> been circulated in the public prints and throughout the country
> ever since my confinement, tending to prejudice the minds of
> the people injurious to my honour and dangerous to my life, I
> still have confidence that your justice and humanity cannot be
> misled by them ...

Donellan went on to outline the history of his marriage, and his
good relationships with the family, Theodosius in particular. He
drew the attention of the court to 'several occasions' when he protected Theodosius against injury. He then addressed the subject of
the missed autopsy.

> These gentlemen arrived about nine o'clock at night when I
> produced to them Sir William's letter and desired they would
> pursue his instructions ... [they] returned and ... informed the
> family that the [body] was so putrid it was not only dangerous
> to approach it but impossible at that time to discover the cause
> of Sir Theodosius's death.

He stressed that Rattray had undertaken to inform Sir William
of what had or had not transpired, but had not done so. He
also described how Bucknill arrived unannounced and that 'he
had understood that I wished to have the body of Sir Theodosius opened and I informed him that it was my wish', but that
he explained that he could not go against the decision of Rattray
and Wilmer without Sir William's permission. He then said that 'I
should nevertheless think myself obliged to him to undertake the
matter if he should wait upon Sir William Wheler and obtain his
consent to do it.'

Until this statement, Donellan's claim that he had asked Bucknill to approach Wheler had never come to light.

Donellan then went on to describe the day of the funeral and the fact that Bucknill and Snow had missed each other, but that Snow had come to the house and 'recommended' the burial.

> The body was therefore buried that evening, but not by my directions or desire ... This, gentlemen, was the undisguised part I took; but such is my misfortune ... but the most trifling actions and expressions have been handled to my prejudice; my private letters have been broken open, and many unjustifiable steps have been taken to prejudice the world and imbitter [*sic*] my defence.
>
> However, depending upon the conscience of my judge, and the unprejudiced impartiality of the jury, I trust my honour will be protected by their verdict.

Donellan did not explain the issue of the bottle-washing, which Judge Buller was later to pronounce was 'above all' the greatest circumstance which 'left [his] guilt without the smallest doubt'.

The variance of his evidence with Anna Maria's is only hinted at in the final paragraph. Was he thinking of his mother-in-law when he talked of 'unjustifiable steps'?

Perhaps a hint was too subtle for the jury.

All Donellan's hopes now rested on a final witness.

Listening all day in court, having travelled from London the day before, the surgeon and anatomist John Hunter was dressed in his usual crumpled suit of clothes. Fifty-three years old, he was famous for his short temper and unkempt appearance; but there was no doubting the luminosity of his reputation.

The list of John Hunter's accomplishments was truly impressive. Having begun studying anatomy in the 1740s and established his own school of anatomy in 1764, he was elected Fellow of the Royal College of Surgeons in 1767 and had served as an army surgeon in France and Portugal. A specialist in venereal disease for at least fifteen years, he had been resident surgeon at St George's Hospital in London for thirteen years and Surgeon General to George III for five. He counted the painter Joshua Reynolds and the naturalist Joseph Banks among his friends.

Hunter's anatomical expertise was second to none: during his 33-year career he had conducted thousands of dissections, and had a vast museum of specimens which were to be bequeathed to the nation after his death. The museum was condemned in a print of 1782 called 'The Resurrection' which shows nine dissected corpses trying to find their respective heads, legs and stomachs – and was also a sideswipe at Hunter as a 'resurrectionist', a man who was not above body-snatching.

Hunter's London home was the original inspiration for the story of Jekyll and Hyde, its frontage as Number 28 Leicester Square being highly respectable, the scene of literary and musical gatherings organised by his wife (although the giraffe in the hallway would have been a mite distracting). The rear – 13 Castle Street – was quite a contrast; it was the entrance to the mortuary and dissecting rooms, guarded by a drawbridge. Corpses from hospitals, street brawls, prisons and executions trundled through there daily, the grisly cartloads a source of terror to local children.

Hunter's Earls Court country house was no less extraordinary. A strange collection of animals grazed the lawns; a crocodile's jawbone hung over the door; and he kept wild cats, including a lion and two leopards, in cages in the grounds. A cart drawn by three Asian buffaloes regularly transported Hunter to London. Hunter was a passionate observer of life in all its forms, with an affection for 'monsters' – a two-headed calf and a bottled set of premature human quintuplets among them.

But in addition to his peculiar passions, Hunter was intelligent and precise, and he did not jump to conclusions or seek popular glory. Unfortunately, it was the scientific accuracy for which he was renowned which was now to prove such a disappointment for Donellan.

Hunter was forthright in his dismissal of Rattray's conclusions:

Q: Can any certain inference, upon physical principles, be drawn from those symptoms described or from the appearances, externally or internally of the body, to enable you, in your judgement, to decide that the death was occasioned by poison?

A: The whole appearances upon the dissection explain nothing but putrefaction.

Q: Are those symptoms you have heard described such, in your judgement, as are the results of putrefaction in dead subjects?

A: Entirely.

Q: Are the symptoms that appeared after the medicine was given such as necessarily conclude that the person had taken poison?

A: Certainly not.

Q: If an apoplexy had come on, would not the symptoms have been nearly or somewhat similar?

A: Very much the same.

So far, so good. Defence counsel Newnham now asked if Hunter had ever known of a 'young subject' dying of apoplexy. Hunter answered that he had, though 'not frequent'.

The questioning now moved to the subject of experiments. Hunter had been known to say that he himself had drunk laurel water and was still alive to tell the tale; unfortunately, however, he was not asked about that now. Instead, Newnham tried to discredit the conclusions drawn by Rattray.

Q: Is any certain analogy to be drawn from the effects of any given poison upon an animal of the brute creation, to that it may have upon a human subject?

A: As far as my experience goes … they are very near the same; opium will poison a dog similar to a man; arsenic will have very near the same effect upon a dog as it would have, I take it for granted, upon a man … I believe their operations will be nearly similar.

Newnham tried again.

Q: Are there not many things that will kill animals almost
   instantaneously that will have no detrimental or noxious
   effects upon a human subject?

A: A great deal depends upon the mode of experiment; no
   man is fit to make one but those who have made many and
   paid considerable attention to all the circumstances that
   relate to experiments.

This was more like it.

A little brandy will kill a cat; I have made the experiment, and
killed several cats, but it is a false experiment. In all those cases
where it kills a cat, it kills the cat by getting into her lungs, not
her stomach … Now in those experiments that are made by
forcing an animal to drink, there are two operations going on;
one is refusing of the liquor by an animal - its kicking or the
working of its throat to refuse it; the other is, a forcing of liquor
upon the animal; and there are very few operations of that kind
but some of the liquor gets into the lungs; I have known it from
experience.

Next Newnham moved on to the specific failings of the autopsy
by Samuel Bucknill.

Q: If you had been called upon to dissect a body supposed
   to have died from poison should you, or not, have
   thought it necessary to have pursued your search through
   the guts?

A: Certainly … that is the tract of the poison, and I certainly
   should have followed that tract through.

Newnham now considered Theodosius's symptoms.

Q: You have heard of the froth issuing from Sir Theodosius's mouth a minute or two before he died; is that peculiar to a man dying of poison, or is it not common in many other complaints?

A: I fancy it is a general effect of people dying in what you may call health in an apoplexy or epilepsy, in all sudden deaths …

Q: Have you ever had an opportunity of seeing such subjects?

A: Hundreds of times.

Q: Should you consider yourself bound, by such appearances, to impute the death to poison?

A: No, certainly not; I should rather suspect an apoplexy, and I wish, in this case, the head had been opened to remove all doubts.

Q: If the head had been opened, do you apprehend all doubts would have been removed?

A: It would have been still farther removed; because, although the body was putrid, so that no one could tell whether it was a recent inflammation, yet an apoplexy arises from an extravasation of blood in the brain, which would have laid in a coagulum. I apprehend, though the body was putrid, that would have been much more visible than the effect any poison could have had upon the stomach or the intestines.

Q: Then, in your judgement upon the appearances the gentlemen have described, no inference can be drawn from thence that Sir Theodosius Boughton died from poison?

A: Certainly not; it does not give the least suspicion.

Newnham concluded his examination here; Hunter's answers were just what he had hoped for. The country's leading authority had suggested that apoplexy could have been to blame for Theodosius's death, and that poison was by no means suggested by Theodosius's symptoms. He had also underlined the point that putridity had obscured what useful information might have been gleaned from the corpse, and emphasised the failings of the surgeons by not examining the brain.

Mr Howarth, he of the florid phrase, took up the cross-examination. Hunter's answers seemed bemused at first, then calmly insistent.

Q: Having heard the account today, that Sir Theodosius Boughton, apparently in good health, had swallowed a draught which had produced the symptoms described, I ask you whether any reasonable man can entertain a doubt but that draught, whatever it was, produced those appearances?

A: I don't know well what answer to make to that question.

Q: Having heard the account given of the health of this young gentleman, on that morning, previous to taking the draught, and the symptoms that were produced immediately upon taking the draught, I ask your opinion, as a man of judgement, whether you don't think that draught was the occasion of his death?

A: With regard to his being in health, that explains nothing; we see the healthiest people dying suddenly … as to the circumstance of the draught, I own they are suspicious.

At this point Justice Buller, evidently deeply irritated by Hunter's dismissal of the other medical witnesses, weighed in:

COURT: You are to give your opinions upon the symptoms only, not upon other evidence given.

Q: I ask whether, in your opinion, that draught did not occasion his death?

A: I can only say that it is a circumstance in favour of that opinion.

COURT: That the draught was the occasion of his death?

A: Not because the symptoms afterwards are those of a man dying who was before in perfect health; a man dying of apoplexy or epilepsy, the symptoms would give one of those general ideas.

COURT: It is the general idea you are asked about now …

whether you are of the opinion that the draught was the
occasion of his death?

A: If I knew the draught was poison, I should say most
probably … but when I don't know the draught was
poison … I cannot answer positively to it.

Q: Then you decline giving any opinion upon the subject.

COURT: You recollect the circumstance that was mentioned
of a violent heaving in the stomach?

A: All that is the effect of the voluntary action being lost, and
nothing going on but the involuntary.

Q: Then you decline giving any opinion on the subject?

A: I don't form any opinion myself; I cannot form an opinion …

But the prosecution was not to be deflected: Howarth needed
this renowned expert's opinion, and he was determined to get it.

Q: If you are at all acquainted with the effects and operations
of distilled laurel water, whether the having swallowed a
draught of that would not have produced the symptoms
described?

A: I should suppose it would; I can only say this, of the
experiments I have conducted with laurel water, it has not
been near so quick … never produced so quick an effect as
described by those gentlemen.

Q: But you admit that laurel water would have produced
symptoms such as have been described?

A: I can conceive it might.

But this was hardly the point. It had not been proved that the
mixture was laurel water – the case was brought on one woman's
sense of smell alone – so to put that supposition now was to ask the
witness to imagine a set of circumstances with the counsel's intention of then drawing a fact from a supposition.

The defence counsel Newnham now interjected in an attempt to
bring Hunter's evidence back on track: he gave Hunter the chance
to infer a fact from a supposition, too.

Q: Would not an apoplexy or an epilepsy, if it had seized
   Sir Theodosius Boughton at this time, though he had
   taken no physic at all, have produced similar symptoms
   too?
A: Certainly.

Newnham also tried to show that there was a significant parallel
between Theodosius's health and his father's:

Q: Where a father has died of an apoplexy, is that not
   understood, in some measure, to be constitutional?
A: Whatever is constitutional in a father, the father has the
   power of giving that to the children ...

Howarth returned to the questioning here:

Q: Do you call apoplexy constitutional?
A: I conceive apoplexy as much constitutional as any disease
   whatsoever.
Q: Is apoplexy likely to attack a thin young man who had
   been taking a course of cooling medicines before?
A: Not so likely, surely; but I have in my account of
   dissections two young women dying of apoplexies.
Q: ... it was very unlikely to happen?
A: I do not know the nature of medicines so well as to know
   that it would hinder an apoplexy from taking place.

Buller appeared to lose his temper at this point.

Here was a witness who, in contrast to former medical 'experts',
was (quite rightly) unwilling to commit himself without knowing
the patient or the medicines that the patient had been prescribed.
But his unwillingness to be swayed, his lack of a commitment, was
not what Buller wanted to hear.

COURT: Give me your opinion in the best manner you
   can, one way or the other, whether, upon the whole of

the symptoms described, the death proceeded from that medicine, or from any other cause.

Hunter was not a man to be bullied, however. He could not give an opinion because he did not have the evidence. He could only say what, in his experience, happened if a person drank laurel water (and it is to be noted that Hunter's opinion was that it would not have the immediate effect described) or if a person had apoplexy. He had testified that a young person could have a stroke and that strokes could run in families. But without a proper autopsy – and he was forthright in his opinion that the autopsy had not been thorough – he could not say if a stroke had occurred.

A: I do not mean to equivocate; but when I tell the sentiments of my own mind, what I feel at the time, I can give nothing decisive.

His answer was perfectly correct, but it was an answer that Buller would use to condemn Donellan.

13

'Against Him Every Circumstance'

'The hungry judges soon the sentence sign, and
Wretches hang that jury men may dine'

Alexander Pope, *The Rape of the Lock* (1712)

THE EVIDENCE CONCLUDED, it was time for Buller to address the jury. Having warned them that they were to ignore any 'false or cruel reports' that they may have read in the newspapers, he focused his opening remarks on the nature of circumstantial evidence. 'It is all circumstantial evidence,' he conceded, 'and in its nature it must be so, for no man is weak enough to commit the act in the presence of other person ... a presumption which necessarily arises from circumstances is often more convincing and more satisfactory than any other kind of evidence ... if the circumstances are such as when laid together bring conviction to your minds, it is fully equal if not more convincing than positive evidence.'

Then, having summed up the evidence, he said that he owed it to the jury and to the public at large to say what his own impressions were, but 'you are not to adopt any opinion because it is mine'.

The first issue, he said, was whether Theodosius had died of poison. They had the evidence, he continued, of 'a great number of very able men in the physical line ... they have no doubt that the death was occasioned by poison'.

He reprised Rattray's opinion that the appearance of the body was not due to putrefaction; he described his experiments and the 'biting upon his tongue when opening the body of Sir Theodosius Boughton', but omitted to say that no other surgeon present felt the same sensation.

As regards Bradford Wilmer, he noted that the surgeon was not able to say how death had occurred, but drew the jury's attention to the fact that Wilmer was 'now clearly of the opinion that Sir Theodosius's death was occasioned by the draught administered by Lady Boughton'. He noted that neither Wilmer nor Rattray were told by Donellan that poison was suspected; and added that both Parsons and Ashe (who had not been present at anything) testified that Theodosius had died of the draught and that Ashe had stressed that 'he can attribute the effects and symptoms which have been spoken of to nothing but poison'.

Buller then turned his attention to John Hunter.

'I can hardly say what his opinion is, for he does not seem to have formed any opinion in the matter,' he began. 'I wished very much to have got a direct answer from Mr Hunter; but he says he can say nothing decisive.'

He then told the jury that, of all the learned medical men who had pronounced their views, four had decided 'positively' that the deceased had died of poison and one had merely expressed a doubt.

This was not accurate. Ashe's opinion was positive, certainly; Parsons had said that the medicine had caused the death, and that laurel water would produce all the symptoms mentioned (which is not the same as saying that the draught *was* laurel water); Wilmer had said that the draught was to blame, but only after listening to Anna Maria, and not basing his view on any medical evidence he had observed; Hunter had stated that apoplexy might be the reason, and would not speculate on laurel water being in the medicine.

Bucknill, incidentally, was left out of the list because, despite being in charge of the autopsy in the churchyard, he had not been asked any question at all about the cause of death, either by the prosecution or the defence. Bucknill, in fact, is something of a mystery character, having appeared, it seems, out of nowhere: his name does not appear on the Medical Registers of 1780 or 1783 despite him saying he 'professed surgery' in Rugby.

Buller then covered the events of the evening of 29 August, saying that Lady Boughton had testified that Donellan had told her that he had been to see Theodosius fishing, a fact disproved by Samuel Frost. Donellan's version of the story – the walk to Hewitt's mill, and the visit of Dand and Matthews – had not been presented in court. Buller commented: 'I can only say that it frequently happens that necessary, strange and contradictory declarations that cannot be accounted for, otherwise than by a fatality which attends guilt.' In other words, there was no explanation for Donellan saying that he had seen Theodosius fishing other than that a guilty man often concocts an unnecessarily detailed story to hide his tracks. But Donellan's *Defence,* of course, claims that he never made such a statement.

The morning of the death was considered next. Buller moved through Anna Maria's testimony sentence by sentence, describing how Donellan immediately asked for the bottles and washed them out. Buller was in no doubt of the motive: 'Was there anything so likely to lead to a discovery as the small remains of medicine in the bottle; but that is destroyed by the prisoner.' Nothing was said of Anna Maria's second deposition to the coroner, in which she claimed that Donellan threw the contents of the bottles 'upon the ground'. Buller moved on to the clearing of the room by Sarah Blundell: 'Why was it necessary for the prisoner to insist upon having everything removed?' he asked. 'Why should he be so solicitous to remove everything that might lead to a discovery?' Later in the morning Donellan, Anna Maria and Theodosia had met in the parlour, where Donellan explained to his wife about the bottles; Buller described this damningly as 'a sudden thought, which occurred to him at the instant, as an excuse'.

The testimony of William Frost next came under scrutiny. Frost told the court that Donellan had gone riding, and that there had been an arrangement for Anna Maria and Donellan to go together, but that he had taken Anna Maria's horse back into the stables where he was some 'considerable time' before she appeared asking him to fetch Powell. Buller did not remark on the apparently missing minutes – at least half an hour – which are unaccounted for in Anna Maria's evidence. Instead, he brought up an issue which did not appear in any evidence presented to the court. Buller said: 'For if Lady Boughton had entertained suspicion of the prisoner's having been in Sir Theodosius's room that morning and had communicated that suspicion to the prisoner, it is natural enough for him to call a person to speak …'

But did Anna Maria's evidence suggest that she suspected Donellan had been in the room? She was not asked that question, and she did not volunteer the information. If she had suspected Donellan of having been in the room either before she gave the medicine, or during the period when she left the room, she never said so. If she suspected Donellan of interfering with the medicine, it must have been before seven o'clock because, in her own words, she only left Theodosius for five minutes (five minutes in which Frost testified that Donellan was out riding) and, by her own admission, the medicine had already been given at that point.

So what was Buller referring to here?

Buller next moved to the subject of Donellan's letters to Sir William Wheler, in particular to the fact that he only showed Wheler's *third* letter to Rattray, Powell and Wilmer when they came to the house on the night of 4 September. Buller said: 'They had heard of no suspicion of poison; they had never seen the first letter which Sir William Wheler had written to the prisoner; it will be for you to consider, whether by showing them the second letter only, in which nothing is said about a suspicion of poison, and keeping back the first, he meant to mislead the doctors.'[1]

Wheler's letter of 4 September was written after the Reverend Newsam had brought him news of the Earl of Denbigh's disquiet. It did indeed say that 'the physic was improper' and 'it is reported all over the country that he was killed either by medicine or by poison … unless the body is opened … we shall all be very much blamed.' Indeed, Rattray did not see this letter: he only saw the one that Wheler sent later that day, and Buller was correct in saying that this one did not mention poison. Rattray said that Donellan was looking for another letter and took out only an envelope, but Rattray could not be bothered with 'such little matters as these', and so did not press the matter. Neither did Wilmer.

But the letter that Rattray saw did specifically say that the body was to be opened. It also said that this was 'to prevent the world from blaming any of us', a phrase which, if the doctors thought this was a routine autopsy, should have at least made them pause to ask what blame Wheler was talking about. According to Rattray's evidence, Donellan said that he had expected Wheler to come that evening, and that he also expected one or both of the doctors to see Wheler the next day. Therefore Donellan would have expected the subject of poison, about which 'the world' was talking, to have been discussed.

Buller commented: 'For what purpose was this letter [i.e. Wheler's first, about poison] secreted? If it were for the purpose of preventing the body being opened and of preventing the doctors from making a full and fair examination, it is then a very strong circumstance in the case.' But he also made the point that, if the jury thought that the first letter was sufficient for the doctors to realise the importance of an autopsy, and that Donellan did not try to 'suppress the suspicions that had been entertained abroad', then they ought to weigh that in their decision.

Buller did at least raise the possibility here that the doctors had been called to an autopsy and had seen a letter asking them to carry it out. But how logical was it that Donellan alone could suppress their knowledge of the poison rumour, if it was being 'entertained abroad'?

Had Donellan deliberately suppressed the first letter that mentioned poison? Why did he not mention it himself, if he could not find the letter? Or was this a ruse to suggest compliance while simultaneously hiding the letter?

The only other witness that night was the apothecary Powell, and here again his somewhat peculiar behaviour is completely ignored by Buller in his address to the jury.

Powell had been with Sir William when Wheler wrote the first of his 4 September letters, the one that mentions poison ('I expect Mr Powell every moment … Mr Powell is now with me') and had seen that Wheler had apparently accepted his word that the medicine was harmless. But he had not been with Wheler when the second letter was written. Was this the reason that he opened the second letter, even though it was addressed to Donellan? (Rattray testified: 'Mr Powell, the apothecary, stood by a great table reading a letter; Captain Donellan turned it up, and saw the direction was to him. Mr Powell said, by mistake he had opened it.') What sort of 'mistake' is this? Powell was not in his own home, so why would he assume any letter in Lawford Hall was addressed to him? He would have recognised Wheler's handwriting on the envelope because he had stood next to him watching him write the first one. Was he anxious about what Wheler had written to Donellan in the second letter? Or did he not trust Donellan to tell the truth?

Buller did not comment on Powell's involvement here and so did not thoroughly explore the issue of who obscured the topic of poison, or if indeed the doctors' contention of not knowing about poison was feasible.

The next subject was Theodosius's health. Here the failure of Donellan's defence became desperately obvious. Buller stated that, from 'Carr's' (this presumably means Kerr's) evidence and Powell's, no mercury was ever given to Theodosius: 'neither of them say a syllable about any mercury ever being given to him'; and it is perfectly correct that Theodosius's health was represented in court as being good, or that his illness was 'trifling'. Buller passed over the matter fairly rapidly now, ignoring Anna Maria's evidence that Theodosius habitually took physic and had been ill 'of a particular disorder', and that in 1777 and 1778 she had written from Bath that she was afraid that he was 'in a bad way'. Similarly he did not remind the jury that Powell testified to having given Theodosius three draughts the week of his death: one on the Saturday, one on the Monday, and one again for 30 August. Why were three prescriptions necessary if Theodosius only had a trifling complaint?

Buller reminded the jury next that the Reverend Newsam testi-fied that Donellan had told him that Theodosius had a swelling in the groin and that he was a 'mass of mercury and corruption'. Buller now asked if that were true, and remarked that there was no evidence either way.

The topic moved on to Bucknill's involvement, at which point Buller became more animated: 'What!' he exclaimed when discuss-ing Donellan's first refusal of Bucknill's autopsy. 'In a case where suspicion of poison had prevailed!' He moved to the day of the funeral, when Bucknill was again rebuffed and told that Snow had given orders for the burial. 'Why should not the prisoner call Snow to prove what passed between them?' he demanded. 'Why did not he communicate to Bucknill the reasons given by Snow?'

Why indeed. Snow remains a mystery.

The final part of Buller's address to the jury wholly concerned Donellan's conduct. He asked why Donellan had behaved as he did at the coroner's court, pulling on Lady Boughton's gown and telling her afterwards not to answer questions she had not been asked; why Donellan had a still, and what it might have been used for; why he said in gaol that Theodosius had been poisoned, and then changed his mind; why he wrote the letters to Sir William Wheler in the way that he did, and why he concealed the second letter from the doctors. He also asked why Donellan claimed to have made a will that meant he would not benefit from Theodo-sius's estate, and then did not produce that will in court. Lastly, he commented that evidence given that Donellan protected Theodo-sius from various scrapes and arguments which were 'at a period very distant' was not relevant to the present trial.

At many points in his summing-up Buller was scrupulously fair, weighing one piece of evidence against another and asking the jury to make up their own minds with the same reasoned objectivity; but the final part bears down heavily on Donellan and Buller's lan-guage becomes more negative. 'He stopped her ... he blamed her ... ' Buller said of Donellan's relationship with Anna Maria at the coroner's court. 'All the conversation respects the bottle,' he noted when reviewing the death, 'and not a word of anything which is likely to be of any use to Sir Theodosius Boughton though he is dying and at the last gasp.' Donellan's remarks to Francis Amos were, he said, 'extraordinary'.

Buller claimed that 'all these are very strong facts to show what was passing in the prisoner's own mind.' But without any letter, note or journal written by them, or without a written confession, it is impossible to know what a person is thinking. However, Buller was asking the jury to consider whether Donellan's actions were contrary to what he was actually thinking or intending: 'It is for you,' he instructed, 'to say that you are satisfied that what he said in one or two of his letters and what he said to the surgeon was his real intention; or whether those expressions were only used to throw a blind upon the case.'

He concluded: 'You must take all the circumstances of the case into consideration, and remember that it is for you to form your own opinions, and decide upon the fate of the prisoner; in the doing of which I am sure you will act according to the best of your judgement and your conscience to find out the truth of the case; and as you find that truth, so you will pronounce your verdict.'

It was twenty-five minutes past six in the evening.

After sitting in court for eleven hours, the jury withdrew.

It took them only nine minutes to 'find out the truth of the case'.

They found John Donellan guilty of murder.

James Boswell, writing in the *Scots Magazine* of 1781, wrote that, after the jury had given their verdict, the Clerk of the Arraigns asked Donellan what he had to say and why sentence of death should not be pronounced upon him.

Donellan answered, 'I am not guilty, My Lord.'

Edward Boughton, writing to his brother on 17 April, said that he was astonished at Donellan's calmness, not only then but during the whole course of the trial. 'Not withstanding his constant denial of the fact to the last,' he wrote, 'never surely did Villain act his part so much like an Ideal.' Donellan's fortitude was not lost on the crowd of spectators, either: one American bystander, Benjamin

Pickman, despite being convinced of Donellan's guilt, wrote to his family back home in Massachusetts that 'his behaviour during his whole trial was such as would have done honour to a man falling in the best of causes'.[2]

Buller began his sentencing.

Rising to his feet, according to Boswell, Buller declaimed:

The offence of which you now stand convicted ... is of the blackest dye that man can commit. For of all felonies murder is the most horrible, and of all murders, poisoning is the most detestable. Poisoning is a secret act, against which there are no means of ... defending a man's life; and as so far as there can be different degrees in crimes of the same nature, yours surpasses all that have ever gone before it ... It was committed in a place where suspicion must have slept; where you had access as a bosom friend and a brother; where you saw the rising representative of an ancient family reside in affluence; but where your ambition led you proudly, but vainly, to imagine that you might live in splendour ... if he whom you thought your only obstacle were removed. Probably the greatness of his fortune caused the greatness of your offence; and I am fully satisfied, upon the evidence given against you, that avarice was your motive and hypocrisy afforded you the means ... the deed ... has been fully proved to the satisfaction of myself and the jury ...

In most cases of murder it has pleased Heaven, by some marks or other, to point out the guilty person; ... in your case, the false accounts given by yourself, the misrepresentations given out to Sir William Wheler, the endeavours you have used to prevent a full enquiry and discovery of the truth of the case, the strange conversations which you have held at different times, and, above all, the circumstance of rinsing out the bottle, leave your guilt without the smallest doubt.

You can receive ... nothing but the strictest justice. But you will soon appear before an Almighty Judge whose unfathomable wisdom is able ... to reconcile justice with mercy ... You will do well to remember that such beneficence is only gained by deep contrition, by sound, unfeigned and substantial repentance. May it please that great and awful Being, during the short time that is allotted for your existence in this world, to work that repentance and that contrition in your mind which may befit you for His everlasting mercy. But the punishment which the public has a right to demand, and which I must inflict upon you, is speedy and ignominious death.

And the sentence I now pronounce upon you is that you be taken from hence to the place from whence you came; that from thence, on Monday next, you be carried to the place of execution, there to be hanged by the neck until you are dead; and that your body be afterwards delivered to the surgeons to be dissected and anatomised; and may God Almighty be merciful to your soul.

According to the *Nottinghamshire Gazette* of 3 April, Donellan heard his sentence with 'extraordinary fortitude and did not display either temerity or cowardice … [he] excited universal sympathy'.

He said only one thing.

Looking at Buller, Donellan replied: 'It is perfectly indifferent to me what becomes of my body.'

14

'With My Last Breath ...'

'Falsehoods of the most flagrant kind have induced a jury to take my life ... ruined by those who ought to have been my friends.'
John Donellan, the day before his execution, 1 April 1781

AFTER THE SENTENCING, John Donellan was taken back to Warwick Gaol, just a few yards' walk from the court house. It was the law that those convicted of a capital offence had to be executed within two days of sentencing, and his hanging was fixed for early on Monday morning.

The *Hibernian* of May 1781 reported that 'whatever he might have committed before his condemnation, he afterwards behaved with the most exemplary propriety'. As Donellan was returned to his cell, he asked the gaoler for a glass of wine and, raising it to his lips, was heard to murmur, 'The Lord forgive them.'

He then sat down and was silent for some minutes, staring pensively ahead of him; and then 'talked a great deal about Mrs Donellan and the children'.

Over the weekend, he was asked if he would like to see his wife. Two different newspapers reported his reply in two different ways. The *Nottinghamshire Gazette* of 4 April, keeping up its hitherto fine tradition of baiting Donellan at every turn, wrote that, although he had been 'tender and affectionate' to Theodosia in previous months, he now would not hear her name mentioned. The *Nottingham Mercury*, however, on 9 April, had a kinder slant, reporting him to have said, 'I do beseech you, let me not hear of this. If she does not come, I shall die more composed.'

However, in Captain Murphy's *Life of Captain Donellan*, published on 1 May 1781, a very bleak and contrasting picture is painted of their relationship through the publication of a letter which was supposed to have been sent by Donellan to Theodosia the day before his execution. Murphy's account is the only source that we have for this letter.

It read:

My Once Esteemed Wife,

Do not think that I am about to reproach you for declining your visits to me in my present ignominious situation. I am better satisfied that you did not even attempt it ... It would be a mockery of feeling to affect a concern for our separation ...

To argue with you on the score of those dark arts which have undone me would be fruitless, because I know your conjugal has ever been subservient to your filial affection.

As to your - mother - ; but I will suppress my indignation, if however you should know my dying sentiments of her, ask our friend W—son, the mournful bearer of this, and he will not hesitate to impart them to you ...

Were I to advise your immediate separation from her, it would have no weight, for my little influence over you has long been at an end!

Mrs H— you well know, has for a series of years treated me with a tender and disinterested regard, let it not surprise you then to learn that I have bequeathed her my gold watch and miniature picture, as the last and strongest token I can give her of my gratitude.

As to our two poor children, if you deem them pledges of our love, cherish them as such, but try to conceal from them their father's unhappy fate. I have been long cogitating unnumbered wishes that pressed me to clasp them in my fond arms, and bid them a last adieu! Thank God, however, I have at length subdued them – the whole world, except my offspring, are welcome to become the spectators of my ignominious though unmerited exit!

If I have omitted any thing that I should have said to you – your own heart, I trust, will urge it for me, when I shall be no more.

Farewell, John.

This is a dreadful letter, a terrible goodbye.

Donellan thinks Theodosia has sided with her mother, the woman of 'dark arts' on which he thinks Theodosia is still to be convinced; he insults her by sending 'the last and strongest token' he can give to his former mistress; and he suggests that any visit of hers would have simply been 'affecting a concern'.

But there are flashes of real feeling, of wounded rejection. Ask the friend who delivers this letter what the truth is, he urges, while then going on to talk of his children with genuine grief.

This is a vengeful letter in more ways then one. Donellan's fury with Anna Maria leaps off the page. How could Theodosia let her 'filial' regard outweigh her respect and love for her husband? he demands. He talks as if Theodosia had not separated from her mother, as Caldecott claimed. Did Donellan realise that Theodosia was living in Northampton? Someone surely must have told him so. And yet perhaps he is talking here of Theodosia's lingering regard for her mother which all his accusations could not really wash away. Or perhaps Theodosia had indeed returned to Lawford for a while, at least until the execution was over.

The sentence about Mrs H——'s 'tender and disinterested regard' comes directly afterwards. 'Here is a woman,' he seems to be saying, 'whose opinion of me could not be coloured by anyone else.' This makes one wonder if John Donellan had maintained his physical relationship with Mrs H all the time he was married to Theodosia; he certainly appears to have kept her as a close friend.

And the gift certainly reached her. Captain Murphy's pamphlet is 'embellished with the head of the unfortunate sufferer engraved from his miniature picture now in the possession of Mrs H'.

How Theodosia received this letter, or who the mysterious 'W—son' was who delivered it, is not recorded.

On the Saturday before his execution, according to Murphy's *Life* and the Coventry newspapers, Donellan had received a visit from 'a Divine' (whether it was the Reverend Newsam or not is unknown) and a similarly unnamed 'particular friend'. They told him that any further denials of his guilt would be looked on by the world as a 'mean prevarication' and would induce people to add insult to his memory.

Donellan surprised them both by answering: 'I cannot help any man's conclusions; I know my own heart; and with my last breath I will assert my innocence. Falsehoods of the most flagrant kind have induced a jury to take my life; but time will do me justice, and prove me an injured man, ruined by those who ought to have been my friends.'

On the Sunday, Donellan spent all day writing his *Defence*, having asked his solicitors, Inge and Webb, to publish his account as soon after his death as they could, also using the notes he had prepared for them before the trial.

Donellan now added various details to that account such as the fact that he paid Wilmer, Powell and Rattray five guineas each on the night of the abortive autopsy, forced to do so because Lady Boughton claimed she had no money. He also said that, on the day of the funeral, the plumber and carpenter had complained that every time they soldered and unsoldered the coffin, the lead became so hot that they could not touch it without burning themselves, and that this was one of the reasons why Bernard Snow had decided not to open it again. Snow was also paid six guineas by Donellan. One wonders what went through Donellan's mind as he recalled the fees (£1,400 in today's money) that he had paid to the men who later helped to incriminate him.

Then he went through the events of the afternoon of 29 August almost minute by minute, accounting for all his time in an effort to prove that he never went to Theodosius's room. He wrote that

Sarah Blundell, Susannah Sparrow and Catharine Amos had all been busy with a household wash in the kitchen when he came in at about five o'clock asking for a ladder to pick fruit on the higher branches of the trees. He records, somewhat poignantly, that Sarah Blundell could have verified his account that Dand and Matthews called to see him, as it was she who announced their visit.

He wrote about the Reverend Newsam, saying that Newsam had agreed with him about the state of Theodosius's health on the Saturday prior to his death, remarking that the boy was 'much altered' and that he had 'ruined his constitution'. To corroborate this, Donellan added that the large amount of mercury that Theodosius had used made him drool uncontrollably, so much so that 'a quantity of water was always running from his mouth and he was obliged to keep a handkerchief continually at his mouth'.

One of Donellan's solicitors, Thomas Webb, published his own account of Donellan's last words in addition to the version he published with his business partner Inge. This one was prefaced with a statement by Donellan which read:

Sunday April 1st, 1781.
This Case has been read over to me this day, being the last day of my life: and it contains nothing but real facts, as far as my knowledge goes, and I solemnly request, and firmly desire, that it may be published as a firm vindication of my honour and character to the world. I also desire that Mr *Webb* [original italics] one of my solicitors, may be the whole and sole publisher of it, as a clear testimony of my being perfectly satisfied with his conduct.
John Donellan.

This little booklet was priced at sixpence. The version written with Inge was priced at 3s. 6d. The first was printed by Wenmans in Fleet Street; the second by John Bell.

There seems to have been some competition between the two lawyers; Webb's booklet is the only one to bear Donellan's seal of approval, and Donellan's script hints that he was dissatisfied with the behaviour of Inge. It is not surprising that the two men whose task it had been to represent Donellan subsequently fought over who had done the better job, once the newspapers began publicly to criticise them. (Inge was listed as coroner and town clerk of Warwick in 1791, so perhaps he moved on to higher things in recognition that he had won this particular contest for public approval.)

Donellan laboured all Sunday to complete his case for his *Defence*, unaware of how his own solicitors would fight over the text once he was dead.

On the afternoon of Sunday 1 April, the gaoler came to tell Donellan what had been arranged for the following morning. On hearing that his body would be taken down after the hanging and put into a rough 'shell' and brought back to the gaol, Donellan asked him to arrange immediately for a black coffin with black nails.

Perhaps Donellan was waiting for an eleventh-hour reprieve during this long, lonely day.

It was, after all, common for a defendant to be convicted and then pardoned even after a sentence had been pronounced. Between 1660 and 1800, only about 30 per cent of those convicted of capital offences were actually executed. Some were transported; others were pardoned as a result of character witnesses; sometimes, evidence that the perpetrator was totally repentant and unlikely to commit further crimes, or a rumour that the jury had been prejudiced, were enough to overturn the sentence. A prominent judge like Buller had it entirely in his power to offer a pardon if he disagreed with the jury's verdict, the pardon usually being conditional on transportation. Perhaps Donellan was even waiting for a confession from Anna Maria, or the news that his young wife had successfully pleaded on his behalf, presented new evidence of some kind and begged for the return of the father of her two small children?

But Theodosia made no such plea. Anna Maria Boughton did not make a confession. And Donellan sat down that evening to write his bitter, angry goodbye to his wife.

As the evening drew on, the gaoler observed Donellan praying 'with great apparent fervency'. When he had finished he seemed composed, and asked after several of his friends. 'I suppose,' he added, 'there will be a vast throng of people to see me executed.'

At seven o'clock on the morning of Monday 2 April, Donellan emerged from Warwick Gaol dressed in deep mourning, and stepped into a coach to be transported to the scaffold.

His last reported words inside the gaol were to the Reverend Musson, chaplain to the prisoners. The revelation, given almost as an aside, is breathtaking.

Donellan told Musson, perhaps at a prompting from the cleric to finally confess, that he had indeed distilled laurel water in the still at Lawford Hall. Who knows why he kept this secret through the long months since September? Perhaps because he knew it would be seized upon as incontrovertible proof of his having poisoned Theodosius – although he maintained now that it had only been to make a lotion to bathe his feet. A friend had given him a book, *Flora* by a Dr Mortimer, he said, and he admitted now to tearing a page from it, but only to refer to while he was making the mixture. Lady Boughton, he added, had used it, too, and found it effective. That Anna Maria Boughton had been given a mixture of laurel water by Donellan had never been mentioned in court.

Although there was a gallows close to the gaol, the use of a coach suggests that Donellan was taken further afield, perhaps to Gibbet Hill, on the road to Rugby. This is a strong possibility, as the hangman would have had other executions to perform that day in other towns in the area and he may have had to leave quickly.

Donellan's coach was followed by a hearse, and the sheriff's officers all dressed in mourning black. The *Nottinghamshire Gazette* reported that on the way to the execution Donellan kept putting his head out of the coach and protesting to the following crowds that he was innocent. He was, he told them, a victim of his mother-in-law's 'diabolical artifice'. Several times along the road, Donellan seems to have lost control of himself in his pleas to the crowds, begging them to join in prayer with him. The newspaper article recorded that there was a 'wildness in his manner that bore the marks of insanity'.

Eventually, the coach arrived at the place of execution; the journey from Warwick Gaol to Gibbet Hill would have taken about half an hour. The land all around Gibbet Hill sloped away to reveal rolling farmland beyond and, somewhere in the far distance across the fields to the east, Lawford Hall. If Donellan had become frantic and panicked in the coach, he was the picture of calm now, seemingly resigned to his fate. He took just a few steps up the ladder to the scaffold. Then he abruptly stopped; but instead of trying to go back down, he began to pray.

The crowd pressed forward. Donellan's hesitation lasted some time; perhaps, as well as praying, he was steeling himself against what was to come, and willing himself not to stumble. Then he negotiated the last few rungs of the ladder. Standing on the scaffold, he listened to the address of the cleric there 'with the greatest appearance of devotion', his head bowed and his hands clasped.

Once the priest was finished, Donellan turned to the waiting crowd, and declaimed: 'As I am about to appear before God, I am innocent of the crime for which I am about to suffer.'

The noose was put around his neck and he was pushed from the platform. A more humane method of hanging, using a trapdoor whose drop would hopefully break the neck of the victim, was yet to be instituted: hanging in 1781 was a prolonged agony of strangulation. Often friends or relatives would rush to the scaffold and pull downwards on the victim's legs to end their suffering.

But no one came to Donellan's aid. He hung for thirty minutes before his body was cut down.

15

Aftermath – The Female Line

'Title and principal part of the family estates devolve to the late Shukburgh Boughton Esq.; the residue, to a very considerable amount, passes in the female line to Theodosia, wife of John Donellan.'

Gentleman's Magazine, 30 August 1780

DONELLAN WENT TO HIS DEATH lonely and unsupported; but in the weeks that followed, many voices were raised in his defence. Newspapers that had previously whipped up public opinion against him now published criticisms of the way that the trial had been conducted. It was the *Northampton Mercury* which devoted the most space to an account of Donellan's life, a report of the trial and, on 30 April, an article on how the defence barrister, Newnham, had failed his client. They listed four mistakes in particular: that Newnham had not cross-examined Bucknill and elicited the information that Donellan had asked him to stay on the afternoon of Theodosius's funeral 'in the presence of upwards thirty witnesses'; that he had not called upon other people who were prepared to say that Theodosius's father had died in the same abrupt convulsions and had 'looked the same' after his death as his son; that he had not cross-examined William Crofts, who had said that Donellan had pulled at Anna Maria's sleeve during her deposition to the coroner; and that he did not cross-examine Anna Maria about Donellan advising Theodosius to keep his medicine unlocked on the chimney shelf in his room.

By its edition of 7 May, the *Mercury's* outrage had increased. It revealed that Donellan had made a will in August 1777 which, it claimed, prevented him from benefiting from Theodosius's estate, and castigated Newnham for not producing it. It fumed that Newnham had not cross-examined Powell, and it questioned the fact that Francis Amos, who had no real evidence against Donellan, had not made a deposition to the coroner. (This may be a case of mistaken identity: it was William Frost who was the best witness for Donellan.)

Two other publications also made a dramatic case against Donellan's convictions. The first was Donellan's own written *Defence*, published by Inge and Webb, in the introduction of which they wrote that they intended to 'justify our conduct … since the trial it has been universally believed that the defence made for the unfortunate sufferer on the trial was a very imperfect one, and that his conviction as chiefly imputable to the neglect of his lawyers.' However, if this was a justification of themselves by the lawyers, it failed miserably, only going to prove just how much useful evidence had been ignored at the trial.

Attached to the end of Donellan's own words was an article whose vociferous, indignant tone fanned the flames of outrage even higher. Donellan's dying words had been astonishing – restrained, patient and respectful while nevertheless casting Anna Maria in a suspiciously bad light – but the accusations in the article that followed, by a 'gentleman who has no personal motives', were sensational.

James Stephen was revealed as the author of the article by his grandson, James Fitzjames Stephen, some eighty years later. He was only twenty-two years old when he sprang to Donellan's defence; brought up in a debtors' prison because of his father's debts, he was already earning a reputation for a brilliant mind and an irascible temper. His zeal for the underdog never left him; he was to become one of the leading members of the Anti-Slavery Society and was appointed Master of Chancery, marrying William Wilberforce's sister in 1800 and being elected as an MP eight years later. In his introduction to the article, Stephen said that he had not known Donellan at all, but, on hearing the case against him, he had been moved to write. 'Public justice is in the interest of every man,' he said; he also hinted that Donellan had 'fallen victim to the laws of his country' instead of being protected by them; and that it was the duty of every member of society to make amends by trying to restore Donellan's name and the honour of his family.

Strong stuff. It would have infuriated Buller, not to mention the solicitors involved on both sides, whom Stephen claimed he did know. Nor could his account have endeared him to the witnesses, especially the medics. Bucknill, he said, was 'adventurous – our modern Hippocrates'; he was 'quite a youth, driven by foolhardiness and ambition', and his whole account against Donellan had been invented through injured pride – Donellan, Stephen said, had smiled to himself when Bucknill announced that he would not be put off by the stench of the corpse because 'it would be a posy to him'.

Rattray's account was no better. The doctor was unnecessarily ghoulish – 'I shall not transcribe his account as the reader may not have dined' – while his conclusions at the open-air autopsy were ludicrously lame: ' ... after opening the stomach, thorax etc. after long deliberation [he] was able to satisfy the whole world that the body had every appearance of putrefaction having been dead eleven days in very hot weather.' The doctor's memory was treacherous, too; Rattray had forgotten to mention the blood in the chest cavity, and the conclusions he drew from his animal experiments had been 'totally unwarrantable'. He was not so much a doctor as an 'oracle', Stephen observed sarcastically, an 'eternal monument to medical fame' who, when forced to admit the impossibility of his evidence, had answered, 'Nothing is impossible under God.' And in referring to Rattray's claim that his gums had bled after smelling the corpse, Stephen dismissed him as a hypochondriac.

Stephen's real fire, however, was reserved for Anna Maria and what he perceived the unnecessarily lenient way in which she had been treated by the court. She was 'full of inconsistencies', he said, 'grossly erroneous' and 'highly improbable'. Her memory had been supplanted by the 'chimera of suspicion' and her entire evidence was based on 'conjectures founded on uncertainty and error'. He ended by saying that it would be charitable to claim that 'she could remember nothing with precision'.

Sir Justice Buller did not escape Stephen's contempt either, particularly for the way that he had dismissed one of the foremost authorities in the land, John Hunter, by equating his expertise with that of lowly country doctors with no experience of dissection. It had been Buller's duty, Stephen contended, to tell the jury of the 'great weight' that should have been attached to Hunter's observations.

Persuasive though Stephen's arguments may have been, they did not apparently convince the man who exposed his authorship of the article, his own grandson, James Fitzjames Stephen.[1] In an essay written in 1863, having asked the reader to suppose that 'Mrs Donellan was the criminal and [Donellan's] conduct was intended to screen her ... the mere possibility ought to have been reason to suspend [the jury's] judgement', he then retracted his apparent support of his grandfather and decided that Donellan was guilty because he had motive, means and opportunity.

Stephen's grandson was not alone in thinking that Donellan was guilty. After the initial furore had died away, Donellan became forever after the man who had murdered his brother-in-law: a simple trawl of the internet today shows that to be the case. As time went on, his guilt began to be regarded as absolute fact.

But what became of Anna Maria, Theodosia and Lawford Hall after Donellan died? And what happened to his children, John and Maria?

It does not appear that Theodosia ever took her children back to live permanently with their grandmother in Lawford Hall. Anna Maria was alone there after the trial, so alone that she asked Edward Boughton, now the Eighth Baronet, if his sister Anne would like to be her companion.[2] Edward did not think much of the idea, explaining that Anne's temper was 'uncomfortable' – but he may well have been protecting Anne's tendency to depression from the gloomy atmosphere at the Hall.[3] Edward, in any case, was in no mood to help Anna Maria. He had just paid part of the bill for the prosecuting lawyers, complaining to his brother Charles that 'expences of the Prosecution come very high'.[4] The cost of the trial had eaten up almost all of the money that he had expected to receive from Theodosius's estate, he grumbled. 'Such is the glorious uncertainty of English law,' he went on, having found out that Theodosia was set to inherit most of the fortune and that 'I am entitled only to Rents from the day of Theodosius's death.'

Edward was an interesting character. As the eldest surviving son of Shukburgh Boughton, he had known all his life that he would inherit the Boughton baronetcy if the line from Mary Ramsey's children failed. (Hence his initial reaction to Theodosius's death – 'wonderful news'; his grandmother Catherine Shukburgh's hopes had been fulfilled.) As a younger man, he had written to his brother Charles in India warning him not to marry 'a Nabob' woman and seek one with a fortune at home, but he did not follow his own advice;[5] he had a lifelong mistress, Salome ('Sally') Davis, once the serving maid at his home, Poston Hall in Herefordshire, and subsequently kept comfortably by Edward while she bore him five children. The daughters lived; the sons died as infants; and when Edward died in 1794, aged fifty-three, Theodosius's title passed to brother Charles, who was still smarting from the humiliating blow of being left only £100 in his brother's will.[6]

Lawford Hall was, temporarily at least, still the residence of Anna Maria, even though it became Edward Boughton's property. But she did not, as it turned out, have to live there entirely alone. Family ledgers in Anna Maria's hand show that she and Theodosia spent several months together there in 1782/3. Instead of a mere list of expenses, as shown in the rest of the accounts, though, Anna Maria includes a lengthy diary entry for 1782, writing that 'Mrs Donellan' came to visit in July, bringing 'her child, a man, and a maidservant'. Theodosia evidently stayed for some twelve weeks,

returned again in November and left again in February 1783. It was
not the first extended visit between the two. Just before Christmas
1781, Theodosia had her mother to stay with her in Northampton.
It had taken Theodosia nearly nine months before she could con-
template the company of her mother after the trial; but she charged
Anna Maria for the privilege – £126 0s. 0d. 'for board of myself and
servants and two horses', Anna Maria noted.

Anna Maria's accounts here are rather touching. They are
really an extended narrative of the time she and Theodosia spent
together, with a slight undercurrent of self-justification, as if she
were determined to correct the idea that they might be estranged:
'March 1783,' she records, 'I went with her and she and her family
set out with me for Bath; her man came a week after and they all
stay'd at my house till I returned to Lawford which was Sunday 21
June, and my daughter and man and maidservant came to Lawford
and her two children … the Monday after they all came she sent
for her other two horses … she took all away on 19th July 1783 …
since then I went to Mrs Donellan's house ye 27th August and
stayed there …' So it goes on, with no rents apparently charged
to Theodosia in Bath 'at my house' but copious amounts flooding
out each time Anna Maria stayed with her daughter – at a rate, in
modern terms, of £330 a week. A daughter referred to only by her
surname, and never her Christian name – a curious relationship
indeed. However close they appeared to be now, it is also interesting that Theodosia maintained her independence, and was not
willing to make Lawford her home again. Anna Maria resolutely
records that Theodosia's home was in Northampton.

Before he died in 1794, Edward Boughton disposed of Lawford
Hall, which had – much to his mother Mary Greville's pleasure –
been part of his inheritance from Theodosius.[7] It is to be presumed
that Anna Maria was spending more time now in Bath, as the
family lawyer, Caldecott, was to record. Whether Edward felt that
Lawford was an unnecessary financial encumbrance, or whether
he agreed with the locals' view that it was 'cursed', is debatable.
The fine house was put up for auction. There is a story that Caldecott attended the auction and bought the house on Anna Maria's

instructions, but when he got back from the sale he told her that he had bought it for himself, not for her – and promptly demolished it.[8] The tale may not be accurate, however: a map of 1787 shows it still standing,[9] though it was indeed taken down some time later (the most quoted date being 1793, the year before Edward died). Nothing now remains of the once graceful Tudor mansion; all the stones of both the house and its walled garden were taken away, some of them going to repair a local road bridge. A less-than-graceful end to the 'fine archway',[10] the parlour where Donellan argued his case over the bottles, and the hallway where Theodosius's coffin had stood on the great table in the oppressive afternoon heat of August 1780. Only the old stable block remains, and is now a private home; but a few tantalising undulations in the fields both to the east and west of the remaining building may hold the key to the exact location of Lawford Hall itself.

Anna Maria would now be living permanently in the fashionable watering hole of Bath, the home of her brother, the doctor Robert Rye. In 1782, the solicitor Caldecott wrote that she was seen about town flaunting her 'wealth' and 'boasting of property'; she had new clothes, he said, a new livery on her carriage, and had been heard to say that she would marry again 'if the opportunity offers'.[11] And we know from her ledgers that she was there again in 1783 with Theodosia. However, the opportunity of marriage did not offer.

Anna Maria died in Bath in 1787 aged fifty-nine. Her past had not been forgotten; the newspaper notices of her death could not resist a hint of notoriety by mentioning that her son Theodosius had died 'after a medicinal draught given by his mother'.

And what of Theodosia, who by 1787 had not only lost both her brother and her husband but the company of her own mother?

Caldecott reported that, fourteen months after Donellan's death, Theodosia was still living 'altogether alone' in Northamptonshire but 'will I believe marry Dr Bree, a young physician, before the year is out'.[12] His belief was misplaced. Robert Bree, born in 1759 in Solihill, was three years older than Theodosia and had matriculated from Oxford just seven years before. He was working as a physician at the General Infirmary in Northampton and in time he would become an authority on asthma, from which he himself suffered. But the romance did not end in marriage, and evidently it was Bree himself who was disappointed in the matter. Anna Maria objected to the amount of money that Theodosia was proposing to settle on Bree, and their relationship foundered.

In March 1783, Theodosia drew up a new will; now possessed of a large fortune, it seems that her primary objective was to protect her two children. Her executor was William King, an alderman of Northampton and probably Theodosia's cousin, the son of Anna Maria's half-brother.[13] The closeness of the Kings to Theodosia was evident in both the will and the fact of Theodosia having fled to Northampton before the trial; King now took on the responsibility, should Theodosia die, of managing all her 'manors, messuages, tenements, hereditaments and real estates' and ensuring that some £6,000 (£377,000) should be raised for Maria when she was twenty-one or on the day of her marriage.

Theodosia's mother was already in Bath, and it seems that Theodosia herself moved there some time before 1785. Whether Anna Maria's health was declining is not known, but Theodosia certainly seems to have taken charge of some of Anna Maria's domestic affairs. 'Hired a cook maid,' she scribbled in a notebook. 'She to have a rate of twelve pound a year to clean the rooms. She came to Lady Boughton's place 5 March and I paid her.'[14]

The year 1787 marked the end of an era with Anna Maria's death. It was six years since John Donellan's trial and execution, and Theodosia's children were now aged nine and seven; but there may have been another family member living in Bath who was in contact with her. A brief reference in family papers in Ireland note that John Donellan's father Nehemiah, who had once been colonel of the 39th Regiment and commander of the garrison at Carrick-fergus – and who had gained his son his place in the army – had died in a private madhouse belonging to Sir Joseph de Burgo at Killaloe, having been driven insane both by a private lawsuit and the scandal of the Boughton trial.[15] However, there is a will in existence for a Nehemiah Donellan who died in Bath in 1787. It makes no mention of Theodosia, but is it too much of a coincidence to suppose that John Donellan's only surviving relative was brought to Bath by the woman who was his daughter-in-law?

Theodosia was probably still in Bath sorting out her mother's affairs when she met Egerton Leigh, son of Peter Leigh, former Attorney General of South Carolina. When the family had lost their estates in the American War of Independence of 1775–83, Egerton had returned to England to find that most of their property in England had gone into Chancery and all that remained was Little Harborough Hall in Warwickshire. Theodosia and Egerton therefore both had possessions in the county, and their friendship blossomed into a romance. It is surprising that Theodosia felt secure with a man who, although well connected, by his own admission did not have a wholesome reputation: he admitted freely that he had been 'deceitful and desperately wicked' in his previous dealings with women.[16] Neither did he seem to be a stable character: his journal shows extreme swings of mood and lurid dreams and visions.[17] Nevertheless, Egerton felt that his life changed dramatically after he met Theodosia; and this is quite some testament to her own calm and strength of character. Indeed, Egerton converted to the Baptist faith and set up a new church in Rugby in the poorest part of town, where Theodosia laid the foundation stone.

The couple were married in Northampton on 12 May 1788.[18] They remained in Bath until 1792, when Theodosia sold her property; from 1792 they seem to have been either at Brownsover Hall or at Cavendish Place in London. Their first child, a little girl called Theodosia Carolina Leigh, died in 1792, and another girl, Theodosia Egerton, died as an infant.[19] Ten months after Theodosia Carolina died, another daughter, Theodosia de Malsburg, was born, followed by a son, Egerton, in 1795. Sadly, Egerton died when he was eleven years old, so the sole remaining child of this marriage was Theodosia de Malsburg Leigh.

During this time, little is known of what happened to Maria and John, Donellan's children. At the time of the marriage they were ten and seven respectively, following which their surname changed to Beauchamp (their grandmother's maiden name). Maria, sadly, becomes clear at only two moments in her life: on the August afternoon in 1780 when Donellan claimed he had spent some time walking with her in the fields near Lawford, and then only again nineteen years later, when she drew up her will. She was then living in Hotwells, near Bristol, briefly famous for its supposedly curative waters. She left everything to her mother and, after Theodosia's death, to her brother John,[20] she died just a few months later, probably from tuberculosis.

John had been given the living of Newbold church, and went up to Oxford while he was still in his teens, matriculating shortly before his sister's death. He gained a Bachelor of Honours in 1802, and was ordained the same year, when he went to live in Dallington, near Northampton. On 23 November 1803, he too drew up his will, leaving everything he owned not to his mother and step-father but to Anna and William King – undoubtedly the same Kings who had helped his mother when she fled Lawford Hall in 1780.[21] John died just two years later, and was buried in Newbold on 26 August 1805. The cause of his death is a mystery: one lurid Victorian account has him committing suicide as a teenager after a local boy told him 'Better a tradesman's son than a murderer's son', but that is patently untrue.[22] However, it is possible that John's real identity caught up with him once he became a curate in a Northamptonshire church, and the attendant rumours were too much for him. Either that or he was simply a victim of natural causes, like his sister six years before him. Here was the end of John Donellan's line, and the son who – if his father had not been found guilty of poisoning Theodosius – would have inherited the Boughton estates.

In the space of fourteen years, from 1792 to 1806, Theodosia and Egerton endured the deaths of five children, and so it is not very surprising that the couple doted on their remaining child, Theodosia. Their daughter, in contrast to her siblings, was destined to live a long life and found a considerable dynasty, but not before she had driven her father to distraction.

By 1811, the Leighs were living at 72 Portland Street, London, and were enjoying a close friendship with their step-cousins, the Rouse-Boughtons.[23] Egerton and Charles seemed to have been close, and Egerton was soon to need Charles's sangfroid in a family crisis. Theodosia fell in love with a young upstart (according to Egerton) called John Ward and, although Egerton banned him from the house, he had his suspicions that she was seeing him secretly. In March and April of 1811 a flurry of letters from Egerton to Charles begged him to act as an intermediary; it appeared that Theodosia was in Warwickshire with Ward and 'I fear that we are too late.' He was right. The headstrong Theodosia had run off to Gretna Green in Scotland some three weeks before, and was already married.[24]

Egerton Leigh was apoplectic. The whole affair reads like a Victorian melodrama, Egerton telling Charles that he felt Ward was after Brownsover Hall: 'It is a most happy circumstance that the property is in Lady Leigh's power.' Actually, John Ward had a complicated distant connection to the Boughton family.[25] Theodosia and John – or perhaps Egerton himself – tried to repair the scandal by posting banns of a forthcoming 'marriage' in the high-society church of St Marylebone, London, as if Theodosia and John were still single. There is no record of that 'marriage' actually taking place, however: perhaps the young couple thought it was too much of a farce. By November, Egerton was almost beside himself with fury, and his letter to Charles reveals a man who was having the greatest difficulty in seeing his daughter as a fully grown woman. 'An infant,' he wrote, 'is seduced to go away with a stranger ... a man thus makes unsatisfactory infancy its prey – No – it cannot be – The son was a material instrument in the seduction – seduction – seduction – My dear Charles, I cannot soften this term.'[26]

But Egerton's misgivings about the suitability of the union proved to be unfounded. John Ward and Theodosia Leigh were married for fifty-seven years. In time, John assumed the name Ward-Boughton-Leigh; the couple had eight surviving children. Their marriage in fact preserved William Boughton and Anna Maria Beauchamp's line, which had looked set to fail when so many of Theodosia's children had perished.

Egerton Leigh died seven years later, on 27 April 1818, aged fifty-six.

It would not have been surprising if the much-bereaved Lady Leigh now retreated into the shadows of widowhood and kept a low profile; but Theodosia Beauchamp Leigh was made of stern stuff. She was sixty-one, but Sir Charles's daughter Lady Templeton suspected that she had had designs on her own father for some time. Several years previously, she had written to him saying that she knew that Theodosia wrote to him, and added, 'Her usual flow of spirits are returned and I make no doubt of it that if Sir Egerton died she would make you tipsy with champagne and then by it persuade you to marry her .. I could not *bear* the thought.' But she need not have worried. The seemingly indestructible Theodosia did marry again, though not to Sir Charles. On 10 February 1823, aged sixty-six, she married Barry O'Meara, who had been surgeon to Napoleon on St Helena.

Despite being what was then perceived as a very old lady, Theodosia was not only still capable of catching a husband but she was as sharp as a tack. She kept up a constant stream of letters to her solicitor, George Harris, complaining most frequently about overspending[27] and ordering him to keep locals off their land so that her new husband could fish, shoot and hunt without their 'molestation' or 'impediments'.

One wonders if the thought crossed her mind of the brother who had spent his last night fishing the same stretch of river some forty-five years before. How different life might have been for her if John Donellan had not been accused of Theodosius's murder. Other Donellan children would have been born; Lawford Hall would not have been demolished. It would have been John Donellan's children who would have established a flourishing line of descendants, not the daughter of Egerton Leigh; and it might have been John Donellan's son who had the living of Newbold church, and not Egerton Leigh's grandson.[28]

Dame Theodosia Beauchamp Leigh, having lived a life of extraordinary drama, died on 14 January 1830, aged seventy-three.

Six days later she was buried in the Boughton family vault at Newbold.

16

What Killed Theodosius Boughton?

'I think your family were always of the opinion that Donellan was innocent ...'

Edward Allesley Boughton Ward-Boughton-Leigh to
Sir Charles Rouse-Boughton, 8 November 1882

'Where there was no poison, there was no poisoner.'

S. M. Phillips, Famous Cases of Circumstantial Evidence (1873)

SAMUEL MARCH PHILLIPS hit the nail on the head when he wrote on the Donellan trial in his *Famous Cases of Circumstantial Evidence*: 'the argument turned upon the breath, the smell of a woman.'[1] A smell which, as James Stephen had pointed out ninety years earlier, Anna Maria had not even mentioned at either of the coroner's inquests. 'But did the deceased die of poison?' Phillips persisted. 'For if he did not, there is an end to the whole. Where there was no poison, there was no poisoner.'

Did Donellan's trial prove beyond a shadow of doubt that the mixture that Theodosius took on 30 August 1780 was prussic acid, distilled from laurel leaves? And did it prove that no other cause of death was possible?

No. The case against Donellan rested solely on Anna Maria

Boughton's testimony that the medicine she gave Theodosius smelled of bitter almonds, but no one could prove that this was true.

No other testimony mentioned such a smell, except for that of Rattray, who claimed to have smelled and tasted something 'acrid' in his mouth at the dissection. None of the other doctors or surgeons mentioned it, let alone proved that the 'acrid' smell was poisonous. Catharine Amos did not say that there was a smell of bitter almonds from Theodosius when she was wiping his mouth, and it is inconceivable that the prosecution did not try their best to get her to say so; similarly, Powell did not say that the recently dead corpse smelled of it. And if Anna Maria's second deposition to the coroner – the one that resulted in Donellan's arrest – was true, then a residue of the mixture had been thrown on the bedroom floor; but no smell was noted in the room.

The trial heard that Donellan had a still, but did not prove that he made laurel water in it. Francis Amos testified that laurel trees grew in the garden, but not that any had been picked for distilling. These are possible sources of poison, but there is no proof that they were the *actual* source.

Hunter testified that the symptoms Theodosius displayed before he died were not certain proof that the cause of death was poison, and he discounted the other medical testimony that had suggested that the autopsy proved poison. Wilmer was adamant that *no cause* could be distinguished. All the experiments which had been done on animals by Rattray, Wheler and Wilmer only proved that laurel water killed animals in a certain way. The jury was then asked to make the leap from the way the animals died to the way that Theodosius had died, based only on Anna Maria's evidence.

Hunter despaired for some time about his performance at the trial, and the unprofessional nature of the other medical witnesses; he warned his students that they should be aware of how the law worked and adjust their answers accordingly. 'A poor devil was lately hanged at Warwick,' he said, 'upon no other testimony than that of physical men whose *first experiments* were made upon this occasion.' In his diary, Hunter recorded various arguments that he had afterwards about Donellan. The Irish inventor Richard Lovell Edgeworth defended Hunter in one such row, saying that ten years earlier he had heard Hunter say that he had swallowed 'enough laurel water to kill twenty dogs and lived to tell the tale'.

As Phillips had it: 'Theodosius was *supposed* to have been poisoned because it was *believed* to have been laurel water; and it was *believed* to have been laurel water because he was *supposed* to have been poisoned … they were but conjectures unsupported by any proof, and formed against all the rules of law.'

James Stephen, in his angry pamphlet published after the trial, quotes a 'learned source' which echoes this point: 'The law never admits an inference from an inference. The question is never as to what *a thing is like* – as in Anna Maria's evidence that it 'smelt like bitter almonds' – 'but the witness must swear to his belief as to what it *is*. The circumstance itself is never to be presumed, but must be absolutely proved.'

Analysing the case in 1825, the medical writer John Gordon Smith said that above all it was the evidence of the scientific witnesses that most prejudiced the outcome. 'It cannot be evidence,' he said, 'on the part of a scientific witness as to the identity of poison, that another person whose opinion cannot be authoritative, such as Lady Boughton, described it to "smell like the taste" of a second substance.'[3]

Even if it were to be accepted that a murder took place, was it proved that Donellan was the murderer?

The classic considerations of murder are motive, means and opportunity. Donellan's motive was given by prosecuting counsel and Justice Buller as 'avarice' – the desire for Theodosius's fortune, which would become the property of Donellan's wife.

But did Donellan actually stand to gain in this way? Undoubtedly Theodosia was the main beneficiary under the terms of her father's will; but a large part of the estate was mortgaged. Donellan had been promised two church livings which were in the gift of Theodosius and worth £500 a year. It is true, however, that once her brother was dead, Theodosia would have been able to give these to her husband, and probably with less fuss. Theodosius had been known to argue with Donellan and resent the way that the older man ruled the show at Lawford Hall; perhaps Donellan felt that Theodosius would get his own back when he became master, and withhold the church livings?

Equally, Donellan may have dreaded the day when Theodosius came into his fortune, not because of the amounts of money involved, which were modest, but because now the whole family would be dependent on a young man who had so far in his life betrayed nothing but recklessness. Donellan may have worried that the money would soon be gone, and the family plunged into debt – protection of his wife in this situation may certainly have been a motivating factor.

Additionally – and this was never mentioned as a motive in court – Donellan may have cared not so much for himself as for his children, to whom he was devoted. He had a son who might one day inherit. He also had a young wife who could have been reasonably expected to produce more offspring. How was he to look after them if his income were dependent upon Theodosius? Donellan perhaps envisaged a lifetime of pleasing the arrogant young baronet, trying to wheedle a few more financial favours in order to secure a happy life for his family.

In the prosecution brief there is a telling little story which never came to court. Sukey Sparrow, the nursemaid, said that she had heard Donellan say to Theodosia that it had been a lucky thing that it had not been he who had given Theodosius his medicine; and later the same day – the day that Theodosius died – she saw him cradling the baby, John, in his arms saying, 'Now, you little rogue, you will be heir to thousands a year.' Did Donellan indeed murder Theodosius, but for the sake of his children?

As for the means, Donellan disputed that he was ever in Theodosius's bedroom after the medicine was delivered the previous evening; but that is not to say that Donellan could not have got another, discarded bottle of Powell's various 'purges', filled it with laurel water and substituted it at some time during the night. Or he could simply have put a second bottle on the chimney shelf at any time in the previous few days: Anna Maria testified that there were two, not one.

Donellan admitted to having a still; he admitted that he had a recipe for distilling laurel leaves; and he admitted – though not to the court – that he had made a dilute mixture 'to bathe his feet'. So he had ample means and opportunity.

Interestingly, an article in the *Coventry Mercury* of 4 June 1781 posed a series of questions to Donellan's solicitor (which one is not specified). The newspaper claimed that Donellan's *Defence* had been published only to make money for Inge and Webb. It also said that Donellan's guilt was expressed freely by them 'In the Three Tuns Inn the morning after Captain Donellan's trial'.

The paper claimed that the unnamed solicitor had declared that there were 'fifty' more incriminating facts about Donellan – one of them being that a carpenter called Burton had been willing to testify, if called, that Donellan sent a servant to intercept a message that Bucknill had sent to Snow on the afternoon of the funeral. On arriving at the house, Snow had been told by Donellan that Bucknill would not return for hours, so Snow had no option but to allow the funeral to proceed.

It was also claimed that 'during his confinement' Donellan had dismissed Theodosius's death, saying that 'a greater piece of work was made about killing one man in England than about killing twenty in Ireland'.

If what was said in the Three Tuns was reported correctly, then it shows Donellan in a bad light. If he *did* intercept a message from Bucknill to Snow, it may have been to get the funeral over with for the sake of the assembled mourners; or it may have been a final attempt to conceal his crime. The remark – again, if true – about killing one man could mean that he simply accepted that Theodosius *had* been murdered; or it could mean that he held other men's lives pretty cheaply.

Donellan's statement in court was not enough to dissuade the jury of his guilt. Only his *Defence*, once he had been sentenced, answered many of the accusations made against him. But by then, of course, it was too late. And there was no defence at all against a legal team so willing to gossip about him in a local inn while he was still alive.

Of the other members of the family, Edward Boughton had a financial incentive to kill Theodosius. Unlike Donellan, he would gain a baronetcy as well as the fortune, and Edward had been convinced that all Theodosius's estates and rents came with the title, until he was disappointed by Dunning's advice and Anna Maria's flat refusal. He also put pen to paper to say how wonderful it was that Theodosius was dead, although, to be fair to him, 'wonderful' had a slightly different connotation in eighteenth-century English – surprising, curious, or shocking in an ironically entertaining way.

Local people, Edward reported in his letters, certainly thought that he was the guilty man: for a while it was rumoured that it was he, not Donellan, who had been locked up in Warwick Gaol.

But Edward Boughton was not short of money. Theodosius's estate and baronetcy were attractive, as Edward's mother showed in her letters, but were they worth murdering for? Edward, after all, had an estate of his own worth hundreds of thousands of pounds, and he also had a family of his own of whom he was very fond. It is not likely that he would have gambled their happiness and security – which he valued so highly that he rejected the usual practice of marrying an heiress to consolidate his fortune – not to mention the reputation and happiness of his own siblings, on a distant cousin's estate in Warwickshire.

The servants at Lawford Hall had plenty of opportunity. They had access to both house and garden. But what possible motive could a servant have for killing Theodosius?

Aside from the usual grumblings of servant about master, one possible motive for murder presents itself. Sarah Blundell was about six months pregnant when Theodosius died. She had hidden the fact well; only when she went into labour did Anna Maria throw the girl out of the house. Was there someone else in the house – one of the servants – who knew very well that Theodosius had seduced Sarah, and was angry enough to revenge themselves on him? Leaving Sarah unquestioned at the time (other than on the issue of the bottles) meant that a possible motive was overlooked.

Anna Maria made her views known – Sarah was a 'bad girl'. Donellan himself had nothing to say in Sarah's favour. But perhaps they both missed the obvious: seduction by the master of the house was a regular hazard for female servants and Theodosius was no slouch at pestering women. Sarah's 'sweetheart' was John Yateman, the footman – but was the child his?

Motive enough for revenge, one might think.

In his opening address to the court, the prosecuting counsel Howarth made enormous play of Donellan's financial motive. 'The attaining of this considerable fortune,' he declaimed, 'beyond a doubt induced the prisoner to plan and execute this abominable crime.' But if this were a motive for Donellan, it was also a motive for Theodosia.

She, too, had means, motive and opportunity. In fact, she had more opportunity than her husband, because she was standing with Theodosius on the stairway when Samuel Frost delivered the medicine into the boy's hands. Samuel said that Theodosius put it in his pocket, but Theodosia could have easily offered to take it upstairs for him. She did, therefore, see the bottle – something that her husband says he did not, except for on the morning of the death. As Theodosius's sister, she was closer to him than Donellan; Theodosius would have trusted her.

It is noticeable that Theodosia did not come to the bedroom that fateful morning when her mother called for help. Anna Maria had been running up and down the stairs calling for the servants. Why did Theodosia not come to see what was the matter? Did she already know? James Fitzjames Stephen referred to the possibility of Theodosia's involvement in his first published work on the subject in 1863. Twenty years later, in a second edition, the implication had been removed.

However, Theodosia had two young children, one of them only a baby. Handling a lethal substance might have posed a danger to her children. If she were the murderer, how had she ordered or distilled the dose?

Alternatively, could Theodosia and Donellan have colluded in the murder? Donellan's outburst in gaol indicated something of the sort ('And who got it for her!'). Did Theodosia know of Donellan's intentions? Did she encourage them? Was it her idea – to protect the fortune and future of her children – or was she simply a bystander, guilty in as much that she did not warn her brother of what Donellan was planning?

After Donellan's committal to Warwick Gaol Theodosia left Lawford on his suggestion, or because she had, independently of his suspicions, fallen out with her mother. This all points to Theodosia supporting Donellan, but as a wife, or as an accomplice?

After Christmas 1780, Theodosia stayed away from Donellan completely. Was she by then more convinced of his guilt, or did she take advice from the Kings that she ought not to associate herself with him? Had she found out about Donellan's continuing relationship with Mrs H? Or was she swayed by the rumours so widely circulating in the area that Donellan was indeed guilty?

One thing seems certain. When Donellan was executed, Theodosia became very ill. She stayed away from her mother, who had really put the noose around Donellan's neck. A woman guilty of plotting in her brother's murder might have felt thankful to Anna Maria for her rank stupidity.

But Theodosia did not act as if she were relieved, or in any way more benevolently disposed towards her mother. She left Anna Maria pleading for companionship among distant branches of the family, and shut herself away in Northampton 'altogether alone'.

Anna Maria Boughton was the witness on whom the whole case rested. It was her testimony that the medicine smelled of bitter almonds that precipitated the laurel-water experiments and the significance being attached to the fact that Donellan owned a still. It was also her testimony that Donellan threw the contents of the bottles 'on the floor' which gave the coroner no option but to arrest him.

Anna Maria had motive, means and opportunity.

If she was as 'covetous' as Donellan claimed, then money was a motivating factor. Within the year Theodosius would come into his fortune, and he had shown no sign at all of being responsible. Was she afraid that the family would be forced into penury by him, and did Donellan's opinion confirm this? She was embarrassed by her son under testimony: he had venereal disease; he had disgraced himself at Eton; and he had brawled in local inns. She seemed to have little control over him, yet this was the young man who would have total control over *her* in eleven months' time. Local newspapers reported that she was present at the open-air autopsy at Newbold, but that she showed no emotion.

Anna Maria, above any other person, had the means and opportunity to poison her son. It was she who gave him the medicine, encouraging him to drink it even though, halfway through, he objected. She sniffed the bottle, testified that it smelled disturbingly like bitter almonds, but still she stood over Theodosius until he drank it all.

What sort of woman could be so cold-hearted as to kill her own son? Was Anna Maria such a woman? Was there evidence that she lacked feelings? John Donellan claimed that Anna Maria had told him that she had once poisoned her husband's pack of dogs. We only have Donellan's word for this, and presumably he brought this up to show that Anna Maria was far from a weak, helpless woman incapable of a vicious act. But did Anna Maria really poison the dogs as revenge because Edward flaunted his mistress and seduced the maids? It is pure hearsay. And even if Anna Maria *were* capable of poisoning a pack of hounds, how did she get the poison? Was she used to handling it, and was it freely available at the house? Or was this all simply an outrageous lie from John Donellan? And is it in any way reasonable to conclude that such an act would make her capable of poisoning her own son?

Throughout this story Anna Maria seems curiously detached from reality. But this is not to be wondered at after the death of her only son: perhaps grief obliterated most of the events of the morning and she found it hard to piece them together properly? Francis Amos is quoted in the prosecution brief as saying that 'on the morning her son died she seemed very much affected and cried a good deal' – something that Donellan never refers to.

What is less comprehensible is, if she was unsure of what exactly happened, why she was so willing to stand up in court and condemn her daughter's husband. 'One of the strangest circumstances attendant upon a death so alarming was the subsequent conduct of Lady Boughton,' observes James Stephen.

Anna Maria showed absolutely no sign of distrusting Donellan before Theodosius was buried, except for her testimony that she had objected to his washing out the bottles. But it is as if she attached no real significance to this act until the coroner's court met; she did not write to Wheler and tell him what Donellan had done, or complain that it worried her. She let Donellan organise everything, just as she had done before Theodosius died. From 1778 to 1780, far from mistrusting Donellan or thinking him a bad influence on her son, Anna Maria let him take charge of the household, and she had sent Theodosius to live with Donellan and Theodosia soon after they were married.

Why would Anna Maria let Donellan handle events after the death if the issue of his washing the bottles preyed heavily on her mind? It took her over a week to find any fault with her son-in-law. In the intense atmosphere of the house, did she simply feel alone and frightened?

Over a week later, she testified that she had feared that she too would fall foul of 'unfair dealings' and gave instructions that, if she died, her body was to be examined immediately. Did she keep silent therefore because she was afraid that Donellan might murder her, too? In the prosecution brief, it is said that Anna Maria became suspicious of Donellan after he washed the bottles out ('at this proceeding her Ladyship began to suspect that he had contrived to put poison into the bottle out of which she had given the draught'). Why not send immediately for Wheler or a doctor like William Kerr, whom Theodosius knew? If she had done so straight away, what could Donellan have done? With Wheler and Kerr or any reputable surgeon in the house, he could not do anything. Did she think he would attack her after they had gone?

'Captain Donellan's temper was very violent,' Anna Maria told her prosecution team in the brief, 'and was of a very assuming disposition in the family concerns, and having no friend there she could consult she was afraid to mention her suspicions to anyone or send for the faculty to open her son's body.'

But even if she were crippled by fright and grief on the day, in the week before the funeral Anna Maria had ample opportunity to visit Wheler, even to ask for some kind of sanctuary with him at Leamington Hastings. It is inconceivable that he would have refused her; the autopsy would have been done there and then, the coroner's court convened, and Donellan arrested all the sooner.

Alternatively, Anna Maria could have confided in her local priest, the Reverend Newsam, who was a regular visitor to the house and had been a close friend of her husband's; he would not have betrayed her confidence, and he was a messenger and friend to Lord Denbigh.

It is also very odd that, if Anna Maria thought Theodosius's death was suspicious in some way, she called for the undertakers within the hour, and not for a doctor to give his opinion.

And why did she not take Powell, especially, to task? She told the court that she had said 'it was an unaccountable thing for the doctor to send such a medicine', but she did not ask anyone to go to Powell and question him further. How could she have been satisfied with Powell turning up at nine in the morning, simply to look at Theodosius and pronounce him dead? If she herself had felt too distressed to talk to Powell, then she could have asked William Wheler or the Reverend Newsam to visit him.

Although at Lawford Anna Maria kept meticulous accounts, and later members of the family wrote that she was perfectly sensible,[2] much was made of Anna Maria's lack of intelligence, and this too could explain her confused testimony. She was regarded as 'all but a fool', even by her own legal team, and she had had to be primed for court by the local JPs – but schooling a witness is not unusual even today. Nervous, distressed, overwhelmed, confused: all this can be understood.

But what is hard to excuse is condemning a man to death as a result. If Anna Maria could not remember, or was not sure of what happened, then it was wrong to testify as if she *were* sure. And it was wrong of her team to encourage her to do so.

What is even more disturbing is that Donellan's own defence team were apparently happy to collude in protecting Anna Maria. They could have, and should have, queried the blatantly awry timings on the morning of the murder. Did Theodosius die within fifteen minutes of being given the medicine, or more than an hour later? Did she leave him for five minutes, or fifty? Did she leave him writhing in pain, or was he just drowsy, 'going to sleep'? Was 'going to sleep' an effect of taking a draught of prussic acid? None of these questions was asked in court.

Powell's whole part in this affair is extraordinary. The apothecary was not questioned at all by Anna Maria or Theodosia or Donellan; his explanations were accepted totally by Wheler. We have no evidence that the other doctors ever expressed any concerns or doubts about him.

Powell was described as an elderly, old-fashioned man by the boys at Rugby School. He certainly had the means and opportunity to have murdered Theodosius, but no discernible motive. As Donellan had told John Derbyshire, to kill Theodosius would have been to rob him of a patient. Unless, of course, he were carrying out the wishes of one of the other members of the family. But it seems far more likely that Powell simply made a mistake. Apothecaries had actually been banned from keeping laurel water for some years; but did Powell still have supplies? Had he inadvertently used laurel water instead of some other innocuous substance?

Powell went to Sir William Wheler before the funeral to explain himself. He was also at Lawford Hall on the night of 4 September, opening a letter from Wheler addressed to Donellan. Perhaps he had reason to be anxious; perhaps he was not really sure that his medicine had been as safe as he was to testify. Was Theodosius's death actually the result of a terrible misjudgement on Powell's part?

Powell was not the only apothecary involved in the case. Bernard Snow, Sir William Wheler's apothecary, apparently gave permission for the funeral to go ahead, and yet was never called to testify at the trial. Why was this? Why would a mere apothecary's word be taken over that of the surgeon, Bucknill, unless both men were in fact acting on the orders of Wheler? Was Snow's absence from the trial due to pressure from Sir William not to testify in Donellan's defence for fear of implicating Sir William himself in the decision to bury Theodosius without an autopsy?

Another possible explanation, given by Donellan in Warwick Gaol, was that Theodosius committed suicide. Donellan dismissed this as absurd almost at once when talking to Derbyshire, but is it possible that Theodosius poisoned himself by accident?

It was common knowledge that Theodosius was careless, irritable and untrustworthy; Donellan also claimed that the boy had told him that he regularly dosed himself up with all sorts of quack medicines. We also have the evidence at the coroner's court that Theodosius had bought two poisons in the weeks before his death: *Cocculus indicus* berries from Bucknill, and arsenic in order to poison rats. Anna Maria testified that Theodosius kept the arsenic in his bedroom.

Both Donellan and Anna Maria said that Theodosius kept more than one bottle of medication on his chimney shelf, and we know that Powell had prescribed four 'purges' in one week. Where were the bottles from those purges and quack medicines? Were they on the chimney shelf, perhaps empty or half empty? Had Theodosius mixed his doses, or added mercury to any of them? Where was the lethal mixture that Thomas Hewitt had brought to him within the last month? Was that, too, standing on the chimney shelf? Had Theodosius decanted it into one of Powell's bottles to prevent his mother from finding out what he had bought?

The prosecution team said in their brief that they had the bottle – but where had they found it?

Is it possible that Theodosius, finding himself ill once again with a blackening swelling in his groin, sickened by the mercury which he had regularly ingested, and frightened by Donellan's assertion that he was ruining his constitution, had taken a dose of his own prescription, either in a desperate attempt to cure himself or out of despair that he would never be cured? Did he buy the arsenic mixture from Hewitt not for poisoning fish, but for another reason? He used a prescription from Bucknill to get it. That points to a medical reason. Why was Bucknill never questioned about this? What exactly was the relationship between Theodosius and Bucknill? These are all questions that were never asked or answered.

If suicide or an accidental dose by Theodosius himself were possibilities, these should have been raised by Donellan's defence team.

The actions of Sir William Wheler, Theodosius's guardian, are also worth considering.

It was only on 4 September that Wheler, the Reverend Newsam and Lord Denbigh showed any interest at all in what had happened, and that was due to rumour. Wheler, distracted by a friend who had suffered a bereavement, was busy elsewhere. Initially, he showed no interest in Theodosius's demise other than to offer routine condolences. And there is no evidence that Anna Maria had contacted either him, Denbigh or Newsam, even though they were the very men who were best placed to protect her if she had any suspicions about Donellan.

Once the rumours began to fly about poison, as Phillips later said, a 'poisoner had to be found'. Wheler knew that it was his responsibility to act. If poison had been used, he must find a culprit, and John Donellan fitted the bill. After all, Donellan was a disgraced army officer, a man of 'gaiety' who had seduced an 18-year-old girl; and he had been a reputed fortune hunter long before he had met Theodosia.

How far did the actual conduct of the trial go to prejudice Donellan's case?

It was quoted for many years afterwards as a dangerous precedent in the use of circumstantial evidence. Despite his experience, Buller was also criticised. Joseph Cradock said that 'Judge Buller's charge at Warwick was imprudent'. He displayed 'harshness and injustice', in the words of Childers.[4] Fifty years later, Buller's name had become 'proverbial as the judge who condemned men before they were tried', according to one popular weekly. In *Biographica Juridica* of 1870, Edward Foss said: 'Yet with all his industry, sagacity and intelligence, Buller was not a popular judge. He was considered arrogant, hasty in his decisions; prejudiced, severe and even cruel in criminal trials.' The *Dublin University Magazine* of 1869 said that Buller had excused Anna Maria's contradictory evidence because 'she was telling the truth according to the best of her ability … and made allowance for her position, her agitation' and added, 'During the whole of this celebrated trial there was not a single fact established by evidence except the death.'

Donellan's defence team were hounded for incompetence after the trial. The jury, despite their protests to the contrary, could not fail to be influenced both by the powerful reputation of the Boughton family and by months of newspaper speculation before-hand. Collusion was hinted at between the Justices of the Peace and Anna Maria; between Anna Maria and the Earl of Denbigh; between Buller and the Justices. Lastly, the jury did not take time to weigh each piece of evidence properly; they came to their decision in only nine minutes. There was no proper defence as we would recognise it – Donellan could not speak or answer evidence as presented in court. And, of course, there was no right of appeal.

Once the rumour of poison spread, no one seemed to have the strength to refute it. Servants ignorant of medicine or perhaps even of Theodosius's true state of health had let the gossip spread through Warwickshire, and possibly even started it; once rumour took its virulent hold, even those most intimately concerned – Anna Maria and Donellan among them – were powerless to say that the boy might have died of a natural cause like epilepsy. The description of the bloated corpse, smelling suspiciously acrid, the tongue protruding as if trying to expel a revolting taste, was out there in the public imagination. It was too late to obscure it. Titillation, scandal and fear were inexhaustible – and so much more interesting than any boringly rational explanation. By the time the case came to trial the impression of poison was reinforced by the images of dogs and horses writhing in agony, and these were then inextricably linked with Theodosius apparently doing the same. Even if Anna Maria had seen her son suffer epileptic fits before, that explanation was a mere candle in the wind, ready to be snuffed out by cries of 'murder'. Worse still, she was now the woman holding a bottle whose contents were held to have been toxic. In panic, and under pressure from Wheler and Denbigh ('we shall all be very much blamed'), did Anna Maria realise that a 'poisoner' must be found, even if Theodosius had died naturally? Donellan protested that it was not poison at first, but in the face of a tidal wave of public opinion he struggled to explain how poison could have reached Theodosius. Anna Maria and Donellan were therefore forced into a position whereby they literally had to fight to the death, each blaming the other. The legal teams merely stood by like ineffectual seconds, skirting round the issue, with no one willing to pursue the possibility that no poison existed at all.

The *American Jurist and Law Magazine* of 1841 put it very succinctly: 'Donellan's conviction,' it said, 'was judicial homicide.'

There are vast differences between the way the case was investigated in 1780 and how it would be investigated today. Today, paramedics would report an unexplained death; and the police would be called to all sudden deaths. An attempt would be made to revive the patient by the ambulance team, and notes would be made of anything suspicious or possibly contributory. The house would be closed off, and nothing in the room would be touched; no one would enter or leave without investigation and permission; and the witnesses to the death would be separated. A thorough search of the room, house, outhouses, stables, drains and rubbish containers would be made. While guarding against unwarranted assumptions, each witness would be a potential suspect.

The body would be properly investigated – first at the scene and later by a Home Office pathologist, especially in such a high-profile case. The corpse would also be preserved in a way that Theodosius was not (an icehouse was never mentioned in relation to Lawford, but it is possible that the Hall did have one).

Crucially, an open mind would be kept today on a motive for murder. Modern toxicology would verify the existence of poison if it had been used; forensic tests by the police and the pathologist would trace the actions of both victim and witnesses. While offering every sympathy to a distressed relative, it would not be unquestioningly assumed that a mother could not murder her son, or – for that matter – that a murder could not be carried out by a sister, a local doctor, a household servant, a guardian, a distant relative who stood to gain financially, or a brother-in-law.

Inanimate objects would also have their story to tell. The clothing of the witnesses would be examined and tested; hand swabs would be taken; even the flooring would be taken up to test for the prussic acid that Anna Maria had first claimed had been thrown from the medicine bottles.

And, as far as this particular case goes, the medical history would be crucial.

Theodosius Boughton had for some time been prescribed mercury, a recognised 'cure' for syphilis. It was given because it was believed that the disease left the body in the increased urine flow and salivation of the sufferer, and applications of mercury to rashes and sores seemed to make them disappear. The side-effects, however, were as well known as the 'cures'.

Inmates of the Bicêtre asylum in Paris, subjected to lotions of mercury, suffered mouth and throat sores, nausea, vomiting and ulcerations of the digestive tract. Mirror-makers commonly suffered tremors, slurred speech and loss of sleep. Many doctors and apothecaries recognised mercurial disease but were loath to give up the money gained from mercury prescriptions.

What was not appreciated at the time was that syphilis, although appearing to respond to the treatment, actually went into its secondary stages and invaded bones, organs, blood vessels, the spinal cord and the brain. Significantly, damage to the aorta was linked to syphilis in 1847; but would a five-year history of syphilis and mercury poisoning have weakened the blood vessels in Theodosius Boughton? And would those blood vessels already be carrying a genetic weakness passed to Theodosius from his father and grandfather?

A forensic pathologist working today, Dr Allen Anscombe, has reviewed the case. He points out that a syphilitic aneurysm would be rare, and that the deaths of Theodosius's father and grandfather do not necessarily suggest a familial predisposition to strokes. In his opinion, the early death of this young man would merit an investigation of at least four possible causes: a history of epilepsy in the family; underlying heart disease; a stroke (which would be unusual in a person of this age and in reasonable health); and drugs.

Dr Anscombe considers that the two pints of 'extravasated blood' found in the chest cavity were misleading for the simple reason that they were unlikely to have actually been blood. A body in a decomposed state contains considerable quantities of fluid; the chest cavity becomes like a watertight container for a while, and the fluid inside it is tinged with a reddish colour. It does not indicate that a major blood vessel has burst. All it indicates is putrefaction.

Hunter was perfectly correct, in Dr Anscombe's opinion, to refuse to be drawn on the cause of death. After ten days' decomposition in hot weather even a modern pathologist, without toxicological examination, would be hard pressed to find a cause. Hunter gave a firm and well-informed response, and was right not to be led into speculation.

Looking at Anna Maria's conflicting testimony, the length of time that Theodosius took to die – *if* prussic acid in the form of laurel water had been administered – would depend upon the dilution of the mixture. A teaspoon of neat prussic acid would cause death within a few minutes; but it is not known how much was (supposedly) given. Dr Anscombe considers it is possible that Theodosius appeared to be sleeping after ten minutes; possible, too, that he was still alive and struggling up to an hour later, if the mixture was diluted.

With the administering of poison not proven, Dr Anscombe next considered the possibility of epilepsy. In this he agrees with Hunter: epilepsy was indicated. After forcing himself to keep an unpleasant-tasting medicine down, Theodosius might have suffered a fit after which he was unconscious or drowsy; and when Anna Maria returned, a second fit might have been in progress.

The effects of severe epileptic fits are, even today, notoriously difficult to determine on the human body: most sufferers do not die, but those that do may experience some sort of asphyxia with attendant paralysis of the muscles; and the electrical storm in the brain may cause the heart to stop beating. During the fits the victim will foam at the mouth, and suffer both rigidity and convulsions. A simple search of the internet today shows examples of fits where the sufferer is rigid, hands clenched, eyes fixed, foaming at the mouth, stomach heaving: all the symptoms described in Theodosius. After a fit, a sufferer will usually sleep; second fits are perfectly possible, and can last thirty minutes, an hour or more; the victim can descend into *status epilepticus*, a life-threatening condition needing immediate medical treatment, where the mortality rate is over 20 per cent.

During a fit, it is not possible for the sufferer to speak (although an occasional muffled word may be heard) – and this corresponds with Theodosius's state. He said nothing, even when Donellan called to him. A poisoned man, even while in agony, retains the ability to speak, but an epileptic does not. If Theodosius had been poisoned, one might have expected him to cry out to his mother, ask her what she had given him and respond to the maids or Donellan. But if he were in a deeply traumatic fit, he would not.

The answer of modern forensic pathology, therefore, is that the only reasonable answer of the surgeons in 1780 was 'cause of death unknown'. Epilepsy, however, was a possibility.

Hunter, derided as he was by Justice Buller as a man 'of no opinion', was absolutely right.

Poisoning is thankfully very rare today. Modern toxicology has seen to that – it is no longer a 'secret weapon'. It was rare, too, in the time of Theodosius Boughton: it was seen as a particularly 'un-English' crime, more common on continental Europe.

But was John Donellan guilty of poisoning?

What was the opinion of the legal world after the event?

Guilty, said James Fitzjames Stephen in 1883, despite the enraged examination of the conviction by his own grandfather. 'Few cases have given rise to more discussion,' he mused, 'but to my mind [there was] so strong a probability of his guilt that I think the jury were right.'

Possibly guilty, reported the *Monthly Review* of 1781, but: 'It was not proved to a jury.'

Guilty, said the *Dublin University Magazine* in 1869, although 'The prisoner was found guilty upon a species of evidence the most dangerous, fallacious and inconclusive.'

Guilty, said William Bentham in 1801 in *The Baronetage of England*: 'little doubt has been entertained of his actual guilt'.

'The public have long since acquiesced in the justice of Donellan's sentence,' agreed the Cornish clergyman Richard Polwhele in 1831, reviewing the life of Justice Buller.

Although still a young man when he died, John Donellan had lived several lives, in each of which ran a thread of contradiction or duality. He was an 'almost man', coming close to success in all he attempted, but each time failing dramatically.

His military career was sponsored by his father even though Donellan was illegitimate; bastard sons could, and did, rise to greatness in the Georgian world. But there would never be that sense of absolute belonging, of a rightful place. The boy might flourish by his own talents, but he would never be a true family member.

Donellan's army career was steady, but his posting to the East India Company put him in a curious position, poised between serving the Crown and rampant commercialism. Britain was involved in the noble cause of securing the vast wealth of India for itself, and its fighting men did the same. A proportion of the spoils was considered payment, and a blind eye was turned; Donellan's mistake was in stepping out from the shadows, boasting of having been some kind of secret agent and sporting a diamond ring that earned him the nickname 'Diamond Donellan'. He drew a picture of himself as a wounded hero in every sense of the word; but, having offended his commanding officer, his dismissal was inevitable. A good soldier but a poor team player, Donellan's contradictions cost him his job.

In London as Master of Ceremonies at the Pantheon, Donellan

inhabited two worlds but was not wholly in either of them. He was supposedly in charge of it; but he failed to stop women like Sophia Baddeley entering and causing a scandal. He was, by all accounts, handsome, although he was small and slight. He dressed well and gambled frequently, but he was also short of money.

In his relationship with Theodosia Boughton the contradictions continue. He seemed to have genuine feeling for her and their children, but his last letter from Warwick suggests that he had kept contact with his London mistress. He moved into Lawford Hall at the request of Anna Maria Boughton and ran the household effectively, but he was not its true master, and never would be while Theodosius was alive.

He lived under the same roof as his mother-in-law, and outwardly at least she was influenced by him and followed his suggestions; but their seemingly good relationship was a lie. Donellan made no bones about his disgust for Anna Maria and she in return was prepared to testify against him. Was the final contradiction – the prospect of living at Lawford, but bowing and scraping to a selfish boy – too much to bear for John Donellan? Did he see a way out of yet another position of insecurity? Perhaps the prospect of finally and incontrovertibly being master of all he surveyed was just too much of a temptation.

However, despite the strains of his various occupations in life, Donellan had never betrayed a truly vicious streak. He had lost his temper apparently more than once with Theodosius, and he was – according to Anna Maria – a bully around the house. But she never accused him of being physically violent or cruel. He was kind and affectionate to his children, and spent time with them. There had been no stories in London of his brawling or threatening anyone: rather the reverse, as it was his good nature and easy way with people that had landed him the job as Master of Ceremonies at the Pantheon.

If he lost his temper now and again with a spoiled womaniser like Theodosius and 'not a very intellectual woman' like Anna Maria, it was not really surprising. He had been deceitful in the past perhaps; a storyteller, a romancer. He had taken advantage of Theodosia. But nothing in his *Defence* document smacks of arrogance or aggression, let alone contempt for human life. It reads well; it sounds measured, intelligent and convincing. But then perhaps that above all was Donellan's one real skill: to tell a good story.

In his dealings with the Armenian merchants in India, it could be imagined how a more cunning and aggressive man could have stolen more while retaining both his reputation and a good relationship with his seniors. His rise further through the ranks was prevented because he lacked a true killer instinct. He complained publicly at being mistreated instead of playing the system; he grovelled to the very man, Colonel Forde, whom he had insulted, and then told the sordid story all over London when he found himself dismissed.

Donellan always seems to have been the man standing in the wrong place at the wrong time. He had tenacity and courage and a charm that won over women – a charm so much more attractive than the low-life brawling behaviour of Theodosius Boughton; but he never seemed to be able to follow through. He won friends, but he did not influence them; he occupied positions of authority but found himself flouted in them; he married an heiress, but was never accepted into the aristocracy.

More than anything else, Donellan's story is that of a man looking in on a world that he could never really enter. His testimonies both before the Board of Trustees of the East India Company and at his own murder trial smack of a man thwarted and misrepresented. Something in his character attracted criticism – jealousy, perhaps. And when he drew opposition, he drew it in a big way.

That the aristocratic ranks of rural Warwickshire closed against Donellan is certain. Privilege, rank and history were the bedrock upon which that society rested; the rise of the common man and the idea of a socialist society were far in the future. An ordinary person might become rich, but they would always be 'of the lower orders'. The nobility owned the land, ran society, ran government. Even criminals in the upper ranks of society could claim 'the privilege of rank' in appealing against sentences against them.

It is impossible to know if John Donellan killed Theodosius

Boughton. But what it is possible to say is that his conviction for the crime was thoroughly unsound.

In time, Donellan's passionate last pleas of innocence faded into obscurity; the details of the case, in all its faults, were forgotten. When the history books were written, Donellan was forever represented as the man who poisoned his brother-in-law.

His wife Theodosia became the matriarch of a long and distinguished line, but Donellan's children vanished. Their deaths are especially poignant. Whatever dreams John Donellan might have had for them, whatever he might have done to secure their future, they both died young – John as a lowly young curate in rented rooms and Maria as a spinster in a spa town, separated from her family. It is not known if either death was a suicide; it seems more likely that both were due to that massive killer of the young in the nineteenth century, tuberculosis.

Most forgotten of all is the young man around whom the whole drama circulated. Theodosius Boughton also had an unrealised future. He might have matured into a man like William Boughton, 'greater in worth than pedigree', a man of 'steady and untainted principle'. With the failings of his youth behind him, he too might have become a Member of Parliament like William, and the county's representative of the monarch as High Sheriff. He might have transcended the reputation of his grandfather and outshone his father; he might have shaken off the recent family histories of mistresses and drunkenness and taken the Boughtons back to the glory days of influence at Court.

But as it is, Theodosius remains forever pinned in place as a kind of laboratory specimen: dissected in public in almost every way possible. The impression of Theodosius we are left with is not the thoughtful-looking, even insipid boy peering out of the engraving which is the only known portrait of him, but of an aggressive, selfish wastrel. The imagined picture of him, teeth clenched and helplessly foaming at the mouth, cannot be eradicated: the details of the autopsy, of his blackened and putrefying body, remain. That is the true tragedy at the heart of this story.

Perhaps, then, the rumour which existed in the nineteenth century is true. On some August nights, it was said, the spectre of Theodosius Boughton, driving an open carriage pulled by two black horses, rose from the River Avon when it was in flood. The carriage and horses rolled dangerously in the current and, standing in the driving seat, Theodosius would be seen using his whip in an effort to spur the horses to the safety of the fields where once Lawford Hall had stood.

But the carriage was always engulfed again by the water; and Theodosius, despite all his desperate efforts, vanished.

Notes

Prologue

1. The *Gentleman's Magazine*, vol. 50 (September 1780), p. 448.

1 Poison

1. The opening address of the prosecution counsel, Howarth, on 30 March 1781.
2. *The Life of Captain Donellan* (London: J. Wenman, 1781), almost certainly by a Captain Murphy. Murphy published his account priced 'only one shilling', claiming that he had been in service with Donellan in India and had 'occasionally associated with him ever since … and has been furnished with the only Authentic Materials of that unfortunate Gentleman'.

2 The Following Days

1. Trial testimony, evidence to the prosecution, 30 April 1781.

3 The Major Players

1. Document 6683/4/3232, Warwickshire County Record Office M. Bloxam (1861); from the testimony of a local man, John Wolf.
2. Samuel Ireland, *Picturesque Views on the Upper or Warwickshire Avon* (London: R. Fouldes, 1795).

3. On the fringes of this cold domestic set-up were cousins living in nearby Bilton Hall. William's sister, Abigail, had married her second cousin Edward: their grandfathers, William and Thomas, had been brothers. To this rather incestuous line, Catherine was fresh blood.

4. Henry Ellis, *Original Letters, Illustrative of English History* (London: Harding, Triphook & Lepart, 1825).

5. Although his staunch royalism had won him a baronetcy, William's behaviour in his personal life was described as 'offensive' by his brother-in-law, William Combe, who challenged his inheritance, claiming that William had been disliked by his own father. CR 1612/492, Warwickshire County Record Office.

6. Ireland, *Picturesque Views*.

7. Thomas, William and Charles.

8. CR 162/479, Warwickshire County Record Office.

9. Mary had since married Sir Henry Houghton, but there is no record of Anne.

10. Daughter Eliza (or 'Meliza') disappeared from the will, presumably because by now she had married a man called Brudenall, by whom she had two sons. It follows that Katherine was still unmarried in 1715.

11. CR 162/486, Warwickshire County Record Office, Boughton *v.* Lister.

12. As above.

13. Parish registers at Warwickshire County Record Office disclose the deaths as infants of four of her children: Charlotte in 1736; Barbara in 1738; John in 1741; and John in 1743.

14. She was probably distantly related to Edward: his great-great-uncle's second wife's daughter by her second marriage. This daughter, Anne, was born in 1683. Edward, the second baronet, had been childless even though he married twice, and his title went to William, his brother. So the fact that William was a baronet at all is something of a fluke.

15. CR 162/486, Warwickshire County Record Office.

16. As above.

17. The full quote reads: 'My father was always esteemed a man of learning and good understanding but at some times when overheated with liquor would remit some indiscreet notions particularly when he lived with the late Lady Boughton his

mother-in-law [presumably this should read 'step-mother', as Catherine had no child called Grace, and in any case it would have meant that Edward had married his half-sister] who used all possible endeavours to keep him in liquor …'

18. When her husband died, Grace 'possessed herself of his personal Estate' (QC's Opinion, 20 January 1739, in CR 162/486, Warwickshire County Record Office) because Edward was still a child; in 1741 the Boughtons did offer her £665 per annum for life; so, though the Listers lost the case, they were not left empty-handed.

19. *Daily Gazetteer*, August 1735.

4 The Major Players

1. CR 1747/1, Warwickshire County Record Office.
2. Collection Database: European paintings: Jacopo Amigoni (1682–1752), the Metropolitan Museum of Art, New York, 'Flora and Zephr', Acc. No. 1985.5.
3. CR 1747/1, Warwickshire County Record Office.
4. Anna Maria had inherited valuable property in Northamptonshire from her mother.
5. CR 162/489, will of Edward Boughton, probate 22 May 1772, Warwickshire County Record Office.
6. 6683/4/330, Rouse-Boughton family letters books, Shropshire Archives, 3 January 1770.
7. As above.
8. See W. H. D. Rouse, *A History of Rugby School* (London: Duckworth, 1898; reprinted 2009).
9. *The Life and Letters of Edward Gibbon* by W. J. Day (Frederick Warne & Co, 1889).
10. According to 'The Little Bottle of Laurel Water', published in *All the Year Round*, the magazine edited by Charles Dickens, on 28 October 1871.
11. Edward Allesley Boughton Ward-Boughton-Leigh to Sir Charles Henry Rouse-Boughton, 8 November 1882.
12. Alan Saville (ed.), *Secret Comment: The Diaries of Gertrude Savile, 1731–1757* (Kingsbridge: Kingsbridge History Society, 1997).
13. 'The daughters of all the gentry of the three counties came hither to be picked up,' Defoe wrote of Bury-Fair. *A Tour Through the Whole Island of Great Britain 1724*.

14. *Sir John Vanbrugh* Ed. W. C. Ward (Lawrence and Buller 1893).

5 *The Major Players*

1. John Donellan, *The Case of John Donnellan, Captain of Foot, in the Service of the United Company of Merchants Trading to the East-Indies, humbly addressed to the Honourable Court of the Directors of the said Company* (London, 1770)

2. Both Donellan's version and the comments of a fellow officer, Captain Murphy, are given in *The Life of Captain Donellan* (London: J. Wenman, 1781).

3. A local tribesman whom Donellan claimed was acting as an interpreter.

4. *The History of the Bengal European Regiment*, written by Lieutenant-Colonel Innes in 1885, claimed that 'Officers participated in profits accruing from trading transactions … presents from native chiefs were viewed as compensation for insufficient pay.' However, although the practice might have been widely accepted, a veil of discretion was drawn over such dealings back home, in an unwritten law of silence that Donellan was now transgressing. Innes may be justly assumed to have been on Donellan's side, as he wrote a play called *Donellan* which was performed at the Strand Theatre in June 1889. The hero, Donellan, is reprieved from a death sentence for poisoning his brother-in-law when the boy's mother herself confesses to his murder. The mother was called Lady Boughton.

5. His *A Picture of England*, published in 1790, shows that Von Archenholz was mightily impressed by both the riches and the poverty of England.

6. See Tobias Smollett, *The Expedition of Humphry Clinker* (1771).

7. Harrington was described by the *Westminster Magazine* as 'a person of the most exceptional immorality'.

8. As reported in 'Nocturnal Revels – The History of King's Place and Other Modern Nunneries, by a Monk of the Order of St Francis [i.e. a member of the Hellfire Club]' (1779).

9. Samuel Derrick produced the first *Harris's List* in 1757, based on a compendium of 400 names kept by the self-styled 'Pimp General of All England', John Harrison (also known as Jack Harris). See Hallie Rubenhold (ed.), *Harris's List of Covent Garden Ladies* (Stroud: Tempus, 2005).

10. See Phillip H. Highfill, Kalman A. Burnim, Edward A. Langhans, *A Biographical Dictionary of Actors, Actresses, Musicians, Dancers, Managers & Other Stage Personnel in London, 1660–1800* (Carbondale, IL: Southern Illinois University Press, revised edition, 2006).
11. Edward Walford, *Old and New England* (1878).

6 The Major Players

1. In the private possession of H. and J. Boughton-Leigh.
2. Newbold-on-Avon Parish Registers.
3. CR 162/490, the will of Anna Maria Boughton, dated 28 September 1778, Warwickshire County Record Office.
4. CR 162/573, Warwickshire County Record Office.

7 'Wonderful News...'

1. 6683/4/331, Shropshire Archives.
2. Published with John Donellan's own written *Defence* (Inge and Webb), see Further Reading on p 264.

8 A Very Long Winter

1. 6683/4/331, Shropshire Archives.
2. M. H. Bloxam, *Rugby: The School and Its Neighbourhood* (London: Whittaker, 1889).
3. William Field, *An Historical and Descriptive Account of the Town and Castle of Warwick* (Warwick: printed by H. Sharpe, 1815). I am also obliged to James Mackay of the Warwick Society for his information on the Shire Hall.
4. CR 162/491, Warwickshire County Record Office.
5. As above.
6. Family letters books of Charles Rouse-Boughton, 6683/4/331, Shropshire Archives.
7. CR162/493, Warwickshire County Record Office.
8. 6683/4/332, Shropshire Archives.
9. As reported in *Dublin University Magazine* (1869).
10. S. M. Phillips, *Famous Cases of Circumstantial Evidence: with an Introduction on the Theory of Presumptive Proof* (Boston: Estes & Lauriat, 1873).

9 *The Trial Begins*

1. Although the Crown Court itself moved to new buildings in 2010.
2. The names of the jurors cannot be confirmed, but the members of the grand jury who had determined before the trial began that there was a case to answer were: foreman the Hon W. William Hewitt; members: Thomas Biddulph, G. Townshend, T. W. Knightly, Miller Sadlier, Christopher Wren, Bertie Greathead, John Grieve, Thomas Webb, Timothy Goodwin, C. P. Packwood, John Halifax, R. A. Johnson, Joseph Charles, John Mallor, Joseph Boultby, Edward Pallas, J. Nobbins Jnr, P. S. Littleton. The sheriff was John Webb.
3. As reported on 11 April 1780 and debated in the House of Commons on the same day; one of them, William Smith, died in the pillory and the other, Theodosius Reade, soon afterwards. The coroner's inquest on Smith brought a charge of 'Wilful Murder by Persons Unknown'.
4. *Mr Cradock's Literary and Miscellaneous Memoirs* (Nichols & Son, 1826).
5. Henry and Thomas Roscoe, *Westminster Hall: Or Professional Relics, and Anecdotes of the Bar, Bench and Woolmark* (London: John Knight & Henry Lacey, 1825).
6. The transcript of the trial, taken in shorthand by Joseph Gurney, was published in John Jay Smith, *Celebrated Trials of All Countries* (Philadelphia: L. A. Godney, 1836).

11 *'Not Particularly Intended for Anatomical Pursuits'*

1. Buller's statement to the grand jury at the beginning of the assizes was reported in the *Northampton Mercury* on 2 April 1781.

13 *'Against Him Every Circumstance'*

1. Buller's reference is confusing here. Wheler's first letter on 2 September was a brief condolence; the second, on 4 September, mentioned poison. The third - shown to Rattray - makes no reference to poison.
2. *The Diary and Letters of Benjamin Pickman (1740–1819) of Salem, Massachusetts* (Unknown publisher, 1928). Sourced from the Generations Network, Inc. 2005.

15 Aftermath

1. James Fitzjames Stephen, *A General View of the Criminal Law of England* (London and Cambridge: Macmillan, 1863).

2. 6683/4/331, family letter books, vol. I, Shropshire Archives.

3. Edward was particularly mindful of Anne's state of mind after her husband (described as a 'base animal' by her mother) died after a fall from his horse. Two other sisters fared rather better. Mary married the Bishop of Durham, and Elizabeth became the wife of Lord Upton Clotworthy, First Baron Templeton, by whom she had four children. Elizabeth's lively observations on Theodosia's life make interesting reading in the family letter books in Shropshire Archives.

4. 6683/4/332, Edward Boughton to his brother Charles on 17 April 1781, Shropshire Archives.

5. Letter of 14 April 1771. His great-nephew, the Twelfth Baronet, Sir William St Andrew Rouse-Boughton, called him a 'damn'd prig' for this 'unask'd for advice'.

6. Charles disputed the will, and was disappointed by a QC's opinion of February 1794 which upheld the entire inheritance for the illegitimate daughters. Edward's daughter Eliza, whom he adored, received all his estates; her sisters Caroline and Lucy were also given generous bequests, and their mother Sally was given an annuity for life.

7. In recompense Edward allowed Anna Maria the use of Brownsover Hall for her lifetime.

8. Frederica St Orlebar's twentieth-century recollection (OR 2315/21 at Bedfordshire & Luton Archives and Record Service). Frederica goes on to say that Anna Maria was so furious that she locked all the Boughton records in a box and sent it to be buried in a sawdust pit at Brownsover Hall, where it was discovered when Anna Maria's great-grandson, Edward Allesley Boughton Ward-Boughton-Leigh, moved out in 1883. The documents in the box, Frederica claimed, included Charles I's original deed granting the Boughton baronetcy. Frederica describes Caldecott as a 'bad, grasping man'.

9. John Cary's *New and Correct English Atlas* (1787).

10. Described by Frederica St Orlebar, as above.

11. 6683/4/332, Shropshire Archives.

12. Caldecott to E. W. Rouse-Boughton, 1 July 1782. Caldecott was informing the Eighth Baronet's family of the legal affairs relating to what had been Theodosius's estate.

13. CR 162/495, dated 28 March 1783, Warwickshire County Record Office. The Kings would later feature heavily in the affairs of John, Donellan's son.

14. CR 1711/58, Warwickshire County Record Office. Theodosia also hired a coach driver and a new set of horses that year.

15. O'Conor Donelan Estate Papers, Document LE10/389, as quoted in www.ballyd.com/history/johnpoisoner.htm. This states that John Donellan was the illegitimate son of Nehemiah Donellan, grandson of James Donellan and nephew of John Donellan, MP for Ardee. The entire reference, however, is noted to have been 'crossed out'.

16. His journal beginning 14 December 1793, held at Rugby Baptist church, tells of a 'Nabob' girl begging him not to disgrace her on her bended knees; as well as the seduction of a 'Devonshire girl' whom he 'shook off with some difficulty', calling her 'a beautiful serpent'.

17. One August morning in 1793 Egerton told Theodosia and the 14-year-old Maria of a nightly visitation by two eagles and a man 'who told me he was David's King'. He attributed his wild dreams to his struggle to overcome his 'vices'.

18. John Donellan's name was eradicated by the marriage settlement drawn up on 10 May. The children were no longer 'Donellan' but 'Beauchamp' and the front cover of the document styled Theodosia not as 'Mrs Donellan' but as 'Mrs Beauchamp'. The settlement made Theodosia's estate worth £12,215 8s. 6d. (£684,000) plus the power to appoint the vicars of Newbold and Great Harborough and receive the tithes (10 per cent of all income). A further document, CR 1711/35 at Warwickshire Record Office, lists an impressive array of jewellery.

19. Her birth and burial is only recorded in the nineteenth-century edition of Debretts.

20. Cat. Ref. Prob. 11/1333, National Archives.

21. Cat. Ref. Prob. 11/1436, National Archives.

22. In *All the Year Round*, 28 October 1871.

23. Sir Charles Rouse-Boughton had inherited the Boughton baronetcy when his brother Edward died. He was later awarded a second

baronetcy for his services in India and, following his marriage to Catherine Hall, the family name was changed to Rouse-Boughton. He referred to himself as the Ninth Baronet Lawford and the First Baronet Rouse-Boughton.

24. The Gretna Green marriage registers record a marriage between 'John Ward of Guilsborough Northamptonshire' and 'Theodosia de Malsburg Leigh of Brownsover Warwickshire' on 15 March 1811.

25. He was related to Caldecott, the family solicitor. His great-uncle's daughter, Merice, had married Abraham Turner, the man to whom Caldecott had confided so many salacious details about Theodosius's father's philanderings. Turner's brother-in-law had married the widow of William Boughton, whose great-grandfather had inherited Bilton Hall from the brother of the First Baronet.

26. All the correspondence quoted here comes from 6683/4/338, family letters of the Rouse-Boughton family, at the Shropshire Archives. Theodosia herself seemed to take a much more relaxed line. Sir Charles's daughter, Lady Templetown, recorded disapprovingly that she had come 'flourishing into town in a barouche and four' and added, 'I should not have expected it from the *position of things.*'

27. 'It would be best to write on a single sheet of paper as the large sheet was charged double'; she complained about a gamekeeper's bill for clothing; she was irked by the expense of a new dairy farm; and in 1829 she told Harris to hurry up and get £1,400 for the Harborough living, 'if not I will sell it to some clergyman for more money'.

28. Theodosius Egerton Boughton Ward-Boughton-Leigh was vicar of Newbold for fifty years until 1902.

16 What Killed Theodosius Boughton?

1. S. M. Phillips, *Famous Cases of Circumstantial Evidence: with an Introduction on the Theory of Presumptive Proof* (Boston: Estes & Lauriat, 1873).

2. Edward Allesley Boughton Ward-Boughton-Leigh to Sir Charles Rouse-Boughton, 8 November 1882: 'Lady Boughton was from her diary and letters the very opposite of "weak" – her diary is well written and well spelt, her business letters well expressed.' If this portrait of Anna Maria is accurate, her behaviour at the trial was all the more extraordinary as she did not have the excuse of being 'all but a fool'.

According to John Derbyshire's trial testimony: 'He said, "It was done amongst themselves; he had no hand in it ..." I asked who he meant by "themselves". He said himself ...'

Q: Who did he mean by 'himself'?

A: Sir Theodosius Boughton ... I said, 'Sure, he could not do it by himself'; he said, no, he did not think he did ...'

3. John Gordon Smith, *An Analysis of Medical Evidence* (1825).
4. Hugh Childers, *Romantic Trials of Three Centuries* (J. Lane, 1913).
5. *Mr Cradock's Literary and Miscellaneous Memoirs* (Nichols & Son, 1826).

List of Illustrations

11. The Pump Room with traders selling their wares, from Bath Illustrated by a Series of Views, print series, 1806. (The Art Archive/Victoria Art Gallery Bath)

12. Edward Boughton (1742–94), who inherited the baronetcy on Theodosius' death. From a private collection.

13. John Donellan, taken from a family archive. From a private collection.

14. *The Pantheon London, interior with John Donellan believed to be figure far left.* Engraving by R. Earlom after M-V. Brandoin, Michel-Vincent, 1772. (The Art Archive/Bibliothèque des Arts Décoratifs Paris/Gianni Dagli Orti)

15. Exterior of the London Pantheon, c.1780s. (Mary Evans Picture Library)

16. The ravishingly pretty Theodosia – Theodosius' sister – aged 17. Taken from a locket in the possession of Mr and Mrs Henry Boughton-Leigh

17. *A Bacchante (Portrait of Mrs Elizabeth Hartley)*, stipple etching by William Nutter after Sir Joshua Reynolds, 1800.(© The Trustees of the British Museum)

18. Nancy Parsons, mezzotint by James Watson after George Willison, 1771. (© The Trustees of the British Museum)

19. View looking along Northgate street in Warwick with the magistrates court to the right and St Mary's Church in the distance, engraving after a drawing by the Revd Mr Streatfield, 1801. Photo: Leamington Spa Art Gallery & Museum

20. The interior of Warwick Crown Court, a new building in Donellan's day, court business moved to new premises in 2011.(© *Country Life* magazine).

21. *John Hunter*, engraving, 1788. (The Art Archive/Private Collection/Marc Charmet)

22. *Judge Thumb* or *Patent Sticks for Family Correction*, cartoon showing Sir Justice Buller, cartoon by James Gillray, 1782 (Mary Evans Picture Library/Castle Howard Collection).

Further Reading

Primary Sources

Donellan, John, *The Case of John Donnellan, Captain of Foot, in the Service of the United Company of Merchants Trading to the East-Indies, humbly addressed to the Honourable Court of Directors of the said Company* (London: 1770; reprinted by Kessinger Publishing Rare Reprints)

'A Defence and Substance of the Trial of John Donellan (*sic*) Esq; who was Convicted for the Murder of Theodosius Boughton, Bart at the Assizes held at Warwick on Friday the 30th of March 1781 Before the Hon. Francis Buller, Esq; founded on the case solemnly attested by the sufferer after his Conviction', Printed for John Bell at the British Library, Strand 1781.

Donellan, John, *The Genuine Case of John Donellan Esquire, as written by Himself; and in pursuance of his dying request* (London: published by Thomas Webb, Solicitor; printed by J. Wenman, April 1781; reprinted by Ecco Print Editions)

Murphy, Captain, *The Life of Captain John Donellan* (London: J. Wenman, 1781; reprinted by Ecco Print Editions)

Smith, John Jay, *Celebrated Trials of All Countries: And Remarkable Cases of Criminal Jurisprudence* (Philadelphia: L. A. Godney, 1836; reprinted by Kessinger Publishing Rare Reprints)

The trial transcript, taken in shorthand by Joseph Gurney, which appears here is the transcript used in this book.

General Reading

Von Archenholz, Johann Wilhelm, *A Picture of England: containing a description of the laws, customs and manners of England* (Dublin: printed by P. Byrne, 1790; reprinted by Kessinger Publishing Rare Reprints)

Baker, Kenneth, *George IV: A Life in Caricature* (London: Thames & Hudson, 2005)

Black, Jeremy, *A Subject for Taste: Culture in Eighteenth-Century England* (London: Hambledon Continuum, 2005)

Cruickshank, Dan, *The Secret History of Georgian London: How the Wages of Sin Shaped the Capital* (London: Random House, 2009)

Harvey, P. D. A. and Thorpe, Harry, *The Printed Maps of Warwickshire 1576–1900* (Warwick: The Records and Museum Committee of Warwickshire County Council in collaboration with the University of Birmingham, 1959)

Linnane, Fergus, *Madams: Bawds and Brothel-Keepers of London* (Stroud: Sutton Publishing, 2005)

Martin, Joanna, *Wives and Daughters: Women and Children in the Georgian Country House* (London: Hambledon and London, 2004)

Porter, Roy, *English Society in the 18th Century* (London: Penguin Books, revised edition, 1991)

Rubenhold, Hallie (ed.), *Harris's List of Covent Garden Ladies: Sex in the City in Georgian Britain* (Stroud: Tempus, 2005)

Swiderski, Richard M., *Quicksilver: A History of the Use, Lore and Effects of Mercury* (Jefferson, NC: McFarland & Co. Inc., 2008)

Websites

British History Online: www.british-history.ac.uk

National Archives: www.nationalarchives.gov.uk

These two websites have been very useful as general reference sources to locate documents, to find street descriptions in London and to provide modern currency equivalents of eighteenth-century amounts.

Acknowledgements

I WOULD LIKE TO THANK the staff at Warwickshire County Record Office, Shropshire Archives, Northamptonshire Record Office, Bedfordshire & Luton Archives and Records Service and the London Metropolitan Archives for their help in piecing together a Boughton family history that became such a wonderful drama; to Joan Adkins for showing me the Egerton Leigh journals at Rugby Baptist Church; to Dr Gillian Russell for her article on the Pantheon; and to Dr Napier Penlington for sharing his thoughts on the Donellan case.

For their technical advice, valuable time and expertise, I am deeply grateful to Dr Allen Anscombe, forensic pathologist, for his opinion on the causes of Theodosius's death, and to Alan Jenkins of Dorset Police for information on modern-day police procedure.

I am hugely indebted to Ann Boughton-Leigh, Henry Boughton-Leigh and Mrs Mark Wiggins for their generous interest in my work and for access to invaluable family portraits and letters. Their kindness has been extraordinary. I also thank Richard Phillips for the provision of the photograph of Little Lawford Hall and its environs; and Reverend Paul Wilkinson for his patience and good humour in showing me the Boughton family monuments at Newbold-upon-Avon church on a very cold day in January 2010.

I owe so much to my agent Laura Longrigg for her enthusiasm, encouragement and insight, and to my editor Peter Carson, both of whom helped to turn a novelist into an historian.

Lastly and very importantly, my heartfelt thanks go to Kate, Charlotte and Roger for their support. I will never forget Roger manfully sorting through hundreds of eighteenth-century letters in search of a single sentence; or the girls leaping about the house at the news that the book would be published. For everything, thanks.

Index

THE DAMNATION OF JOHN DONELLAN